13
Things
Mentally
Strong
Women
Don't Do

Also by Amy Morin

*13 Things Mentally
Strong People Don't Do*

*13 Things Mentally
Strong Parents Don't Do*

13

Things

Mentally

Strong

Women

Don't Do

OWN YOUR

POWER,

CHANNEL YOUR

CONFIDENCE,

AND FIND YOUR

AUTHENTIC

VOICE FOR A LIFE

OF MEANING

AND JOY

AMY MORIN

WILLIAM MORROW
An Imprint of HarperCollins*Publishers*

13 THINGS MENTALLY STRONG WOMEN DON'T DO. Copyright © 2019 by Amy Morin. All rights reserved. Printed in the United States of America. No part of this book may be used or reproduced in any manner whatsoever without written permission except in the case of brief quotations embodied in critical articles and reviews. For information, address HarperCollins Publishers, 195 Broadway, New York, NY 10007.

HarperCollins books may be purchased for educational, business, or sales promotional use. For information, please email the Special Markets Department at SPsales@harpercollins.com.

FIRST EDITION

Designed by Bonni Leon-Berman

Library of Congress Cataloging-in-Publication Data has been applied for.

ISBN 978-0-06-284762-1 (hardcover)
ISBN 978-0-06-291107-0 (International edition)

19 20 21 22 23   RS/LSC   10 9 8 7 6 5 4 3 2 1

To all the women who strive to become a little stronger today
than they were yesterday

CONTENTS

INTRODUCTION   1

CHAPTER 1   They Don't Compare Themselves to Other People   9

CHAPTER 2   They Don't Insist on Perfection   31

CHAPTER 3   They Don't See Vulnerability as a Weakness   53

CHAPTER 4   They Don't Let Self-Doubt Stop Them from Reaching Their Goals   75

CHAPTER 5   They Don't Overthink Everything   97

CHAPTER 6   They Don't Avoid Tough Challenges   119

CHAPTER 7   They Don't Fear Breaking the Rules   141

CHAPTER 8   They Don't Put Others Down to Lift Themselves Up   165

CHAPTER 9   They Don't Let Others Limit Their Potential   189

CHAPTER 10   They Don't Blame Themselves When Something Goes Wrong   215

CHAPTER 11   They Don't Stay Silent   239

CHAPTER 12   They Don't Feel Bad about Reinventing Themselves   265

CHAPTER 13   They Don't Downplay Their Success   289

CONCLUSION   313

ACKNOWLEDGMENTS   319

REFERENCES   321

13
Things
Mentally
Strong
Women
Don't Do

INTRODUCTION

I grew up driving an ATV and catching night crawlers to use as fishing bait. I never liked dolls. I wasn't interested in makeup. And I hated to shop.

But my skinned knees, messy hair, and dirty fingernails made for a wonderful childhood. My parents convinced me I could do whatever boys did—and I certainly tried. Whether it was racing the boys at recess or arm wrestling them into submission, I was able to keep up most of the time. But I wasn't trying to prove anything. I was just having fun.

The first time I recall encountering the word "sexist" was when I was in the seventh grade. My algebra teacher always asked a sports-related bonus question that had nothing to do with math. But if you got the answer correct, he added five points to your test grade. It was frustrating that five points hinged on knowing who ran the most yards in Sunday's football game or who scored the most points in last year's NBA playoffs. But no one complained.

One day, I was sick and had to stay home from school. I missed an algebra test, so I had to stay after school the following day to make it up. The bonus question was about a Major League Baseball player. Fortunately, I loved baseball, and I knew the answer. My teacher handed the graded test back to me the next day at the beginning of class. Written across the top of the page in red ink were the words "0 bonus points. You only got this right because one of your friends told you the question ahead of time."

I was horrified that my teacher thought I cheated, but I didn't say anything to him. I didn't know what to say. So I brought the test home and showed my dad.

My dad promptly wrote a note back to my teacher: "Amy owns more than 10,000 baseball cards and she watches baseball games on TV with me every week. But because she got your bonus answer correct, you accused her of cheating. She knew the answer fair and square. But what's not fair is that you ask sports-related questions that have nothing to do with math. Clearly, you are trying to give the boys an advantage since most 13-year-old girls aren't following professional sports that closely."

I gave the note to my teacher the next day and quickly took my seat. When he was done reading it, he announced to the class, "I can't give you bonus questions anymore because someone's father thinks I'm sexist." That was the last time my teacher ever gave us a bonus question, and that was the first time I really thought about sexism.

It occurred to me that he didn't assume my friends told me any of the math questions ahead of time—just the sports question. And he assumed I couldn't possibly know the answer to an obscure baseball question unless I cheated. I can't help but wonder if he would have made that same assumption if I was a boy.

That happened twenty-five years ago, and I'd like to think teachers aren't still giving boys an unfair advantage in the classroom. But research shows it's still happening, and we'll talk more about those specifics later on.

I'd also like to think students and parents wouldn't be so tolerant of something like that these days. Back then, no one said anything—and neither did their parents. We tolerated it. Had my teacher not accused me of cheating, I don't know if my father would have raised the issue.

My ideas about sexism have certainly shifted since the seventh grade, and thankfully so have our culture's. Still, women continue to face unique challenges in today's world. I've seen it in my therapy office as well as in my own life.

My Interest in Mental Strength Is Personal

When I landed my first job as a therapist, I was excited to help people overcome the challenges they faced. I was armed with a master's degree and knowledge I'd gleaned from my textbooks, college lectures, and internships. During my first year as a therapist, however, my mother passed away suddenly and unexpectedly. My quest to learn about mental strength became personal.

I started studying everyone who came into my therapy office on a deeper level. I realized that some people were more likely to get better than others. They bounced back faster, they were hopeful about the future, and no matter what problems they faced, they persisted. I wanted to know what specifically made these people tick.

Then, in a cruel twist of fate, on the three-year anniversary of my mother's death, my twenty-six-year-old husband, Lincoln, died of a heart attack. Being a twenty-six-year-old widow was a surreal experience. The grief was overwhelming at times, but I knew that allowing myself to experience painful emotions was part of the healing process.

By then, I was armed with new knowledge about mental strength. I had discovered that people who persevered in life didn't just have healthy habits—they were also intentional about avoiding the unhealthy habits that would keep them stuck.

I was starting to see clear patterns in the people I worked with. Those who were intent on reaching their greatest potential refused to indulge in counterproductive bad habits. The key to their progress wasn't just what they did. It was more what they *didn't* do.

I applied what I'd learned to my own life as I worked through my grief. It took several years for my heart to heal. I was fortunate enough to find love again, when I met Steve. But shortly after we got married, Steve's dad was diagnosed with terminal cancer. I found myself thinking things like "This isn't fair. Why do I have to keep losing my loved ones?"

But I knew that allowing myself to indulge in self-pity was one of those bad habits that would drain my mental strength at a time when I needed it the most. So I wrote a letter to myself reminding me of all of those bad habits that could keep me stuck in a place of misery. When I was done, I had a list of thirteen things mentally strong people don't do. I read over the list many times in the following days, and the reminders of what not to do gave me some solace. I decided if *I* found that list helpful, maybe others would too. So I published it online, hoping my message on mental strength might resonate with someone else.

Within a matter of days, the article went viral. It was read by more than fifty million people. Before I knew it, media outlets like *Forbes* and CNN were asking me about my list. My article didn't explain the context of the list, however, so everyone assumed I'd written it because I'd mastered everything on it. But the truth was, I still needed a reminder to avoid those thirteen things.

I was grateful to have the chance to write the book *13 Things Mentally Strong People Don't Do,* to explain the story behind the viral article. And when readers kept asking me how to teach kids to be mentally strong, I was thrilled to be able to write *13 Things Mentally Strong Parents Don't Do.*

Since I began talking about mental strength, I've fielded many questions from women, especially in light of the #MeToo revelations. And while the principles of mental strength are the same for everyone, women experience different cultural pressures than men. Consequently, there are some specific bad habits that we're more likely to engage in, struggle with, and experience, compared to our male counterparts.

The 3 Components of Mental Strength

Mental strength is a lot like physical strength. When it comes to growing stronger and becoming better, good habits are important. But your good habits will only get you so far in life if you're performing bad habits right alongside them.

If I wanted to grow physically strong, I might lift weights. But if I really wanted to see some muscle definition, I'd need to give up eating too much junk food. Otherwise, my workouts wouldn't be all that effective. The same can be said for your mental muscles. You need good habits, like gratitude, to grow stronger. But if you really want to see results, you also have to give up bad habits, like comparing yourself with other people.

It's important to note that having a mental illness doesn't mean you're weak. Just like someone with diabetes could choose to become physically strong, someone with depression can choose to become mentally strong. An illness can make building muscle more complicated, but it's still possible.

You aren't either mentally strong or mentally weak. Everyone possesses mental strength to a certain degree. And no matter how strong you are, there's always room for improvement.

It's important to keep working your mental muscles too. If you grow lax about building strength, your mental muscles will atrophy.

There are three parts to mental strength:

- **Thoughts**—It's important to develop a realistic inner monologue. Thinking overly negative thoughts like "I'll never succeed" will drag you down. But you also don't want to think in an overly positive way. Saying things like "This will be easy" could cause you to enter a situation unprepared.

- **Feelings**—While it's healthy to experience a wide range of emotions, you don't have to let your feelings control you. If you wake up in a grumpy mood, you can take steps to feel better. When you're angry, knowing how to calm yourself down can prevent you from doing something you regret. The more mental strength you build, the more aware you'll become of your emotions and how those emotions affect your choices.

- **Behavior**—No matter what circumstance you find yourself in, it's important to take positive action. Whether you go to the gym when you're tired or you speak up in a meeting when you're filled with self-doubt, your choices can change your life. Even if you can't solve a problem, you can always choose to make your life or someone else's life better.

All three aspects of mental strength are interrelated. If you think, "I don't have anything valuable to say," you'll feel awkward about speaking up. That, in turn, will likely affect your behavior, as you'll probably stay silent. Consequently, your belief that you don't have anything to add to the conversation will be reinforced.

We all get caught up in negative patterns like this in our lives. Building mental strength disrupts those unhealthy cycles and helps you develop better habits so you can live a more fulfilling life.

Why the Focus Is on Women

I wanted to write a book for women that portrays strength in an accurate light. While many people refer to Navy SEALs as the epitome of mental toughness, women, who tend to be more nurturing and place more value on relationships, can also exemplify mental strength. You don't have to suppress your emotions, deny your pain, or push yourself to your physical limits to be strong.

Studies show women find that mental strength plays an important role in their lives. In 2015 and 2016, Kellogg surveyed six thousand women across the globe about inner strength. Here are a few of their findings:

- 92 percent of women said inner strength is important in today's world.
- 90 percent of women consider inner strength to be the key to success.
- 71 percent of women feel that with more strength they could reach their full potential.
- 82 percent of women wished they possessed greater reserves of inner strength.

Clearly, women want to be mentally stronger, but many aren't sure how to build their mental muscles.

I wrote this book for women with two goals in mind:

1. Empower women to build their mental muscles so they can become the strongest and best versions of themselves.

2. Encourage women to create a ripple effect that will inspire others to become mentally stronger.

I've interviewed women from across the country, and in this book, I'll share their stories, challenges, and strategies. I'll also share case studies from my therapy office that show what happens when women give up the bad habits that rob them of mental strength.

The following thirteen chapters aren't meant to be a checklist of things you either do or don't do. We all engage in these unhealthy practices at one time or another—especially when we encounter adversity.

There have probably been times in your life when you felt strong, powerful, and unstoppable—but those instances may feel few and far between. You've probably also caught glimpses of how strong you could be, like in those moments when you almost make a brave move. Wouldn't it be nice to draw upon your inner strength all the time so you can reach your greatest potential? This book is meant to help you do just that.

I'm not going to tell you that you need to be doing more grueling activities to live a better life (there are too many messages out there already insisting you *should* be doing more to improve yourself). Instead, I'll explain how to give up the bad habits that are draining you of the strength you've already tried so hard to build. I'll teach you how to work smarter, not just harder, so you can become the best version of yourself.

1

They Don't Compare Themselves to Other People

Every flower blooms at a different pace.
—SUZY KASSEM

Cara began therapy because she felt like she wasn't as happy as she should be. She was a twenty-eight-year-old nurse, and she loved her job in the pediatric unit of a hospital. She had been with her boyfriend for almost a year, and she felt confident that he was "the one." She had a great relationship with her parents and her older brother and she had plenty of friends.

She was doing well financially, thanks to the house she inherited when her grandmother passed away. Without rent or a mortgage, she'd paid off her student loans early.

Despite having everything she wanted, she felt dissatisfied—and that caused her to feel guilty and ungrateful. She worried that her displeasure was a slap in the face to her parents, who had sacrificed so much to give her the tools she needed to build a great life.

"I know most people would give anything to have my life. So I just don't understand why I'm not over-the-moon happy," she said.

We spent several weeks talking about her discontent and the discrepancy between the way she felt and the way she thought she *should* feel. She was convinced her friends were happier than she was, and she thought she must be doing something wrong.

When she talked to a friend who was married with two children, Cara questioned whether her own life was progressing as fast as it should be. When she spent time with another friend who worked out all the time, Cara felt like "an out-of-shape hippo."

"Part of me thinks I should make friends with miserable people so I can feel better about myself," she joked. And while that was an option, it wasn't likely to help much.

As long as she thought she *should* be happier, she wasn't going to enjoy her life. To stop feeling that way, she needed to stop comparing her happiness level with the level of happiness she presumed her friends had achieved.

She had to put the focus back on her own goals if she wanted to feel content. Turning life into a happiness competition was backfiring.

My work with Cara focused on reframing her thoughts. When she thought things like "My friend has a better life than I do," she would remind herself, "My friend has a different life than I do, but it's not better or worse. Just different."

Cara also had to accept that her friends might be happier than she was sometimes. But life is full of ups and downs and thinking she was in a competition to be the happiest was never going to give her a sense of inner peace.

As Cara became more aware of her emotions and as she practiced reframing her thoughts, she recognized that she didn't need to be as happy as her friends in order to live a great life. During one of her last sessions, Cara said, "Rather than measure happiness against my friends' zest for life, I'm practicing being happy for them when they share their passions and excitement. It helps me feel more content about my own life."

Do You Compare Yourself to Others?

We all compare ourselves to others sometimes. After all, how do you know if you're good at basketball or terrible at math unless you have someone to stack yourself up against? And while comparisons can help you identify some of your strengths and weaknesses, measuring your worth against others is detrimental to your sense of self. Do any of the following points ring true to you?

- ❐ I think other people are happier, more attractive, and have better lives.
- ❐ I treat life like it's a competition and I view the people around me as competitors.
- ❐ I feel envious when other people succeed.
- ❐ I spend a lot of time thinking about whether others are financially better off than me.
- ❐ When I meet new women, I immediately begin assessing how I stack up against them.
- ❐ I feel best about myself when I feel more attractive than the women around me.
- ❐ When I scroll through social media, I often size up other women to see if they look happier, thinner, or more fortunate than I do.
- ❐ I find myself trying to keep up with my friends because I think they are living better lives than I am.
- ❐ I fear being the dumbest, poorest, or least attractive person in the room.
- ❐ I feel insignificant or insecure when I meet women with impressive job titles.

Why We Do It

Cara had grown up with her closest friends. When they were young, they shared their dreams for the future and they talked about all the different things they could achieve as they aged. But after they graduated from college, they had to pick their own path. As they embarked on different journeys, Cara questioned whether she had taken the "best" path. During one of her appointments she said, "We all just want to be happy, right? So if someone else is happier than you are, it must mean they've got life better figured out."

Cara's belief that there was one best route to happiness had to be addressed. Deep down, she believed that she was competing against those around her for the best life. She thought being happier than her friends meant she was winning. And when she felt like her pals were happier than she was, she felt like a loser.

It's easy to get caught up in the comparison trap like Cara did. Social media has made it easier than ever to look around and size yourself up against other people. And for many women, comparisons have become a hard habit to break.

THERE'S CULTURAL PRESSURE TO BE BETTER

Imagine you're a student in a class. You take a test and the professor reveals you earned a C. Take a minute to imagine how you'd feel about that C. Now, imagine you learned that everyone else in the class failed. How would you feel about that C now?

Or what if you learned everyone else in the class actually got As and your C was the lowest grade? Would that change how you feel about your grade? If you're like most people, your feelings about your grade would be at least partially influenced by how others performed.

Most of us do this same thing in everyday life—we look around to see how other people are doing. And to an extent that makes sense. How do you know if you're smart unless you compare yourself to others? Or how do you know if you're a good golfer, a bad bowler, or a great cook? Without someone to compare yourself against, it's impossible to tell.

The same can be said for money. Are you rich or poor? Well, that depends, right? Compare yourself to people across the globe, and you're probably wealthy. Measure your net worth against pro athletes or celebrities, and you might feel poor.

Looking to other people gives us information about ourselves. We learn a lot about our talents, strengths, and weaknesses by understanding how we stack up against others.

One of the sneaky ways companies try to convince women to invest in their beauty products is by showing beautiful women who seem happier, healthier, and wealthier. They want you to compare yourself to their models and actresses and feel as though you fall short. They promise that if you buy their products, you'll enjoy a better life.

There's a lot of pressure for women to be beautiful. Media images and beauty products emphasize the importance of a woman's appearance. The beauty industry created what Renee Engeln, a psychology professor at Northwestern University, calls "beauty sickness." In her book *Beauty Sick,* she says, "A nonstop barrage of marketing tells us that all we need to do to release that more beautiful version of us is spend money. The right mascara could change your life, we're told. The right wrinkle cream could stop time. A ten-pound weight loss could fundamentally change the nature of your romantic relationships and erase every neurosis."

Engeln asked over two hundred college women to write down all the thoughts they had while looking at magazine advertisements from women's magazines. Some images featured products only, such as an ad for lip gloss, while others included models. Over 80 percent of the women looking at the images that featured models made at least one social comparison. Here are some of the comments women made:

- I think I would be happy if my thighs were that thin.
- God, she's pretty. Why can't I be that pretty?
- I wish I had a perfect flat stomach like hers.

She worked with researcher assistants to code all the thoughts the women in the study listed and she learned that those with the highest levels of body dissatisfaction made the most social comparisons. She concluded, "When you're already feeling vulnerable about how you look, your tendency is to constantly seek out more information about your appearance."

SOCIAL MEDIA DRIVES COMPARISONS

Instagram is filled with fitness gurus with six-pack abs. Facebook ads trumpet business experts who seem to have it all. And Pinterest touts the crafty wizards who make party hosting, house decorating, and baking look easy. So it's hard not to look at these other women and think, "Why can't I be like that?"

Maria is one of the women I interviewed for this book. She said, "I'm so glad we didn't have social media when I was a kid. I watch my fifteen-year-old daughter spend hours trying to capture the perfect selfie to put on Instagram. When I ask her why she spends so much time on one picture she says, 'I want people to think I look pretty. But I'm not as pretty as most girls, so it takes a long time to find a picture that makes me look better than I do in real life.'"

Of course, it's not just young women who draw social comparisons on social media. I spoke to a thirty-eight-year-old woman who said, "I'm constantly looking at my Facebook friends' pictures, and I think I'm secretly trying to find flaws, like gray hairs or wrinkles. Rather than looking at their pictures and being happy that they're enjoying their vacation or a night out, I'm just looking at them to see if they look better than I do."

Men aren't necessarily immune to drawing social comparisons on social media, but women spend more time on social media sites. Women are also more likely to use social media that relies heavily on images, such as Facebook, Pinterest, and Instagram, while men are more likely to use Twitter and LinkedIn.

Social media can warp your perspective on other people. A 2012 study found that the more time people spent on Facebook, the more likely they were to conclude that other people had better and happier lives than they did.

A 2015 study found that a woman's mood and body image are likely to decline after just ten minutes spent browsing Facebook, where ten million new photographs are uploaded every day. Looking at social media images was linked to lower levels of body satisfaction, because participants were comparing their face, hair, and skin.

Why It's Bad

Cara took for granted that she knew everything about her friends, because they'd known each other for a long time. She assumed their lives were as rosy as they appeared to be on Facebook.

So one week I asked her whether she'd told her friends that she was coming to therapy. She admitted she hadn't. I asked her if she posted on social media about how she thought everyone else was happier than she was. Again, she admitted she hadn't made that public either. It led to an interesting conversation about how her friends may be struggling with similar issues, and they just hadn't told her about it—and they certainly hadn't shared their personal problems on social media.

That helped Cara see she was putting her attention in the wrong place. Rather than focus on what she wanted to achieve, she'd become distracted by her friends' success. Her preoccupation with her friends' presumed level of happiness created unnecessary turmoil and angst.

Comparisons aren't necessarily based on fact, and they can be never-ending. There will always be someone who is doing better than you or has more than you do. Wasting your energy comparing yourself to others won't motivate you to do better. Instead, it'll drag you down and hold you back.

WOMEN FEEL BAD, MEN GAIN INSPIRATION

There are two types of social comparisons: upward and downward. Upward social comparison is when you look at people who seem superior—wealthier, healthier, or happier. You might compare your body to that of a fitness model, or you might compare your home to the mansion down the street.

Looking at people who seem more fortunate than you wreaks havoc on your psychological well-being. It can lead you to believe you are less worthy, less capable, less attractive, and less likable than others. Studies show that upward social comparisons fuel depression and envy.

On the other hand, downward social comparisons involve looking at people who are less fortunate. Perhaps you think about your friend who is heavier than you are to feel better about your body. Or maybe you drive past a neighborhood that looks a little shabby and revel in the fact that you have a nicer place.

You might think comparing yourself to the less fortunate is good for you. After all, won't it make you feel grateful for what you have? Not likely. Studies show downward social comparisons may boost your self-image momentarily, but in the long term, looking down on others fuels worry and sympathy, which will cause you to feel worse.

Ultimately, it doesn't matter whether you're measuring yourself against those who have their acts together or you're comparing yourself to individuals who are less fortunate. Either way, you'll limit the amount of mental strength you're able to build.

While men aren't immune to comparing themselves to others, studies show that women compare their appearance to others more readily than men do. And women are more likely to make upward comparisons that worsen their body image.

A 2012 study conducted by researchers at Marquette University examined who men and women were most likely to compare themselves to. Through a series of questions, researchers discovered that women are more likely to compare their faces and bodies to idyllic-looking women. And they are more likely to think they'll never be able to achieve similar results. The researchers suspected this stems from the emphasis society places on beauty for women.

Men, on the other hand, were more likely to compare their bodies to their future selves. So rather than wish they could look like a more attractive man, they're more likely to imagine how they could achieve similar results. Unlike women, who feel they'll never be able to look like an idyllic woman, men are more likely to be hopeful that they have the power to improve their appearance.

So, when a man looks at a picture of a muscular man or a man with an ideal physique, he's likely to feel inspired. He might think more about working out or changing his diet so that he could look similar someday. When a woman views images of attractive women, she's more likely to feel bad about herself because she won't think she has any hope of achieving similar results.

In addition, the research is clear that the more comparisons women make, the worse they feel about their bodies. And the worse they feel about themselves, the more likely they are to compare themselves. It's a vicious self-perpetuating cycle.

But you probably didn't need a study to tell you that. When was the last time you looked at celebrities in a magazine or workout gurus on social media and thought, "Wow, I'm good-looking!"?

YOU'RE ONLY GETTING A SMALL SNAPSHOT OF SOMEONE'S LIFE

By 1996, Mindy McCready had reached a level of fame most singers only dream about. Her debut album, *Ten Thousand Angels,* sold more than two million copies and contained four chart-topping singles.

In addition to her skyrocketing music career, her personal life seemed perfect too. She was engaged to Dean Cain—the actor who played Superman on the hit TV show *Lois & Clark: The New Adventures of Superman.* They were a beautiful couple who appeared to have it all.

But within a few years, her life spiraled downward. The relationship with Dean Cain ended and her music career fizzled. She began making headlines for all the wrong reasons: DUI, prescription drug fraud, and driving with a suspended license. Then, in 2005, her boyfriend, Billy McKnight, beat her so brutally that he was charged with attempted murder.

McCready and McKnight later reunited long enough for her to become pregnant with her first child. But the relationship didn't last and McCready attempted suicide several times.

She later began a relationship with David Wilson and became pregnant with her second son. Her struggle with substance abuse continued and her relationship with Wilson was an on-again, off-again romance.

Then, in 2013, Wilson was found dead from a presumed self-inflicted gunshot wound. McCready's children were placed in foster care because of her substance abuse issues, and a judge ordered her to be committed to a treatment facility.

When she was served paperwork that proposed her sons be sent to live with her estranged mother, McCready couldn't take any more. She stepped out onto her porch and shot herself. She was only thirty-seven.

I can't help but wonder how many women compared themselves to McCready at one point or another. She was beautiful, talented, and famous. For quite a long time, she was living an enviable life.

I have no idea whether she was a tormented soul from the start or a series of tough circumstances sparked her downward spiral, but I do know most of us would never want to trade lives with her now, knowing everything she went through.

Mindy McCready isn't the only story of someone who appeared to have it all on the outside yet seemed to be secretly crumbling on the inside. I suspect there are lots of people out there who have wished they could "be funny like Robin Williams," or "sing like Kurt Cobain." It's easy to think someone has a great life from the outside, but you never know what sort of battle they're fighting on the inside. It's not fair to compare the way your life really is to the way you perceive someone else's life to be.

What to Do Instead

Cara was an intelligent woman who recognized that comparing herself to other people wasn't helpful. Yet at the same time, she said, "I just can't help it. I look at what my friends are doing and I begin to question what I'm doing—even little things like how I'm spending my Friday night or what I'm making for dinner."

Since many of Cara's social comparisons stemmed from social media, she agreed to take a break from it for a week to see what would happen. When she came to a therapy appointment after her one-week fast from Facebook, she said, "I noticed I wasn't so worried about what everyone else was doing when I wasn't on social media."

She didn't want to give up social media altogether, but she did agree to monitor her use. Simply becoming more aware of the way social media affected her mood and her thoughts helped her to become more proactive in reducing her social comparisons.

Cara recognized that her attitude began to shift, and she said, "Just like there's plenty of sunshine for everyone—and one person soaking up sun on the beach doesn't affect how much sun you get—there's plenty of happiness to go around."

There are three main things you can do to stop falling into the comparison trap:

1. Reduce the likelihood that you'll compare yourself to others.
2. Address the exaggerated and unfair comparisons you make by changing your thinking.
3. Deal with the discomfort that you experience when other people have more than you.

CREATE A RICH-ENOUGH LIFE THAT YOU WON'T CARE WHAT OTHERS ARE DOING

A 2017 study published in *Body Image* found that women are less likely to be affected by social comparisons when they have something on their mind. Every participant in the study was a woman who had acknowledged that looking at media images caused her to feel bad about herself.

When the women were given a task to do as they viewed images of idyllic women, however, their mood and body image were not affected by the pictures.

Prior to looking at images, the women were asked to rate their mood and their satisfaction with their appearance. Then they were divided into three groups: group one was asked to memorize a complex eight-digit number while viewing images of attractive models; group two was asked to memorize a simple number as they viewed attractive models; and group three viewed pictures that didn't depict people.

After viewing the pictures, the women were asked to rate their mood and their attractiveness again. Researchers found that the women who were preoccupied trying to memorize a complex number were not affected by the images they saw. Their moods remained stable and they rated their attractiveness the same.

The women who only had a simple number to remember didn't fare as well. After looking at the pictures, their moods declined and they rated themselves as less attractive than before.

So what can we glean from this study? When you have a lot going on in your own life, you'll be less affected by the lives of those around you. That's not to say you should fill your life with busyness and distractions, but it does mean that creating a rich, full life could prevent you from wasting your time worrying about whether someone else is doing better.

When you're comparing yourself to other women—whether you're scrolling through social media to look at fitness images or you're looking around at the women in front of you to size up how they're dressed—catch yourself. Think about better things you could be doing with your time, such as getting to know people on a deeper level, reading a book, learning a new skill, or practicing a hobby. Remind yourself that you can take steps to create a life so rich that you won't be distracted by others' perceived good fortune.

ACKNOWLEDGE THE DIFFERENCE BETWEEN
THE INSIDE AND THE OUTSIDE

Imagine you're creating a collage on a shoebox. The outside of the box reflects how other people see you. Perhaps you'd add pictures of some of your favorite hobbies, activities, or interests. Or maybe you'd depict yourself smiling, happy, and hardworking.

Now picture yourself decorating the inside of the shoebox to reflect how you feel on the inside. Perhaps you'd show your secret fears, hidden insecurities, and darkest thoughts. Maybe you'd depict some of those negative tapes that play over and over in your mind.

Take a second to imagine how the outside of the box would look different from the inside. Would people be surprised to learn about the things on the inside of the box? If you're like most people, there's a good chance that even your closest loved ones would be stunned by what's in your box.

You might even decide to do the exercise with a real box. Add magazine photos to your box so you'll have a physical representation of the difference between how you feel on the inside and how others see you on the outside.

I've done this exercise with many people in my therapy office over the years. And almost everyone feels as though their loved ones don't really know the depths of their suffering.

Keep that in mind when you're tempted to compare yourself to other people. You only see the outside of their shoebox. You have no idea what the inside of their shoebox actually looks like.

Social media has come to represent a new way for people to display the outside of their shoebox. Most people only share their greatest moments, happiest memories, and biggest achievements with the world. It's become easy to think we know someone's insides based on what we see on the outside.

The fitness guru you idolize may spend all of her time working out and not have time to spend with friends and family. Or the woman with a really adventurous spirit might not have a stable family life. Keep that in mind the next time you're tempted to compare how you perceive someone from the outside to your own feelings or traits.

PAY ATTENTION TO THOSE LITTLE JUDGMENTAL WORDS THAT MAKE A BIG DIFFERENCE

Factual comparisons are automatic. You can't help but notice when someone is thinner, taller, or has longer hair than you. The judgments you make about those facts are optional, however. And it's those judgments that have the power to cause you to feel bad.

I'm five foot four. When I meet someone who is six foot four, I can't help but notice that person is taller than I am. I notice that fact automatically, and I don't have much control over it.

But I do have control over the judgments I form about the fact that I'm shorter. Thinking "No one ever takes me seriously because I'm so short" is a choice. Making that inference will affect my mood and my behavior.

Facts don't make you feel bad. The conclusions you draw from those facts, however, could cause you to feel bad. Your goal doesn't have to be to prevent all comparisons. Instead, make it a goal to become less affected by the comparisons you make.

Here are some words to be on the lookout for:

- **"Should" and "shouldn't."** *I should be earning more money. I shouldn't dress like such a slob.* "Should" outlines the difference between reality and your expectations. Practice accepting what it is, rather than insisting things be different.
- **"I wish."** *I wish I had as many friends as she does. I wish my husband treated me like her husband treats her.* Be careful what you "wish" for, and practice acknowledging the good things you have going on in your own life already.
- **Words that end in "-er."** *My friend is richer. My boss is prettier. My sister is smarter.* Be aware when you're drawing clear comparisons, and ask yourself whether it's a fact or an opinion.

So rather than sort people into categories like "better or worse" or "good or bad," try sorting your thoughts into "facts and opinions." When you say, "She drives a more expensive car than I do," you might be stating a fact. But saying, "Everyone likes her car better. My car is an embarrassment," is stating an opinion. Simply acknowledging to yourself the difference between facts and opinions can serve as a good reminder that the judgments you form about those comparisons are simply your opinion.

THINK OF PEOPLE AS OPINION HOLDERS, NOT COMPETITORS

My former client Brandi began therapy because she was feeling overwhelmed. She had managed her demanding job and busy social life well until one of her coworkers embraced minimalism. This coworker had sold many of her possessions, downsized her home, and traded in her car for a bicycle. Upon seeing what her coworker had done, Brandi said, "Ever since I saw my coworker make changes in her life, I can't stop thinking about what my life could be like if I got rid of my stuff. I wish I could have fewer things that tie me down."

It was the first time I'd ever heard anyone express envy toward someone who had less than they did. I asked her what stopped her from becoming a minimalist, and she said, "I wouldn't even know where to start."

I suggested that, rather than envy her coworker from afar, Brandi talk to her coworker about her journey to minimalism. By asking questions about what her coworker learned or what she enjoyed giving up, Brandi could learn more about what it means to be a minimalist.

Brandi agreed to strike up a conversation and after talking to her coworker, she said, "It actually doesn't sound like that much fun. She does laundry all the time because she doesn't have a lot of clothes. She has to go to the grocery store every day because she has to carry groceries in her backpack while riding her bike. I wouldn't want to get rid of all of my sentimental items either. I think I'd regret it later."

Brandi was only able to come to that conclusion once she began seeing her coworker as an opinion holder, not a competitor. They weren't in a race to see who could own fewer items or who could feel the freest. Instead, they had different ideas about how to live their best lives.

Thinking of other people as your competition puts you at odds with them. You'll begin to view everyone as a rival, and you'll constantly ask yourself if you're better than those around you.

Changing that mind-set could help your self-worth (as well as your relationships). If someone has something you want, view them as a role model, not your competition.

A 2018 study published in *Computers in Human Behavior* found that people who think "This person has a view on an issue that I am dealing with" enjoy better mental health than those who think "This person is better able to achieve the task than I am." Researchers found that viewing others as opinion holders fosters optimism and inspiration, as opposed to depression and envy.

When you look at other people as having a different opinion, as opposed to being better than you, you'll learn from them. With this mind-set, you can learn something from everyone.

So rather than allow yourself to go down the rabbit hole of thinking someone is luckier, better, or happier, ask yourself the following questions:

- What information does this person have that could be helpful to me?
- What can I learn from this person?
- What opinions, ideas, or areas of expertise does this person have that are different from my own?

Career

When it comes to your career, it's easy to think you should be making as much money as your friend or that you should be advancing as fast as your coworker. But your career path is yours and yours alone. Every industry, company, and team is different. And it doesn't often make sense to compare your experience at your place of work to someone else's.

You don't have 100 percent control over your career. You can't control whether your boss gives you a promotion. You can't make people sign up for your services. You can't prevent an economic downturn. So, when you're making a comparison about your and someone else's career and saying things like "She got the job because she's better than I am," that might not be an accurate statement.

This doesn't mean you have to tolerate discrimination in the workplace, however. Take the gender pay gap, for instance. Many people say women earn less because they take more time off when they have a baby or they work fewer hours because they're the primary caregivers for children or elderly family members. But studies have found that somewhere between 5 and 7 percent of income disparity between men and women may be due to discrimination.

If you're making less than a male coworker who has less experience, inquire about the discrepancy. You might learn there's a legitimate reason why your coworker earns more. But if you suspect women are being paid less than men due to gender discrimination, advocate for equal pay.

Family

Remember when your mom would hand your sibling a brownie that looked bigger than yours? You might recall saying, "That's not fair!" after you saw such injustice. Comparing what you were given to what other family members had is a normal part of childhood. Comparisons don't necessarily end when we grow up, however. In fact, they can get worse as we grow older.

Maybe your sister got better grades and now earns more money than you do. Or perhaps your grandmother always reminds you that your cousin is the most successful person in the whole family.

If you have family members who still say things like "Well, your sister was able to find a job right after college," gently remind them that you're two different people. Just because you share DNA and a history together doesn't mean you're comparing apples to apples. Each individual has a unique set of skills, talents, and life experiences. And, even more so, make it clear that you aren't in a competition with anyone—including your siblings.

You also might be tempted to compare your family to other families. Perhaps you hear about another family's vacation and think, "I wish our family could get along well enough to have a great vacation like that." Or maybe you see another family's holiday photos on social media and you wish your family's celebrations were warm and fuzzy too.

But just like each individual is unique, each family unit is different too. Invest your energy into treasuring the relationships you have rather than wasting time wishing your family could be more like someone else's family.

Social Life

A twenty-four-year-old woman named Beth responded to my request to interview women for this book. When I spoke to her she said, "All my friends are coming forward in the #MeToo movement, and they're sharing their stories. They're braver than I am. I was molested when I was a kid. I haven't told anyone. My friends don't even know what happened."

Beth had felt a lot of shame over the years because of what happened to her. Now she felt even more shame because she didn't want to come forward like her friends did. I urged her to seek therapy to talk about everything she'd endured and her concerns that she wasn't brave enough. Comparing herself to her friends could have serious implications for her mental health, because her choice to stay silent didn't mean she was a coward (we'll talk more about that in chapter 11). She just had a different journey than they did and it was up to her to decide what was best for her.

Your friends have a big impact on the way you see yourself. It's important to keep things in proper perspective and recognize that your friends' choices, successes, or failures shouldn't be used to measure how you feel about yourself.

In my therapy office, I often see people who surround themselves with friends who reaffirm their beliefs. Someone who feels bad about herself may choose friends who are doing better in life, so her beliefs about being a loser are somewhat reaffirmed. On the other hand, I sometimes see people who choose friends who are struggling because it helps them feel better about themselves.

Carefully consider why you choose to surround yourself with certain people. Do you choose a variety of friends? Or do you pick certain types of friends?

Whether you look to your social circle to determine who has the most fun, or you compare your friend's marriage to your romantic relationships, comparisons hurt your friendships. It's impossible to enjoy your friend's company when all you can think about is the fact that she's more fortunate or more attractive than you are.

Refusing to Compare Yourself to Others Makes You Stronger

My entire tenth-grade geometry class was struggling to find the surface area of cylinders and the volume of pyramids. After most of us bombed a test, one of my friends asked the teacher, "Can you just grade on a curve?" My teacher said, "No. When I was a kid, my math teacher graded on a curve. So rather than do my best, I only had to do better than everyone else." Getting the highest grade in the class wasn't a challenge for her.

She made a good point. Striving to be better than other people is different than striving to do your personal best. When you compare yourself to someone else, you might be satisfied as soon as you think you're "winning." But you might sell yourself short.

Take Katie Ledecky, for instance. She's the greatest swimmer in the world—perhaps the best athlete in the world. She's set eleven world records.

If she'd compared herself to the other swimmers, she may have been content as soon as she knew she could win. But Ledecky is constantly trying to improve herself, even when she beats her competitors by ten seconds or more. Her goal isn't just to win—she strives to do her personal best.

If she'd focused on her competition, she may have ended up copying the other swimmers. For example, most of the other swimmers pace themselves early on. But Ledecky does the opposite. In an interview with the *Washington Post,* she said, "I'm always afraid I'll get to the end and have too much left. I'm trying to manage myself so I don't kill myself [at the start]. It's about finding a balance. And it's about having the confidence to know you've done the work so you can get in there and race the whole 800 or 1,500." Clearly, being a trailblazer has paid off for her.

Life isn't a competition. Trying to outshine everyone will drain your mental strength. When you give up comparing yourself to other people you'll be free to focus on your best effort. You won't feel threatened that other people are somehow going to beat you.

Strive to become your best self, rather than better than someone else. Decide that the only person you should compare yourself to is the person you were yesterday.

Troubleshooting and Common Traps

A common trap is thinking that your comparisons drive you to become better. Your secret comparisons, however, aren't the same as healthy competition. Competition is only healthy when everyone is aware that they're playing the game. Weight-loss challenges, for example, work well when everyone is competing for a specific goal. Learning that your coworker lost a pound more than you might push you to do better next week, but that's very different than secretly envying your coworker's physique from afar.

When you compare yourself to other people inside your own head, no one else is playing with you. You're trying to keep score against people who aren't competing against you.

The other downside to competitions is that they don't last forever. And once the competition phase is over, most people's motivation rapidly declines.

Another common trap is trying to escape the discomfort you might feel when someone seems superior. You might avoid talking to a friend who lands a great job, or you might skip going to the gym when your sister successfully loses all of her baby weight, because working out reminds you that you aren't as thin as you'd like to be. But avoiding your discomfort doesn't make it go away. In fact, your jealousy, sadness, or anger can grow worse if left unattended.

When you feel uncomfortable, acknowledge it. Take a deep breath and admit that you're feeling bad. Depending on the situation, you might even come clean with the person you're comparing yourself to. Saying "I am happy for you, but your success also reminds me of how much work I need to do" could clear the air.

WHAT'S HELPFUL

- Recognizing when you're comparing yourself to others
- Reframing your comparison language
- Accepting your discomfort
- Separating factual thoughts from judgments
- Competing against yourself

WHAT'S NOT HELPFUL

- Using words like "should," "wish," or "better"
- Using downward comparisons to temporarily boost your mood
- Viewing everyone as your competition
- Using social media to compare your life to the lives of other women

2

They Don't Insist
on Perfection

It's important to be willing to make mistakes. The worst thing that can happen is you become memorable.
—SARA BLAKELY

Shelby was a thirty-five-year-old woman who began therapy because she was experiencing anxiety. She'd been a stay-at-home mother for the past eight years, but once both of her children started school, she reentered the workforce.

At first, she was happy to be back at work. She liked her job, and she felt good about the money she was earning. "It felt great to be able to get out of the house and to be able to help contribute to the household again," she said.

But within a few months, things changed. She felt overwhelmed and stressed out. "I feel like being a stay-at-home mom for all those years turned me into a wimp," she said.

Shelby wanted to impress her employer, so she arrived at work early. She stayed up late packing lunches, doing laundry, and cleaning the house after the kids were asleep. Then, when she was done with all that, she dove into the unfinished paperwork from her job.

When she called my office to set up her initial appointment, the receptionist asked her what concern she wanted to address in therapy. Shelby said, "I don't think I was cut out to be a working mom."

Shelby spent several sessions talking about the reasons she shouldn't be a working mom. She said things like "I'm grouchy more often" and "I'm not making home-cooked meals for my family. My house isn't as clean as I want it to be, and it stresses me out."

She explained that her mother had always been a stay-at-home mom. She said, "I don't think my mom ever slept. She kept our home spotless. She made homemade bread for our sandwiches. And I never once heard her complain."

I also learned that Shelby had been a star athlete and a stellar student as a child. "I went to college on a tennis scholarship and I had a 4.0 GPA in school," she said.

Shelby's parents had always showered her with praise for being athletically and academically gifted. They were proud of her accomplishments, and it was important to her to please them.

School and sports came relatively easy to her. When she got married and had children, she excelled at being a stay-at-home mom. But now that she had reentered the workforce, she discovered there weren't enough hours in the day to be a perfect mother, perfect wife, and perfect employee.

For the first time in her life, she felt like she couldn't fix it. When she wanted to do better in school, she just studied longer. When she wanted to do better on the tennis court, she practiced harder. That wasn't an option now, because there weren't any more hours left in the day to become a better mother, a better wife, and a better employee.

Rather than cut herself some slack, however, Shelby was trying to double down. She was anxious because she wasn't able to squeeze thirty hours' worth of work into a twenty-four-hour day. She thought falling short of her goals and feeling exhausted reflected a lack of mental strength.

Shelby was hoping I could offer some relief. "Isn't there a pill I can take that will help?" she asked.

"What exactly would you hope a pill could do for you?" I replied.

"Well, I'm not sure if I'd rather have some sort of antianxiety medication that would calm me down, or a pill that would pump me up so I could get more done in less time," she said.

But there wasn't a magic pill to fix Shelby's stress. Instead, the key to feeling better was learning to give herself a break.

As a working mom, trying to accomplish all the things she was able to do as a stay-at-home mom came at a price—it cost her sleep and time with her family, and it was taking a toll on her psychological well-being.

Shelby's treatment involved several strategies: changing the way she evaluated herself, reducing her workload, and incorporating self-care practices into her life. Shelby handed some of the household chores to her family. The kids packed their lunches and did the dishes. Her husband became more involved in helping too. And Shelby changed her constant inner dialogue that told her she needed to be perfect.

Shelby had to accept that she had to lower her expectations of herself, not raise her performance. Cutting herself some slack wasn't easy, but once she gave herself permission to do less, she began to feel better.

Do You Insist on Perfection?

Some perfectionists have unrealistic expectations for themselves, while others strive to reach idealistic standards established by other people. Either way, striving for perfection isn't healthy. Do any of these statements sound like you?

❏ When I look in the mirror, I notice all the things I'd like to change about myself.

❏ When I'm working on a goal, I focus on the results more than the journey to success.

❏ If I try something new and I'm not good at it, I give up.

❏ Criticism feels like a personal attack—even when it's constructive feedback.

- When I'm finished with a project, I notice the small imperfections more than the things I like about it.
- I procrastinate sometimes because I fear my work won't be perfect.
- I struggle to call a project complete because I think I could always improve it somehow.
- I don't like people to see my home when things are out of place.
- I spend a lot of time thinking about how to improve my appearance.
- I experience anxiety when I feel like I'm not in complete control.

Why We Do It

Shelby revealed that she felt best about herself when other people told her she was doing a good job. She said, "No one ever says you're doing great work when you're in the middle of the pack. You have to be the best to really stand out."

But she also recognized that praise for being the best wasn't satisfying. In fact, it was a double-edged sword.

The more she accomplished, the more others expected from her, and she worried that she'd make a mistake that would ruin everything.

Like many women I've worked with, Shelby worried constantly about disappointing people or falling short of her goals. No matter how hard she worked, she never felt quite good enough.

The pressure to look, act, sound, and be perfect manifests itself in many ways. While the pressure may start out as external, many women adopt an internal dialogue that promotes perfection.

WOMEN ARE EXPECTED TO DO IT ALL WITHOUT BREAKING A SWEAT

Out of the dozens of women I interviewed for this book, one issue came up in almost every conversation—almost all the women mentioned feeling as though they were under a lot of pressure to do everything and to look good while doing it.

Leann, a fifty-four-year-old woman I spoke to, summed it up by saying, "I'm expected to work full-time, run the house, organize calendars, send emails, do all the shopping, and communicate with the school. I'm looked at as if I'm a bitch when I ask for help. Women are expected to work two to three full-time jobs. Men are expected to work forty hours and mow the lawn."

So while women have successfully entered the workforce, their domestic duties haven't shifted. In most households across the globe, women are still expected to manage the bulk of the household duties regardless of whether they have a full-time job.

Studies consistently show women tend to do the majority of domestic tasks, meal preparation, and childcare duties. Even in same-sex couples, one partner tends to take on the masculine chores while the other tends to handle more of the feminine duties. And the one with the feminine duties tends to take on the bulk of the household responsibilities.

A fifty-year study that spanned nineteen countries, from Australia to Israel, found a general movement toward gender equality between 1961 and 2011. In countries where housework was already more equal—like the Scandinavian countries, the United States, Canada, and Australia—researchers noted a slowing of gender convergence after the late 1980s.

In countries where men are more likely to be the main breadwinners, women spend much more time on household chores. On average, women in Spain and Italy do the most housework. Italian women spend four hours and twenty minutes on household chores per day—while their husbands spend seventeen minutes.

In Germany, women spend three times more time cooking and cleaning than men. That's an improvement from the 1960s, when women spent fourteen times more time doing household chores than men.

To put those numbers in perspective, women in the United States were doing seven times as much housework as men in 1965. As of 2010, women were doing twice as much housework as men.

It's unlikely that women enjoy cleaning more than men—laundry and dishes aren't fun for anyone. Women, however, feel pressure to have a cleaner house, because they're judged for the mess. Many women feel like heaps of dishes and piles of laundry mean that they're bad wives, mothers, or people.

In the past fifteen years, hundreds of women have come into my office to talk about how overwhelmed they have felt by their household duties. I can only recall a couple of men who've expressed similar sentiments. Many of the women came to therapy looking for strategies to become more efficient or more productive, because they felt inadequate in a world that insists women can "have it all."

The pressure women feel to be perfect isn't confined to their home's cleanliness, of course. There's also the added burden to look perfect. I interviewed a twenty-one-year-old college student about college life and she said, "I wake up two hours early just to get ready in the morning. Boys can roll out of bed and walk into class with pajama pants on and no one cares. But I feel like I have to do my hair, wear makeup, and always look a certain way if I want to be taken seriously."

A poll conducted by *Today* found that the average U.S. woman spends fifty-five minutes per day getting ready. That adds up to two weeks per year. Author Renee Engeln discusses this issue in *Beauty Sick* and says, "A *Women's Health* survey covered that finding with what felt like disingenuous shock. Their answer to the problem of too much of women's time being taken up by beauty? Timesaving tips like swapping out a regular hand lotion for a hand salve that lasts longer."

Of course, the survey conducted by *Today* only refers to a woman's daily hair and makeup routine in the morning. If you added in how much time women spend in other beauty rituals, such as getting their hair colored, nails painted, and body hair waxed, the annual number of weeks wasted on primping and grooming would likely skyrocket.

For women, looking good isn't just about vanity. In 2016, researchers from the University of Chicago and the University of California at Irvine found that women who don't invest as much time and money into their appearance may be at risk of losing a substantial amount of money. As in past studies, researchers found that attractive people tend to earn higher salaries. But their research also found that grooming practices accounted for nearly all of the salary differences for women of varying attractiveness. Their makeup, hairstyle, and clothing made a big difference. For men, the difference was negligible.

Michelle Obama addressed the double standard in dress codes when she spoke at Apple's Worldwide Developers Conference in San Jose, California, in early 2017. When talking about her experiences going to events with her husband, she said, "People take pictures of the shoes I wear, the bracelets, the necklace—they didn't comment that for eight years he wore the same tux, same shoes. He was proud of it too; he was like, 'Mmm! I'm ready. I'm ready in ten minutes, how long did it take you?'"

Managing household duties and looking beautiful is a burden. Many women feel compelled to try to meet unrealistically high expectations that drive them to try to be perfect.

PERFECTIONISM STEMS FROM TWISTED THINKING

A 2009 study published in the *Journal of Occupational and Organizational Psychology* found that a higher proportion of women than men felt as though they did not meet their own high standards with workplace and family commitments. At work, 38 percent of women said they felt they weren't meeting the high standards they set for themselves, compared to 24 percent of men. And at home, 30 percent of women felt inadequate, compared to 17 percent of men.

While some women feel pressure to be perfect to please others or to meet society's unrealistic expectations, others feel tension from within to be perfect. Of course, for many women, it's a mixture of both.

Take, for instance, Gwyneth Paltrow. She has won an Academy Award and Golden Globe Award for best actress. Despite that, she continues to struggle with feeling like she's not good enough. In an interview with the *Daily Mail* Paltrow said, "I never think I'm thin enough or toned enough or my boobs are big enough or whatever it is. We all carry around these things based on how society expects us to look."

Paltrow talked about her perfectionism in an interview with *Vogue* in

2010. She said, "Sometimes I think I'll have to check myself into a mental asylum, it gets so bad. I hate myself for it. It's like, what's wrong? Relax." Clearly, no matter how much fame, money, or beauty you possess, when you're a perfectionist, you'll never feel like you are good enough.

There are many reasons why women convince themselves they have to be perfect. Here are some other reasons deep-rooted inadequacies cause women to strive for perfection:

- **Desire to be loved and accepted**—Perfectionists often think if they can just be "good enough" somehow they'll be loved and accepted by other people.
- **Biological disposition**—Perfectionism runs in families, and researchers think there may be a genetic component that makes certain individuals more susceptible than others.
- **The way your parents raised you**—If your parents always praised you for getting perfect grades as opposed to studying hard, or for scoring the most goals in the game as opposed to hustling hard, you may have learned that a perfect outcome matters more than anything else.
- **Sensationalism of success**—The "go big or go home" slogan has become a mantra for many people in their pursuit of money, fame, and success. Anything short of perfection may feel like utter failure.
- **Trauma history**—Childhood trauma can also lead to perfectionism. Someone may think if she can be perfect she won't be abused. Or an individual may feel like she can prevent herself from being hurt again if she is able to maintain complete control over everything all the time.

Why It's Bad

Shelby wanted to be the perfect mother, wife, and employee. But the irony was, her perfectionism left her grouchy and overwhelmed—far from the idyllic woman she strived to be.

One day she said, "I think I should just quit working." When we explored her desire to quit, it wasn't because she thought quitting was really best for her family; it was because she felt inadequate. Although she was doing her best—and doing a great job—she didn't want to do anything if she couldn't do it perfectly. And for a long time, she believed her quest for perfection was an admirable trait.

Much like Shelby, many women think perfectionism is a badge of honor. But expecting more from yourself than you're able to give is a serious issue that can prevent you from living a fulfilling life. For many women, the quest for perfection takes a physical, financial, emotional, and social toll on their lives.

WOMEN ARE DYING TO LOOK PERFECT

I interviewed a twenty-three-year-old woman named Simone who had a lengthy history of being a perfectionist. Growing up, she'd been an honor student, a star athlete, and an overall model citizen. She said, "From the outside, I'm sure everyone thought I was just a happy overachiever, but I was miserable on the inside. I felt like if I made a mistake, I was going to ruin my life." She developed an eating disorder during her teen years—something that often goes hand in hand with perfectionism in young women.

She said, "I was anorexic. But for a long time people actually said I looked good. It was my doctor who first suggested I might have a problem." She now refers to herself as a "recovering perfectionist," but she says it's still a struggle to cut herself some slack. "Whenever I start to feel like things are getting a little too chaotic in my life, I feel my perfectionist tendencies start to kick back in. It's as if I think not eating gives me some kind of control in my life," she said.

Like Simone, many women go to great lengths to try to obtain the ideal image of beauty. And quite often, those lengths include dangerous diets, binging and purging, compulsive exercise, or fasting. A 2008 study conducted by the University of North Carolina at Chapel Hill found that 65 percent of women between the ages of twenty-five and forty-five report disordered eating behaviors. An additional 10 percent of women reported symptoms consistent with eating disorders, meaning that a total of 75 percent of all American women endorse unhealthy thoughts, feelings, or behaviors related to food or their body size.

A 2013 study published in the *Journal of Eating Disorders* found that women who wanted to be the smallest size were more concerned about making mistakes, were more worried about maintaining organization, and had higher levels of self-doubt than everyone else.

Perfectionism and other body image issues often go hand in hand as well. Rather than just accept they have a few body parts they don't love, many women are striving for perfection. A study by RealSelf.com found that one in five American women is considering plastic surgery at any given time. And the trend to seek help from a cosmetic doctor has risen 200 percent since 2000. A whopping 90 percent of women between the ages of eighteen and twenty-four are unhappy with at least one body part. And that number only declines slightly with age. Eighty-five percent of fifty-five- to sixty-four-year-olds say they're unhappy with at least one body part.

That's not to say women who seek plastic surgery or those who go to great lengths to improve their appearance aren't mentally strong. If you feel undergoing a procedure will help you feel better so you can do better, more power to you. But even if plastic surgery could make you look perfect, it won't repair self-esteem issues.

I interviewed a woman named Brittany who works in the magazine publishing industry. She said, "I've learned so much about women because we deal with models every month in our magazine. Even the most gorgeous models feel insecure inside. That gave me a new confidence to realize that we're all a little bit scared."

UNREALISTIC EXPECTATIONS LEAD
TO A DOWNWARD SPIRAL

You idiot. You just embarrassed yourself. You messed up again. You're never going to reach your goals. Being bombarded with that type of negativity from anyone would take a toll on you. But when that criticism comes from your own brain, you'll never be able to get a break from it.

Women who have high expectations are able to appreciate their success. When they reach a new milestone or achieve something new, they celebrate. Perfectionists, on the other hand, never feel satisfied. They focus on mistakes, worry they could have done better, and evaluate improvements they need to keep making. Ironically, their feelings of never being good enough create a downward spiral that prevents them from becoming their best.

Here are some other downsides to being a perfectionist:

- **Self-defeating behavior**—A 2016 study published in *Personality and Individual Differences* found that perfectionism leads to self-defeating behaviors, like binge eating, procrastination, and interpersonal conflict.
- **High risk of burnout**—Students and athletes who are perfectionists are at a greater risk of burnout. A 2017 study published in *Learning and Individual Differences* found that college students who were perfectionists experienced worse self-regulation, less engagement, and lower achievement than other students.
- **Fear of trying new things**—Perfectionists tend to use "avoidance coping." That means they avoid doing things where they might fail, or they avoid doing things when they think they might make a mistake.
- **High risk of mental health problems**—Perfectionists are more likely to experience anxiety, depression, eating disorders, and other mental health issues.
- **Greater risk of death**—A 2011 study published in the *Journal of Health Psychology* found that people who rank high on the perfectionism scale are 51 percent more likely to die earlier than those who rank low in perfectionism. Perfectionists heal slower from heart attacks, and their recovery is slower when they have issues like Crohn's disease and ulcerative colitis.

- **Less likely to be successful**—The top people in any field aren't usually perfectionists. Instead, the people who accomplish the most are more likely to take risks, learn from their mistakes, and accept that failure is part of the process.
- **Greater risk of suicide**—A 2014 study published in *Review of General Psychology* found that perfectionist professionals— including doctors, lawyers, and architects—are more likely to kill themselves. No matter how successful they are, failure, regret, and the fear of making mistakes may push them over the edge.

What to Do Instead

During one of her appointments, Shelby said, "I read an article about work-life balance for women. I think I just need to work harder to find that balance." She was convinced she could learn productivity tips and skills that would help her feel less frazzled and irritable. It was as if she even wanted to be a perfectionist at balancing life and work. What she didn't realize, however, was that working harder wasn't the solution. There wasn't a magical work-life balance that existed just beyond her reach.

In order to feel better, Shelby had to change the message she was telling herself. Instead of insisting she had to be the perfect mother, worker, and wife, she had to accept that being a working mom meant she was going to have to give some things up, and she couldn't do her best unless she was caring for herself.

There are many things you can do to overcome perfectionist tendencies. But before any of those things will work, you have to recognize that being a perfectionist hurts more than it helps.

IDENTIFY WHAT PERFECTIONISM COSTS YOU

Perfectionism often leads to self-sabotage. It sounds ridiculous on the surface, though. After all, why would you purposely ruin your chances of reaching your goals if you're intent on being perfect? It's an easy way to get rid of the tension and anxiety that you might feel over making a mistake.

I once worked with a woman who was a successful perfectionist in almost every area of her life. But she wasn't able to lose her baby weight after giving birth. She said, "I stay motivated for a few weeks, but then I end up blowing it. I eat everything in sight for several days. Why on earth can't I seem to reach my goal weight?"

When we explored her tendencies more closely, we discovered that she was terrified of failure. When she made healthy choices and saw progress, she felt anxious that she wouldn't be able to keep it up. She'd think, "I wonder how long this will last." or "What happens if I mess up?" To relieve her anxiety, she started eating. Then she didn't have to wonder how long she could maintain the "perfect diet."

She wasn't consciously doing this to herself. It just sort of happened. It took some digging for us to identify the pattern and the perfectionist tendencies that went into it.

Not everyone actively sabotages themselves, though. Some perfectionists procrastinate to their own detriment. They have six half-finished novels tucked in a drawer that they can never finish because they feel they're not good enough.

No matter how perfectionism rears its ugly head in your life, it's important to identify what your perfectionism costs you. Here are some questions to consider:

- Do you avoid going out with your friends when you don't feel you look good enough?
- Do your insecurities hurt your romantic relationships?
- Do you expect your kids to be perfect?
- Do you spend more than you can afford on clothing or cosmetics?
- Do you avoid inviting people into your home because you worry your house doesn't look good enough?

You can't change your expectations of yourself unless you recognize the specific ways perfectionism is doing more harm than good. Invest time into creating your list, and think about the ways perfectionism plays out in all areas of your life.

ASK YOURSELF, "WHAT WOULD IT MEAN?"

When you find yourself thinking that you have to be flawless—either because you want to achieve the standards you've set for yourself or because you want others to view you as perfect—think about what it would mean if you fell short. Ask yourself, "What would it mean?" a few times, and you'll uncover the meaning behind your desire to be perfect.

I used this strategy in my therapy office with a woman who felt she had to be perfect at her job. Despite positive reviews from her supervisors, she felt like she wasn't good enough. She worked longer and longer hours, but the more she worked, the less competent she felt. To help uncover the meaning behind her perfectionism, I asked her, "What would it mean?" several times until we got to the heart of the issues. Here's what we uncovered:

- **Original thought:** This report isn't good enough.
- **What would it mean if your report wasn't good enough?:** If my report isn't good enough, my boss will think I'm stupid.
- **What would it mean if your boss thought you were stupid?:** It'd mean I'd never get promoted.
- **What would it mean if you never got promoted?:** It'd mean I'm incompetent.

Her perfectionism masked her fear that she was incompetent. She convinced herself that if she could do better, somehow people would finally see that she was worthy of her job—even though deep down she didn't think she was smart enough or good enough to be there.

We all have a desire to be loved, be accepted, and be seen as competent, worthwhile people who have something to contribute. Perfectionism often masks the deep-rooted fears that somehow, we aren't good enough.

Another young woman I worked with tried hard to impress others. She invested countless hours and dollars into looking her best, and she constantly worried about how she was perceived. On the day before hosting a social event, she was especially stressed out about all the things she had to do to prepare. So we explored the meaning behind her perfectionist thoughts. Here's what it all boiled down to:

- **Thought:** I have to impress everyone for this party.
- **What would it mean if you didn't impress them?:** People might think I don't fit in with them.
- **What would it mean if people thought you don't fit in?:** They won't want to associate with me.
- **What would it mean if people didn't want to associate with you?:** I'm unlikable.

So she concluded that her best hope in attracting friends and romantic partners was to appear perfect on the outside, because deep down, she worried people wouldn't like her.

When you think you have to be perfect, ask yourself, "What would it mean if I wasn't?" Each time you ask that, you'll peel back another layer. Eventually, you'll uncover the core insecurity behind your quest for perfection.

OWN YOUR FLAWS

It sounds a bit cliché to say your imperfections are what make you unique. But sometimes, those things that make you different can help you succeed.

Take Cindy Crawford, for example. As a child, kids made fun of her for having a mole on her face and her sister teased her that it was an "ugly mark." She wanted to get it removed but her mother talked her out of it.

Ultimately, her mole became a characteristic that helped launch her modeling career. In an interview with *Into the Gloss,* Crawford said, "It's the thing that made people remember me, and it made a lot of women who also have beauty marks identify with me. They set you apart."

Having ears that are larger than you'd like or a scar on your arm from a bicycle mishap in the third grade might not land you a modeling contract. But, those things might give you a bit of character and aren't things you need to hide, fix, or change.

I work with a lot of people who have been told to "make a list of all the reasons you like yourself." While it's great to remind yourself of your good qualities, it's also important to acknowledge your imperfections. Creating a list of flaws isn't about shaming yourself. But it can be an exercise in honesty and courage.

Break your list down into two parts; things you can change and things you can't (or aren't going to). Your eye color, height, and shoe size fall into the "things you can't change" category. But, the things you can change will likely go beyond your superficial characteristics.

Maybe you are passive-aggressive toward friends when you feel offended. Or perhaps you have little patience for that coworker who asks a lot of questions. We all have some not-so-perfect habits.

Practice accepting the imperfections you can't change so you can put your energy into the things you have control over. Rather than waste time worrying that your toes are too ugly for sandals, work on something you can change, like how much money you spend.

You might decide that list is for your eyes only, but sharing it with someone else can be empowering sometimes. You don't have to announce your flaws publicly, but admitting them to someone—whether it's your spouse or your friend—can reinforce to you that people still love you, flaws and all. In fact, those closest to you already know you aren't perfect.

WRITE YOURSELF A KIND LETTER

Most of us wouldn't tolerate a friend, coworker, or loved one calling us names and putting us down all the time. Yet we often verbally abuse ourselves. Whether you repeatedly call yourself a loser or you constantly focus on all of your flaws, beating yourself up for your imperfections will take a toll on you. The best way to combat that negative voice in your head is to replace it with self-compassion.

Kristin Neff, a professor at the University of Texas at Austin and one of the world's top researchers on self-compassion, says, "Having compassion for oneself is really no different than having compassion for others." It's about treating yourself with kindness and recognizing that suffering, failure, and imperfection are part of the shared human experience.

While there are many ways to be kinder to yourself—and to give yourself a break from thinking you have to be perfect—one of my favorite exercises is to write a letter to yourself. Similar to the way you might write an encouraging note to a friend who is going through a tough time, write some encouraging words to yourself.

It could be a few simple sentences like:

"Life is hard sometimes, but you've got this. Even though you'll want to give up or there will be times when you feel like you've messed everything up, you'll be OK. Life isn't about never making a mistake. It's about moving forward, flaws and all—and enjoying each step of the journey along the way."

Stash your letter in your purse, put it in your pocket, or hang it on the bathroom mirror. Read it often—especially when you're having a hard time. Reading over your kind words can help you develop a kinder inner dialogue. Rather than beat yourself up for your mistakes, you'll train your brain to talk to yourself more like you'd speak to a trusted friend.

Career

As I approached college graduation, I applied for a handful of jobs. To my delight, I was invited to interview for every position I applied for. To my further delight, I was offered a job at all five places.

I chose the one that had the best hours and highest starting salary. After a few years, I applied for a new job. I got an interview and a job offer shortly after.

I can remember saying, "I've gotten every job I've ever applied for," as if that were something to brag about. It wasn't. For starters, there was a social-work shortage, so many employers were thrilled to have applicants (for all I know, I was the only person who applied). Second, getting every job you apply for probably means you aren't striving to reach your greatest potential.

Rejection means you're reaching for something bigger and better. It says you're stepping outside of your comfort zone and stretching yourself to see how far you can go.

But it can be tempting sometimes to try to avoid failure, so you can maintain a perfect record. Being rejected or being turned down is tolerable.

Keep in mind, at the end of your life no one will be there to hand you an award for "never failing." And it's not likely that people will remember you as "the woman who always got the jobs she applied for." However, they may admire you for being brave, stretching beyond your comfort zone, and striving to do your best.

Family

Perfectionism can easily spill over into your family relationships. After all, your children are an extension of you, right? And if you want to live a perfect life, you'll need a perfect partner to complete the package.

But expecting your family to be perfect wreaks havoc on your relationships. Whether you put pressure on your children to get straight As, or you insist your partner do a better job of washing the car, your insistence on perfection won't actually get you there.

In fact, the more you expect others to be perfect, the more likely they are to fail to meet your expectations. If you expect more from people than they give, they'll usually try their hardest for a while. But once they see it's a lost cause, they'll give up. They'll stop trying to reach your standards, because they'll know they're doomed to fail anyway.

Be mindful of how you react when your partner forgets to pick up milk on the way home from work. And pay attention to the way you respond when your child gets a bad grade. Responding too harshly to your family members' mistakes won't motivate them to do better. Instead, you'll push them away and harm your relationships.

Social Life

One of my former clients began therapy because she felt frustrated by her social life. She said, "I think I need new friends who aren't losers."

When I asked her why she thought they were losers she said, "I like to make plans a few weeks in advance so I can get it on the calendar, but most of them can't plan that far ahead. When it comes to making reservations or buying tickets for an event, I have to do all the work." There wasn't any real reason that she needed so much advance notice—other than she liked to plan far ahead.

She thought she was well organized and a great "planner," but she was actually quite anxious. In an effort to control her anxiety, she tried to control everything around her. She had little tolerance for those who didn't do what she wanted according to her schedule.

Treatment involved letting go of her expectations that her friends be perfect. She had to see that social gatherings weren't always going to be perfect either—at least not to her standard of perfection. Most of her friends were spontaneous, and they didn't care if they had reservations at the best restaurants, or if they had tickets to every event. They just wanted to spend time together and have fun without feeling as though it had to be planned months in advance.

Sometimes, lowering your expectations of other people can go a long way toward preserving your relationships. If you insist other people behave in a way that will meet your need for perfection, you'll be disappointed. Recognize that other people have different standards, and that your friends aren't under any obligation to meet the expectations you have set for them.

A Willingness to Be Imperfect Makes You Stronger

As a young, beautiful blond woman, Sophie Gray seemed to have everything. She was an Instagram model with over four hundred thousand followers, and every day she posted pictures of her six-pack abs and diet and fitness tips. Her audience responded with hashtags like #LIFEGOALS and #PERFECTBODY.

But Sophie felt like she was living a lie. As she poured everything she had into making it look like she had the perfect life, she was looking at other people's Instagram accounts with envy. And she felt like her own life was falling apart.

She was secretly struggling with crippling anxiety. One day it all came to a head. She had a panic attack in the airport and couldn't force herself to get on a connecting flight. She and her boyfriend had to rent a car and drive thirty-eight hours home.

She knew a lot of her fans had anxiety too, and she felt as though her six-pack ab photos probably weren't helping them. "I don't want to compound anyone's pain and anxiety with my portrayal of a so-called perfect life or body," she told *Marie Claire* magazine. "I want to reach out in understanding and compassion to my followers who are living with anxiety and help them through it too. And that way, I will feel that every experience I have with my own 'troubles' is worth it."

Sophie decided to start showing real pictures of herself online—sometimes without makeup. She started keeping her midriff covered, and decided to show what her real life is actually like.

On her blog, she explains how much better she feels now that she doesn't succumb to the pressure to maintain the façade of perfection. Instead, she's focused on being real and helping people love themselves for who they are, not how they look.

Giving up the idea that you need to be perfect doesn't mean you'll sell yourself short. You can still have high expectations for yourself. But you can also love yourself for who you are—flaws and all. True mental strength is about cutting yourself a break sometimes. It involves forgiving yourself when you make a mistake and knowing that you'll be OK, even if you fail.

Troubleshooting and Common Traps

It can be hard to expose your flaws if you have built up an image of perfection. If you fell into the role of the perfect daughter as a child, it can be hard to break out of the mold. When parents say things like "Susan has always been such a good girl," or "Susan has always been the one we can count on," it can be tempting to make sure you're always living up to those expectations.

No one wants to risk falling from their family's good graces or to disappoint their parents. But sometimes, you have to stop trying to fill the role of the perfect child. It may mean saying no to certain things your parents ask of you, or it could mean talking about some of your mistakes or failures in front of them.

Another common trap is postponing happiness. Too many women think "I'll enjoy life when I get promoted" or "I'll be happy when I finally start my own business." But life is happening right now. Enjoy the journey and embrace the imperfections along the way.

Many perfectionists have perfected the art of hiding their inner turmoil. Consequently, they don't tell their doctors or therapists about their struggles because they fear letting down their guard. If you struggle with perfectionism to the point that it interferes with your daily functioning, seek professional help. It can be very treatable, and the sooner you get help, the sooner you can start feeling better.

WHAT'S HELPFUL

- Identifying what perfectionism costs you
- Asking yourself, "What would it mean?" to get to the core issues
- Admitting your flaws to yourself and someone else
- Writing a kind letter to yourself and reading it often
- Recognizing when you expect too much from other people

WHAT'S NOT HELPFUL

- Expecting other people to be perfect
- Using harsh words to criticize yourself
- Assuming that you must be flawless to succeed
- Hiding your flaws from others

3

They Don't See Vulnerability as a Weakness

Vulnerability is the last thing I want you to see in me,
but the first thing I look for in you.
—BRENÉ BROWN

Veronica began therapy because she wanted help managing her anxiety. When I asked her what types of things made her anxious, she said, "Almost everything—work, social situations, family gatherings, you name it."

Although she said *everything* made her feel anxious, the more she talked, the more it became clear that her anxiety usually spiked when she was in social settings. Then, as our hour-long conversation came to a close, she stood up and casually stated, "Oh, I should probably mention I have Tourette's syndrome. See you next week!"

Doorknob confessions are rather common in therapy. Just as people are about to leave—often with their hand on the doorknob—they blurt out a major revelation and sprint out the door. So when Veronica returned the following week, I asked her to tell me more about her Tourette's at the beginning of the session.

She said, "Oh, it's not a big deal. I have a few facial tics, but people never really notice." She'd found some clever ways to disguise her tics, which consisted mostly of slight grimaces and nose scrunching. Sometimes she rubbed her eyes. At other times, she'd scratch her nose. I'd noticed she was fidgety during our first meeting, and I'd suspected it was anxiety related. But she did a great job of keeping her tics well hidden.

Veronica had a history of vocal tics too—constant throat-clearing. Her vocal tics only became apparent when she was feeling really anxious, so to keep them at bay, she avoided things that caused a dramatic spike in anxiety, like public speaking.

Veronica said, "I'm concerned other people will think my tics are a big deal. I'm used to them, but I worry other people will think I'm crazy." She avoided social situations whenever possible and when she couldn't avoid a situation, she went to great lengths to disguise her tics. Consequently, only a fraction of her attention went into the conversation. The bulk of her energy was spent trying to prevent people from noticing her facial tics.

It was no wonder she was anxious. She was harboring a secret.

The only people she socialized with were the friends and family members who knew she had Tourette's. She felt lonely and isolated. She wanted to get involved in a romantic relationship, but she shied away from dating because it just felt "too scary."

It was important for Veronica to socialize, and the best way to overcome her fears was to face them head-on. But before she could do that, she needed to know that she didn't have to hide her tics from everyone she met.

She agreed to try being more open about her Tourette's with others, just as an experiment. She had no idea how people might react, since she hadn't told anyone about it since she was a kid.

She began by saying to a supervisor, "You may have noticed I look fidgety sometimes. I wanted to explain that it's because I have Tourette's and when I get nervous, my facial tics get worse." To her relief, her supervisor was kind and supportive. That was a big deal for her, because she had feared her tics would be perceived as a weakness, and any weakness in the workplace would be considered a disadvantage.

From there, she told a few of her coworkers. No one overreacted or made a big deal out of it. Some of them knew others who had tics or Tourette's, and others asked her questions or revealed some of their hidden struggles too.

With each successful revelation, Veronica gained a bit of courage and confidence in her ability to socialize. She felt less pressure to disguise her tics and no longer felt like she needed to withdraw from social activity.

During one of our final sessions, she said, "I kept thinking other people were going to make it a big deal. But hiding it for a long time and then making a 'big announcement' actually meant I was the one making it a big deal."

Do You View Vulnerability as a Weakness?

Many people think vulnerability is a weakness, but letting down your guard doesn't mean you're soft. In fact, a willingness to put yourself out there means you know you're strong enough to risk being hurt. Do any of the following points sound like you?

- ❏ I have a lot of acquaintances but I don't form deep friendships.
- ❏ I prefer to keep conversation superficial and I don't like to talk about myself or my past, even with people I know well.
- ❏ I have trouble trusting people.
- ❏ I think if people knew the real me, they wouldn't like me.
- ❏ There are certain parts of my life that I think I need to keep hidden from everyone.
- ❏ I fear if I let anyone get too close to me, they will hurt me.
- ❏ I rarely share my true opinions, because I fear people will judge me.
- ❏ Sometimes, I become too needy in relationships because I'm terrified of being abandoned or hurt.
- ❏ I fear loving someone more than they love me.
- ❏ I avoid putting myself in situations where I may fail or be rejected.

Why We Do It

Veronica said being a girl with Tourette's was particularly tough growing up. Since it's a condition that affects more boys than girls, she didn't know any other girls who had it. She said, "Boys with Tourette's often become class clowns as kids. They draw even more attention to themselves as a way to cope. As a girl, I felt like that wasn't an option. I feared being the weird girl, or the girl who stood out for all the wrong reasons."

Becoming an adult with Tourette's introduced new issues. She said, "Some of my mother's friends or people from my hometown who know I have Tourette's have asked if my kids will get Tourette's. The men I know who have Tourette's never get asked that question. In fact, if I asked them about it, I'm sure none of them would even know whether Tourette's is genetic."

Veronica had never even been in a long-term relationship, and she wasn't sure she wanted to have kids. As a woman, however, she felt like there was a huge value placed on her reproductive capabilities. She feared that letting people know she had Tourette's would lead to more conversations about whether she was "genetically worthy of reproducing." So, rather than address the issue, she thought it was easier to hide her tics.

While you may not have a condition like Tourette's that you hide from the world, you probably have at least one vulnerability you keep secret. Maybe you feel self-conscious about your math skills. Or perhaps you grew up with a parent who was an alcoholic. Whatever it is, there's likely a part of you or your past that you mask, hide, or cover up.

NO SELF-RESPECTING WOMAN WANTS TO LOOK WEAK

I have a friend who used to work for a major financial corporation. The company's female vice president gave birth to her baby on a Friday. She returned to work the following Monday.

Not taking a single day of maternity leave was a badge of honor for her. She prided herself on the fact that she was physically and emotionally capable of returning to work immediately after giving birth. It was as if she feared that spending time with her new baby or taking time to care for herself would be viewed as weakness. My friend who worked in the same institution said she never felt pressure from her employer to do that. In fact, she said many of the bosses seemed shocked she returned to work.

But perhaps this supervisor felt she had to fight back against the entrenched notion that women are the weaker sex. But she went too far. Her effort to prove she wasn't needy, incompetent, or helpless could have crossed the line into unhealthy.

Despite the fact that "self-care" has become a self-improvement buzzword, acknowledging that you need to care for yourself can still feel like a weakness. Have you ever denied that you were sleeping when someone calls and wakes you up? Have you ever forced yourself to go into work when you were sick because you thought staying home would be too wimpy?

Your game face serves a purpose. It might intimidate your opponent if you're an athlete. Or it might help you get through a doctor's appointment when you're learning bad news about a family member's test results. Pretending you're OK may prevent painful emotions—and the people who evoke them—from hurting you.

Many women learned to put up protective barriers in childhood. When the bully picked on you and then made fun of you for crying, you learned to pretend those harsh words didn't sting. Or when you told your friend a secret and she told the whole school, you stopped trusting anyone with personal information ever again. Those little moments taught you about people and how much you could allow them into your life.

Your childhood relationships with your caregivers also play a major role in how vulnerable you're willing to be. If you grew up with loving, trustworthy parents who taught you excellent emotional and communication skills, you'll likely be able to trust other people.

If however, your parents, teachers, and caregivers were cold, distant, or abusive, you may expect people to treat you poorly. And you might have concluded that growing close to people is pointless, since they'll only hurt you in the end.

You carry those beliefs into adulthood—about when it's safe to let your guard down or when it's OK to let people in. If you were hurt too much or too often, there's a good chance you'll become overprotective of yourself as an adult.

WOMEN ARE JUDGED HARSHLY FOR BEING EMOTIONAL

One of the women I interviewed for this book was a twenty-six-year-old named Heather. When I asked her about her experiences in the workplace, she told me about the pressure she felt to never show emotion in the corporate world. She said, "I am the kind of person who wears her heart on her sleeve. But I learned really early on that you can't show when you're scared or sad at work. I'm a crier. And when someone hurts my feelings, I can't help it, I cry. So I have to go into the bathroom and cry so no one sees, and then I have to try and make it look like I wasn't crying before I can go back out there. But that's hard when you've got mascara running down your face."

While both sexes feel pressure to have a tough exterior, women feel that pressure in a different way. In general, girls are taught it's OK to cry, but boys are told to toughen up. As adults, women tend to cry more than men. In some parts of the world, women only cry a little more than men, but in American culture, women tend to cry a lot more than men.

Yet women aren't supposed to cry in public—especially in the workplace. Crying at work can be the kiss of death, which means women carry the emotional burden to fight back tears in the workplace.

Kimberly Elsbach, a professor at the UC Davis Graduate School of Management, has conducted extensive research on women crying in the workplace. She discovered that women are often viewed as "weak, unprofessional, and manipulative" when they shed tears at work. They are judged harshly by both men and women.

It's a strange dynamic. We tell little girls it's OK to cry, and in general, most people would acknowledge that crying is healthy. But at the same time, we say, "Just make sure you don't do it in public—especially in the workplace." Emotional expression in the office is forbidden—mostly because it seems to make other people feel uncomfortable.

Sadness isn't the only emotion that comes with a stigma attached for women. Anger brings about another whole set of issues. In general, people are tolerant of angry men, but not angry women.

A 2015 study published in *Law and Human Behavior* examined the perceptions of angry men versus angry women. The experiment involved 210 undergraduate students who participated in a computerized mock-jury simulation that took place over an instant-messenger program.

Participants were told they were assigned to six-person virtual juries with others in the study. They were presented a real-life murder case and asked to deliberate in a chat room with the other jury members. Throughout the deliberations, they reported their verdict and their level of confidence in their decision.

Unbeknownst to participants, the chat room was scripted by the researchers. In each chat, four of the other jurors agreed with the participant's verdict and one juror disagreed. The juror who disagreed (referred to as the holdout juror) was either a man named Jason or a woman named Alicia. The holdout juror either showed no emotion or used clear expressions of anger, like typing, "SERIOUSLY, THIS JUST MAKES ME ANGRY," and "OK, THIS IS GETTING REALLY FRUSTRATING." During the discussion, one juror would switch their verdict to agree with the holdout.

Following the deliberation, participants reported their final verdict, and they weighed in on how confident they felt about their decision. They also completed a survey to report how they perceived their co-jurors.

When the holdout was a male who expressed anger, participants were more likely to doubt their own opinion, even when they were in the majority. But if the holdout was a woman who expressed anger, the participants were more likely to become increasingly confident in their opposing view. The participants found the men's anger to be powerful and persuasive. Yet the women's anger worked against them.

Unfortunately, many women have found this to be true in the workplace as well. When a male raises his voice in a meeting, he's viewed as a leader. When a woman raises her voice, she's seen as "out of control." In an effort to avoid being dubbed the "emotional crazy woman" in the office, many women put up protective barriers that prevent anyone from detecting their emotions.

Acting as if you're happy all the time—but not overly happy—may provide some benefits. But refusing to be vulnerable has some downsides too.

Why It's Bad

It had become second nature for Veronica to disguise her tics and avoid social situations where people might notice. Consequently, she couldn't put much energy into forming and maintaining relationships—all of her effort went into trying to hide her secret. It kept her from developing close bonds with new people.

One week she said, "I'm envious of my childhood friends. They've all developed lots of new friendships over the years. But I feel like I'm stuck. I can't really get close to anyone new."

When you refuse to let people in and keep them from knowing the real you, most likely all of your relationships will stay superficial at best. And, in the same way, if you are afraid of embarrassing yourself, you'll struggle to step outside of your comfort zone and reach your greatest potential.

PUTTING UP A TOUGH EXTERIOR PREVENTS MEANINGFUL CONNECTIONS

My former client Dawn had a history of unhealthy relationships, and she assumed it was because she was attracting the wrong type of men. "I choose the wrong people every time," she said.

She talked about her current relationship—a rocky romance with a man named Craig. She was convinced Craig was cheating on her. Whenever they weren't together, she called or texted him incessantly to accuse him of talking to other women.

In response to her constant accusations, Craig avoided spending time with her. He sought solace from his friends and family—which in turn reinforced Dawn's notion that Craig didn't love her.

Dawn had fallen into a pattern that many people who fear vulnerability get into—the more emotional she felt, the crazier she acted. Behind all the yelling, accusations, and threats was a big ball of anxiety that told her she was going to get hurt.

Dawn had orchestrated this tug-of-war type of pattern in every relationship she'd ever been in. Her frantic fear of abandonment led her to push people away. Essentially, she made her biggest fears come true in every relationship she was in.

Dawn's anxiety stemmed from her refusal to be vulnerable in her communication. If she could just say, "I'm feeling anxious right now because I think you don't want to be with me. I could really use some reassurance," Craig may have been able to reassure her. Then they could grow closer and have a healthier relationship. But she had to be willing to express her emotions.

Dawn's assumption that she attracted the wrong men wasn't accurate. Instead, she was pushing the good men out of her life with her behavior. Like many women I've worked with, Dawn struggled to form meaningful connections because her insecurities prevented her from developing healthy attachments.

While there are many ways your fear of vulnerability can harm your relationships, here are a few common examples:

- You never get too close in romantic relationships because you fear being rejected.
- You don't tell your loved ones when your feelings are hurt.
- You don't invite acquaintances to social engagements because you fear they don't like you as much as you like them.
- You avoid telling people about your personal life because you fear they won't like you.

If you think being vulnerable makes you weak—no matter how it manifests itself—your relationships will never be as close as they could be. Whether you struggle with romantic intimacy or you have few close friends, you'll keep people at a distance to prevent them from being able to hurt you.

A FIXED MIND-SET WILL KEEP YOU STUCK

A refusal to be vulnerable hurts more than just your relationships, however. It can also interfere with your ability to live life to its fullest.

Avoiding failure and preventing mistakes often stems from a fear of vulnerability—and it's something women may be more prone to than men. According to Carol Dweck, author of *Mindset,* women are socialized to develop a fixed mind-set. They learn that their mistakes stem from character flaws, rather than behaviors that can be improved.

Dweck's research has found that gender differences in the reaction to failure can be found in young children. Boys are more likely to assume a bad test score means they didn't pay attention in class. Girls, on the other hand, are more likely to assume they got a bad grade because they aren't smart enough.

Dweck says this difference stems from the way adults respond to girls differently than boys. Her research found that teachers were more likely to give boys effort-based feedback when they fail and ability-based feedback when they succeed. So if a boy fails, a teacher may be more likely to say, "You need to study harder next time." But when a boy succeeds, the teacher is more likely to say, "You are smart."

Girls, however, are more likely to receive feedback that their failures stem from their lack of ability while their successes are due to good behavior. So a teacher is more likely to tell a girl, "Math comes hard to you," when she fails and is more likely to say, "You do well on tests because you pay attention in class," when she succeeds.

So it's no wonder women fear being vulnerable. If you think a single error means you are incompetent, you'll be much more likely to prevent failure or hide your mistakes.

A fixed mind-set prevents people from reaching their greatest potential. Here are some dangers:

- **You'll avoid challenges rather than overcome them.** Instead of applying for a promotion or running for PTA president, you'll stay within your comfort zone to avoid the sting of failure.
- **You'll react to criticism rather than learn from it.** Whether you lash out in anger at someone who gives you feedback or you ignore criticism that you don't like, you can't learn from other people unless you're willing to consider what they have to say.
- **You'll feel threatened by others' success rather than find inspiration in it.** If you believe natural talent is something you're born with, you may grow resentful of people who seem to be given more abilities than you.

What to Do Instead

Veronica wanted to get out into the world and meet new people. Putting herself out there meant she had to risk getting hurt, however. Some people might not understand her condition. They might look at her strangely, ask rude questions, or make assumptions about her. But, putting herself out there also meant she might form some amazing relationships with new people.

To help give her the push she needed, she wrote a letter to herself about all the reasons why it was a good idea to be more vulnerable. Then, before heading out to a new situation, she read the letter before she walked out the door. She reminded herself that even if someone wasn't accepting of her, she'd be OK.

Putting yourself in a position to be judged by other people is hard, but it's worth it. You don't have to face all your fears at once. Instead, you can take small steps toward becoming a little more vulnerable every day.

IDENTIFY YOUR PROTECTIVE ARMOR

The fear of vulnerability manifests itself in many ways. So while one person may become a perfectionist (like we talked about in chapter 2) to ward off feeling incompetent, someone else may act like a prickly pear to prevent people from getting too close. No matter what form it takes, these shields are meant to minimize hurt and pain.

Consider the protective armor you use to keep yourself safe. You may have one strategy you use at the office and a completely different shield you use at a home. But those strategies have likely become second nature, and you may have no idea that you use them.

We all create rules that protect us from being hurt. For example:

- If I don't speak up in meetings, no one will think I'm dumb.
- If I avoid talking about my childhood, no one will ask about my parents.
- If I exceed my boss's expectations, she won't see I don't belong here.
- If I act like I'm not interested, no one will see that I'm too scared to try.
- If I cry when he starts to talk about things I don't want to hear, he'll stop.

A helpful way to uncover some of the armor you use is to ask yourself these questions: What's the most painful emotion I could ever experience? What do I do to avoid that emotion?

Someone who thinks embarrassment is intolerable may sit quietly in the back of the room and avoid being the center of attention at all costs. Meanwhile, someone who thinks loneliness is the most difficult emotion may jump into a new relationship as soon as one relationship ends.

You can also uncover some of your protective armor by thinking about your anger. Anger is a powerful protective shield. It feels better to be angry than sad or hurt. Anger gives you energy, but just below the surface, fear, embarrassment, and pain often lurk.

If someone criticizes you and you lash out and call them an idiot, you might be masking the pain their feedback stirred up. Or, when you yell at your partner, you might be sidestepping the issues you don't want to discuss. While there's nothing wrong with being angry, it's important to consider how anger might be covering up more painful emotions.

OWN YOUR STORY

If anyone has a right to crawl under a rock and not come out again, it'd be Monica Lewinsky. The whole world knew she'd had an affair with the president. Her conversations about their intimate moments were secretly recorded and broadcast all over the globe.

If that weren't bad enough, she had to testify about the sexual acts she engaged in with the president while under oath. Every gory detail was discussed and scrutinized, right down to the infamous blue dress.

Unfortunately for Monica, the story broke in 1998—around the same time most households gained access to the internet. It was one of the first stories to reach people around the world with a single click. She was vilified, taunted, and cyberbullied—long before we had a name for cyberbullying. The paparazzi followed her relentlessly as she was shamed and humiliated for her actions.

After leaving the White House, Monica had trouble finding a job—organizations didn't want to be associated with the president's mistress. When she tried selling handbags, the media accused her of trying to capitalize on her notoriety. She laid low for years, but the media firestorm continued on and off for a decade.

Eventually, she went to grad school in England, where she got her master's degree in psychology. Upon returning to the United States, she struggled to find work and she found herself in a dark place. She avoided the public eye as much as possible but floundered in her attempts to move forward.

Then in 2010, she heard about Tyler Clementi—a freshman at Rutgers University whose roommate secretly broadcast him kissing another man via webcam. Tyler was shamed and humiliated on social media and a few days later, he jumped off the George Washington Bridge and killed himself.

Monica understood the depths of the anguish Tyler must have felt, because she too had her most private moments circulated around the globe. In an article for *Vanity Fair,* Monica said, "In the wake of Tyler's tragedy, my own suffering took on a different meaning. Perhaps by sharing my story, I reasoned, I might be able to help others in their darkest moments of humiliation."

She went on to say, "I turned forty last year, and it is time to stop tiptoeing around my past—and other people's futures. I am determined to have a different ending to my story. I've decided, finally, to stick my head above the parapet so that I can take back my narrative and give a purpose to my past."

Shortly thereafter, Monica decided to speak up against the culture of humiliation. She's since given a TED talk that's been viewed twelve million times.

As Brené Brown, a top researcher on shame, says, "Courage starts with showing up and letting ourselves be seen." And that's exactly what Monica was willing to do. She bravely stood up and owned her story. She put herself out there and risked further ridicule, but she did so to encourage others to create a more compassionate world in hopes that fewer people will ever have to experience the shame and humiliation she felt.

While your story may not include public humiliation on a global level, you still have a tale to tell. And just like Monica, you can choose to find purpose in the struggles that you've endured—rather than hiding behind your own vulnerabilities and not letting them come out.

Perhaps you pick a different path so you can choose a different ending to your story. Or maybe you're willing to talk about what you've learned so you can prevent others from repeating your mistakes. Whatever your story is, owning it requires you to be vulnerable. You have to acknowledge your mistakes, face your fears, and risk being hurt.

BE CONSCIOUS ABOUT BEING VULNERABLE

During an initial therapy appointment with a client, a woman once said to me, "Whenever I'm on a first date I always say I was molested as a child. Then I find out right away if my date can handle my past." Needless to say, she hadn't had much luck in the romance department.

Upon getting to know her a little more, it became clear that she wasn't just telling potential suitors about her history of sexual abuse. She told friends, acquaintances, coworkers, and virtual strangers about her horrific past. She thought broadcasting her abuse meant she was authentic. In reality, however, she was blurting out her story because she hadn't healed.

She felt like she was carrying around a deep, dark secret, and she thought people could tell there was something wrong with her just by looking at her. So, in an effort to relieve her anxiety, she shared private details of her abuse history with almost everyone she met.

While someone else might say, "Hi, I'm a lawyer," this woman was essentially announcing, "Hi, I'm a wounded person with a painful past." She felt relieved as soon as she got it off her chest, but other people weren't sure how to handle that information. Some withdrew, while others expressed sympathy. But either way, it took a toll on her relationships— romantic and otherwise.

Therapy helped her heal some of the emotional wounds that she'd never properly addressed. And part of the healing process was learning to recognize that her history of abuse was something that happened to her; it wasn't who she was. Over time, she became more comfortable in her own skin and she felt less compelled to tell everyone she met about her traumatic past. She learned that she could keep details of her life private without harboring a huge secret.

There's a big difference between privacy and secrecy. Privacy is voluntary. Secrecy isn't.

Be conscious about who you are sharing private information with and when you're sharing it. You don't have to be vulnerable with everyone you meet. You should form a trusting relationship first before sharing too many details of your private life. When you can do that, you'll own your story, rather than allow your story to own you.

PRACTICE BEING VULNERABLE

No one ever wakes up one day and suddenly becomes proficient at being humble, listening to criticism, or letting down their guard. Allowing yourself to be vulnerable is a skill. And like any other skill, it takes practice.

Here are some questions to ask yourself to help you become more vulnerable:

- **What gets in the way of being vulnerable?** Are you afraid it will feel too uncomfortable? Do you fear what other people will think? Are you not sure how to begin? Identifying the obstacles will help you overcome them.
- **Who are people I can become more vulnerable with?** Carefully select the people whom you might want to become more vulnerable with—a partner, a close friend, or a family member is usually a good place to start.
- **What's one small thing I can do to be vulnerable today?** For some people, inviting a neighbor out for coffee might take a great deal of courage. After all, she might say no. For others, asking for help is a big step. Identify something you can do and take action.
- **How can I take care of myself when I'm being vulnerable?** Think about the healthy strategies you'll use to take care of yourself when uncomfortable emotions get stirred up. Going for a walk, taking some deep breaths, writing in a journal, and watching a funny movie are just a few things you might do to manage your emotions in a healthy way.

You don't have to start out becoming more vulnerable by opening old wounds or digging into the darkest parts of your past. Instead, you can be more vulnerable in your everyday conversations with people. Here are some phrases that you could incorporate into your conversations to reflect your vulnerability:

- I'm sorry.
- I need help.
- I made a mistake.
- I'm scared.
- My feelings are hurt.
- I was wrong.

With practice, becoming vulnerable becomes a little bit easier. That's not to say you won't get hurt sometimes, but you'll gain confidence in your ability to handle discomfort and you'll be on track to living a richer, fuller life.

Career

The idea that you should "never let them see you sweat" makes sense—especially in the workplace. Masking your weaknesses, suppressing your emotions, and insisting you have everything handled comes at a price, however. After all, it's sort of silly that we pretend as if emotions, personal issues, and past experiences don't play a role in the workplace.

You might be tempted to think vulnerability has no place in the office, since women who get dubbed too emotional aren't viewed as credible. But you don't necessarily need to shed tears in a meeting to be more vulnerable in the office.

It's possible to be vulnerable at work without baring your soul to your boss or wearing your heart on your sleeve. Vulnerability at work may mean:

- Speaking up in a meeting when you have an idea about how to improve things
- Apologizing when you've hurt someone
- Showing compassion to someone who is struggling
- Trying something new, even when you know you might fail
- Announcing your latest entrepreneurial venture on social media
- Telling people about your new product idea
- Reaching out to a contact to discuss a possible collaboration

Family

When one of my former clients heard that her toddler was using the potty at daycare, she was upset. She'd been trying to toilet train her son at home to no avail. He'd shown no interest in toilet training. She said, "I think the daycare workers are rushing him so they'll have fewer diapers to change during the day."

She immediately started researching alternative daycare options. "I want to find people who have my child's best interest at heart," she said. But none of the daycares she contacted had any openings.

After a few days, she calmed down a bit and asked to meet with the teacher to discuss her concerns. She learned that her son had shown interest after several of his toddler friends began toilet training. The workers cheered for kids each time they successfully used the restroom and her son seemed to want to get in on the action.

After hearing the story, my client felt embarrassed. She'd jumped to a conclusion that the daycare workers were lazy or that they were trying to outshine her somehow. But underneath her anger was hurt. She'd felt like an incompetent parent and she thought the daycare workers were upstaging her. Listening to the teacher took vulnerability.

It can be especially hard to be vulnerable when you feel like your role as a mother, wife, daughter, or sister is being threatened. And while your instinct may be to become defensive, you may lose out on opportunities to grow better and become stronger.

When you feel hurt, avoid jumping to conclusions and lashing out in anger. Take a deep breath and make a conscious effort to be more vulnerable.

Social Life

Technology has changed the way we interact with people. Social invitations are often sent over text message or social media. And rather than ask, "Do you want to go shopping with me?" many people are inclined to say something more like "I'm going shopping. Let me know if you want to go." Wording it this way means you don't have to face rejection.

And while it also means you don't have to put someone on the spot, saying "You can join me if you want" is also a way to protect yourself. If the other individual doesn't respond or she says she's busy, it can sting less than hearing an outright "No."

There are many ways to become more vulnerable in your relationships. Here are just a few examples:

- Say "I love you" first.
- Send a note to someone to tell them how much they mean to you.
- Speak up when your feelings are hurt.
- Apologize when you've messed up.
- Share your failures and embarrassing moments.

Being Vulnerable Makes You Stronger

From *21 Jump Street* and *Hangin' with Mr. Cooper* to *The Talk* and *Love, Inc.,* Holly Robinson Peete has been a TV icon for thirty years. She's married to former NFL quarterback Rodney Peete, and together the couple has four children.

But their journey hasn't always been easy. And Holly isn't afraid to talk publicly about the struggles the family has experienced.

In 2000, one of their twin sons was diagnosed with autism. The added strain of raising a child with special needs brought their relationship to the brink of divorce.

In a 2010 interview with *Redbook* magazine, Holly says she and Rodney grew distant and describes the role she played in their turmoil. "I needed help, but I kept pretending I didn't. So Rodney would come home, and I would just be so independent, like, 'Do what you need to do. I'll take him to school, I'll do this and that.' Rodney never had a chance to be involved. I was asking him to be involved, but then I wouldn't let him do it."

Holly and Rodney sought help from a therapist and their relationship improved. She says, "It's the whole corny 'What doesn't kill you makes you stronger' thing. The problem with autism is that you don't know if things are going to come out fine. You just have to tweak the expectations. And that's what I knew I needed Rodney for—I needed a partner for that journey."

She didn't have to tell anyone about their family's struggles. She is a famous actress and he's a successful retired NFL athlete. They could have acted as if their lives were glamorous and easy.

But she chose to be open about the difficulties they faced. She wanted to help other families who have experienced the challenges that come with raising a child with special needs.

Her willingness to be authentic and vulnerable has won her so much favor in the public eye that she was offered a spot on reality TV, in a show called *For Peete's Sake*. Although Holly has caught some criticism for being "boring" from people like talk-show host Wendy Williams, she's made it clear that she's sticking to her values and showing what life is like for a busy family raising a child with special needs.

Getting real about the struggles you face and the emotions you experience won't just help you. It might also help someone else who is just beginning their journey.

If you go through life always playing defense—trying to protect yourself from pain—you'll never create your best life. To live your life to its fullest, you need to be willing to put yourself out there and risk being hurt sometimes. Being vulnerable will help you build strength, and the stronger you become, the more confident you'll be in your ability to take emotional risks.

Troubleshooting and Common Traps

After you've shared something deeply personal or had an honest conversation with someone about your feelings, there's a good chance you'll wake up the next morning in a state of panic, thinking you shared too much. But a "vulnerability hangover" is normal if you're new at this. Keep in mind that your fears and catastrophic thoughts are likely overblown. Remind yourself that being vulnerable can help you in the long term.

With that said, there will be times that you may cross the line into becoming too vulnerable. Perhaps your coworker used something you said against you when you were both applying for the same promotion. Or maybe you became too close to someone too fast who you realized wasn't a good person to let into your life. Refuse to let your errors lead you to build a permanent wall around yourself. Learn from your mistakes and cut yourself some slack.

Another common trap people fall into is confusing acting tough with being strong. Suppressing your emotions or denying your pain is about acting tough—not being strong. It takes strength to acknowledge your weaknesses and admit to your mistakes. Finding the courage to put yourself out there is a sign of strength, and the process will help you continue building mental muscle.

WHAT'S HELPFUL

- Identifying the protective armor you use to protect yourself from emotional wounds
- Owning your story without letting your story own you
- Practicing vulnerability on a regular basis

- Incorporating vulnerable language into your everyday conversations

WHAT'S NOT HELPFUL

- Maintaining a tough exterior so people can't hurt you
- Suppressing your emotions all the time
- Avoiding social and emotional risks because you think you can't handle rejection and disappointment
- Lashing out in anger to mask your pain

4

They Don't Let Self-Doubt Stop Them from Reaching Their Goals

You do not need to pay attention to those voices within you that create pain, or make you feel less competent, smart or able.
—SANAYA ROMAN

Dominique had been a standout artist in high school, but she never really thought about making a living with her artwork—at least not until she was preparing to reenter the workforce after being a stay-at-home mom.

She loved making her children personalized books with bright, colorful pictures. Her friends often asked her to create books for their kids too. She was always happy to do so and she refused to accept any money for her work.

Now she was thinking about launching a business as an illustrator, but she wasn't sure her work was good enough to charge people for it. After months of thinking about it, she just couldn't force herself to get going.

Her inability to take action had become a source of contention in her marriage. Her husband wanted her to start making an income to help take some of the pressure off him. Dominique wanted to earn money, but she wasn't sure self-employment was the right move.

That's how she landed in my therapy office. She felt stuck and she felt bad that her fear was affecting her family. "I'm not sure I can run my own business," she said.

When I asked her what she wasn't sure about, she said, "I have no idea how to operate a business. I'm not sure I'm even that good of an artist. And I don't know if I can actually earn money."

So I asked her, "What would you think if someone was starting a similar business and they said, 'I know everything there is to know about running my own business. I am the best artist ever and I am sure I'll get rich.'" Dominique smiled and said, "I'd think that person was overconfident and might not know what they're talking about."

That opened the door to a conversation about the dangers of arrogance and overconfidence. We discussed how a little self-doubt is normal—and how it might actually be an asset.

Then Dominique asked, "Do you think I can do it?" To her dismay, I said, "It doesn't matter whether *I* think you can do it. If this is important to you, it matters that *you* think you can do it." She needed to learn how to trust her own judgment.

After a long pause, she said, "I think I can do it. But I have a nagging voice in my head that keeps whispering, 'You're going to fail.'" So we developed a plan:

- **Increase her courage.** Dominique needed some courage to balance out her self-doubt. I suggested she write down all the evidence that pointed to the fact that she could succeed. Everything from "My husband has faith I can do it" to "My friends love the illustrations I made for them" went on the list. I encouraged her to read that list whenever she felt like backing out.
- **Learn more about owning a business.** Dominique needed to learn more about the practicalities of operating a home-based business, like what tax records to keep and how to market herself.

She decided to join the local organization for women business owners to gain more knowledge. Learning from others gave her more confidence that she could succeed.

- **Take action, one small step at a time.** One of the best things about Dominique's business is that it didn't cost anything to launch. She identified how she could get going—build a website, identify a target audience, create social media pages for the business, etc. Focusing on each small objective could prevent her from feeling too overwhelmed.

I only saw Dominique a few more times over the course of the next few months. But with each visit, she had progress to report. By the end of our time together, her website was up and running and she was reaching out to self-published children's authors to offer her services. And while she still felt a little self-doubt about her business venture, she was determined to try.

Do You Struggle with Self-Doubt?

The conversations you have with yourself will either fuel your confidence in moving forward or rob you of the mental strength you need to take action. And while everyone struggles with self-doubt sometimes, some people talk themselves out of reaching their goals. Do any of the following statements sound like you?

- ❑ I seek other people's advice often because I don't trust my own judgment.
- ❑ I have trouble working when someone is watching me because I'm afraid I'm doing something wrong.
- ❑ Before trying something new, I think of all the reasons I'm likely to fail.
- ❑ I often imagine embarrassing myself.
- ❑ I talk myself out of doing things outside of my comfort zone.

❐ I need reassurance from other people before I take a risk.

❐ I call myself names and put myself down.

❐ I feel like other people have more faith in me than I have in myself.

❐ I think my lack of confidence is a sign that I shouldn't move forward with something.

❐ I have trouble making decisions because I second-guess whether I can succeed.

Why We Do It

During one of her therapy appointments, Dominique talked about some of the reasons she doubted herself. She said, "I entered an art contest in high school. I didn't win anything, not even an honorable mention in any category. That made me think perhaps I wasn't as good as I thought I was."

Although Dominique had received plenty of praise and positive feed-back for her artwork over the years, it was the criticism, mistakes, and past failures that she remembered most readily.

Self-doubt sinks in when we think about negative experiences from the past or when we're imagining bad things happening in the future. Quite often, those mental images or memories are exaggerated or distorted, yet we believe them to be true.

WE'RE TAUGHT BOYS ARE BRILLIANT
AND GIRLS TRY HARD

Although self-doubt can stand in anyone's way, women are more likely to struggle with confidence. One of the main reasons for this is that children are brought up believing that boys are brilliant and girls try hard.

A study published in the journal *Science* found that by age six, girls believe that men are smarter and more talented than women. It's no wonder that girls are less likely to dream big.

In the first part of the study, children were told a story about a person who is "really, really smart." Then the children were shown photos of two women and two men and asked to identify which one they thought was the really smart individual. The people in the photos looked to be about the same age, appeared equally happy, and were dressed professionally.

At age five, both boys and girls were more likely to associate brilliance with their own gender. Boys chose mostly men and girls chose mostly women in the photo lineups.

When they asked six- and seven-year-olds, however, there was a significant shift in their answers. Almost all of the children guessed the brilliant individual was a man. The results were the same when they were given images of children instead of adults.

Interestingly, the answers changed when they asked the children to select the child who looked like they did well in school, as opposed to being brilliant. Girls were more likely to choose girls, which meant their perception of brilliance was not based on academic performance. Researchers suspected the girls may have assumed brilliance stemmed more from innate talent or IQ, rather than hard work and achievement.

In the second part of the study, the children were given an option to play one of two board games: one for children who are really, really smart or one for children who try really, really hard. The five-year-old girls and boys were equally likely to pick the game for smart kids. But at ages six and seven, girls opted for the game for people who try hard more often, while boys continued to prefer the game for smart children.

The authors of the study said, "These stereotypes discourage women's pursuit of many prestigious careers; that is, women are underrepresented in fields whose members cherish brilliance."

Where do girls get the notion that women aren't brilliant? The stereotype emerges about the same time kids go to school. Is it possible our public education system reinforces the idea that girls try hard but boys are more likely to be gifted with brilliance?

Historically, many of the great artists, scientists, and leaders have been men. So, many of the brilliant people kids learn about are likely to be men. And while many toy manufacturers are trying to break down gender stereotypes, we have a long way to go for little girls to see that they can be something beyond a princess when they grow up.

If that idea was embedded in you as a young child—even subtly—it's clear why you might experience more self-doubt than your male counterparts. It's no wonder that girls might not aspire to be as ambitious as the boys.

THERE'S A DISCONNECT BETWEEN WHAT OUR PARENTS TOLD US AND WHAT SOCIETY SHOWS US

A thirty-two-year-old woman I interviewed for this book said, "I feel like I am caught between a generation of women who had limited rights and a future generation where there will be more equality. I'm told I can do whatever I want. At the same time, I was raised by a generation of women who valued serving their husbands and clearing their dinner plates. I have certain rights that I am thankful for, but I also see discrimination, which makes me realize I still face barriers that make it hard to succeed."

Most young women were likely told, "You can be anything you want." Their parents, teachers, and other adults promised them that girls are just as good as boys.

But society may not have caught up with that notion quite yet. Women are grossly underrepresented in leadership positions. Women are more likely to play supporting roles in most aspects of society. Men are more likely to be physicians, CEOs, and presidents.

While we've certainly seen women gain more opportunities, they still face uphill battles in many areas. That disconnect between what generations of women have been told and what we're actually seeing raises some questions.

A survey by Kellogg found that 57 percent of women say they listen to their self-doubt too often. That means many women probably aren't seeking the opportunities that could help them reach their greatest personal and professional potential.

The emphasis on achievement also plays into self-doubt. It sounds inspiring to tell girls that they can be anything they want, but unless we tell them how to deal with mistakes, failures, and setbacks, we're not giving them the skills they need to succeed.

Why It's Bad

Dominique spent her whole life dreaming about ways to make a living as an artist. Yet her self-doubt took a toll on her ability to create. She said, "Ever since I started thinking about starting a business, I've felt anxious. And my anxiety crushes my creativity."

Initially, she assumed her anxiety was a sign that she shouldn't turn her art into a business. She justified this by saying, "I should just keep it a hobby." But, deep down, she knew there was nothing she'd rather be doing. And if she could earn money doing what she loved, she'd be living her dream.

It's easy to do what Dominique was doing—convince yourself that your self-doubt is really your intuition telling you that you shouldn't move forward. But just because you question whether something is going to work out doesn't mean you shouldn't try.

SELF-DOUBT TAKES A PSYCHOLOGICAL TOLL

Annette is a twenty-eight-year-old woman whom I interviewed for this book. When I asked her about self-doubt, she said, "I have a big voice in my head that tells me I can't do anything right, and it all started when I got into a bad relationship." Two years ago, she got involved with a man whom everyone warned her about. She didn't listen and kept dating him. "It turned out to be a huge mistake. He had a bad temper and he hit me. But the verbal abuse was worse. Every day he told me I'd never make it on my own and that I couldn't live without him."

About a year into the relationship, Annette found the courage to leave. She said she was terrified to leave because she was afraid of what he might do to her, but she was even more scared about what might happen if she stayed longer.

She said, "He's not here to verbally abuse me anymore, but I still hear his voice. I hear him tell me that I'm not good enough and I start telling myself I can't do anything right. It sticks with me. It didn't help that some of my family members couldn't wait to say 'I told you he was a bad guy,' after I left him. They were right. They did tell me and I didn't listen. Now, I don't dare to trust my own judgment most of the time."

Even if you've never been subjected to domestic violence, you've likely been told by at least one person that you weren't good enough or that you'd never make it. Sometimes, those words get ingrained in our brains and continue to haunt us.

You think, feel, and behave differently when you are confident versus when you are filled with self-doubt. Over time, serious self-doubt takes a toll on your mental health. A 2002 study published in *Personality and Individual Differences* found that self-doubt leads to:

- **More discomfort with uncertainty.** Uncertainty is part of life. But people who struggle with self-doubt feel uncertainty is intolerable.
- **Greater need for approval from others.** High self-doubters are so apprehensive about making a wrong decision that they often ask others to make decisions for them.
- **Lower self-esteem.** People who mistrust their judgment feel bad about themselves. Their doubt affects their performance, and failure causes their self-esteem to plummet even further.
- **Higher degrees of anxiety and depression.** High self-doubters believe they have little control over outcomes in their lives, and they are more likely to experience chronic anxiety and depression.
- **More procrastination.** Self-doubters put off doing work that requires decision-making because it's too anxiety-provoking. They also tend to waffle back and forth, which delays the completion of their work.

SELF-DOUBT BECOMES A SELF-FULFILLING PROPHECY

When you believe that you can't do something, there's a good chance that you're right. Repeatedly telling yourself that you're going to fail is the fastest way to ensure that you won't succeed. Unfortunately, women tend to sell themselves short.

A 2003 study conducted by researchers at Cornell University found that women underestimate their abilities while men overestimate their abilities. When participants were asked about their scientific abilities, women rated themselves a 6.5 on average and men rated themselves a 7.6. After answering questions about science, women predicted they got 5.8 out of 10 questions right while men estimated they got 7.1 right answers. In reality, their average was almost the same; women got 7.5 out of 10 right and men scored 7.9.

The students were invited to participate in a science competition before they learned how they'd performed. Only 49 percent of women signed up for the competition while 71 percent of men expressed interest.

This could explain why women are less likely to apply for promotions. When women think they can't do something, they don't bother trying. And they underestimate what they're capable of doing.

Self-doubt may also be one of the reasons women are less likely to negotiate higher salaries. If you don't believe in yourself, it's hard to ask for more money.

Whether you want to quit smoking or you want to improve your relationship, self-doubt will talk you out of succeeding. It becomes a vicious cycle that is hard to break.

Here's an example of an unhealthy pattern self-doubt creates for a woman who is giving a presentation at work:

- **Thought:** I'm going to embarrass myself when I give this presentation.
- **Feelings:** Fear and dread.

- **Behavior:** Half of her mental energy is devoted to criticizing herself during the presentation. She looks around the room to find people who look like they're unhappy with her performance. She confirms to herself that no one is interested in what she has to say, and she ends the talk early.
- **Conclusion:** Following the presentation, she thinks, "I knew I couldn't do it." Ultimately, her belief that she's a poor public speaker is reinforced, and she'll continue to struggle with self-doubt.

Here's another example, of a woman on a date:

- **Thought:** I am terrible at making small talk. I can't think of anything interesting to say.
- **Feeling:** Anxious.
- **Behavior:** Brings up random subjects because she can't stand a second of awkward silence.
- **Conclusion:** After the date, she recognizes she rambled on about a lot of things without ever really being able to ask questions that would help her get to know her date better. She concludes that she's a terrible conversationalist.

Self-doubt can cause you to make mistakes or to conclude that you're never going to succeed. This way of thinking makes it harder to make good choices and the cycle perpetuates itself. Sometimes, it's difficult to recognize those patterns—let alone escape them.

What to Do Instead

During one of her therapy appointments, Dominique explained all the reasons why she was convinced she didn't belong in the business world. She said, "Businesswomen are supposed to be confident. I'm not sure of myself, so I don't think launching my illustration business is going to work."

On one hand, Dominique was right. If she didn't feel her illustrations were good enough, she would have a hard time charging people for her work. But, on the other hand, a little self-doubt wasn't entirely bad. As long as she turned her self-doubt into positive action, it could fuel her business.

Our work together wasn't about erasing all self-doubt. If we waited until she felt 100 percent confident, she'd never get moving. Instead, we focused on moving forward despite the self-doubt she continued to experience.

Doubting yourself won't necessarily hold you back. Believing your self-doubt and feeling helpless about your situation, however, will prevent you from reaching your goals.

MONITOR YOUR EMOTIONS

Your thoughts feed your emotions. Thinking about bad things happening, like getting into an accident or getting fired from your job, will likely trigger feelings of fear. Imagining yourself enjoying a wonderful life or thinking about your next vacation might conjure up feelings of happiness.

The reverse is also true. Your emotions influence your thoughts. If you're feeling anxious about something, you might start thinking about all of the things that could go wrong. When you're feeling excited about an opportunity, you might imagine the best-case scenarios.

This is why it's important to be aware of your emotions and how those emotions are influencing the way you look at a situation. Studies show that feelings of anxiety—even when your anxiety is completely unrelated to the task at hand—will cause you to play it safe. For example, if you're worried about your grandfather's recent lab tests, you'll be less likely to take a risk at work.

A 2001 study published in *Behavior Research and Therapy* demonstrated how anxiety from one area of your life can spill over into other areas. Researchers asked students to predict how they thought they'd do on an upcoming exam. Students who were experiencing high anxiety about something, even when it had nothing to do with the class, predicted they would do worse on the exam. Their unrelated anxiety increased their self-doubt in other areas of their lives.

Anxiety isn't the only emotion that can increase your self-doubt. Sadness may also cause you to play it safe.

A 2004 study conducted by researchers at Carnegie Mellon divided participants into several groups. One group watched a sad clip from the movie *The Champ*—the scene where the mentor dies. After watching the clip, participants were asked to write about how they would feel if they were in that situation. This self-reflection exercise was used to induce sad feelings.

Then some participants were asked to set prices for highlighters they were selling. Others were asked how much they would pay to purchase the highlighters.

When compared to the control group, the sad participants in the selling group sold their highlighters for less money. In the buying group, the sad participants spent more money to purchase the highlighters than the other groups.

Even though their sad feelings had nothing to do with the task at hand, the sad groups showed a significant difference in their economic choices. The researchers suspected the sad participants settled for less because they doubted their ability to handle rejection.

So if you're going through some rough times, you might not dare try anything new or negotiate for a higher salary because you think you can't handle one more blow to your self-esteem.

Simply being aware of your emotions—and labeling your feelings as sad, happy, or anxious—can help you realize that your self-doubt may be irrational. Learning to say to yourself, "OK, I'm feeling anxious right now so I might be underestimating myself," or "I'm sad today so I might be overestimating how painful rejection will feel," could help you gain a more realistic perspective.

COLLECT THE EVIDENCE

Not all self-doubt is exaggeratedly negative. If I tried out for a professional soccer team, "There's no way I'm going to make the team" would be an accurate statement to think. But if I applied for a job as a therapist and walked into the interview thinking, "There's no way they're going to hire me," that may not be accurate.

So before you declare all of your self-doubt absolute truth or totally ridiculous, consider the facts. Ask yourself, "What's the evidence this is true?" and "What's the evidence this isn't true?" Looking at the evidence on paper can help you decide whether you need to change the way you think or change the way you behave.

A woman who believes she can't succeed if she goes back to college part-time might draw a line down the middle of a piece of paper and collect evidence that looks like this:

Evidence I won't succeed in college	Evidence I will succeed in college
I haven't studied in over ten years.	I'm motivated to do well.
I have trouble with self-discipline.	I'm excited about getting a degree.
I was only an average student in high school.	I completed a certification program last year.
I am disorganized.	I can create a plan to keep myself on track.
I'm not very good at writing papers.	I can ask for help writing and editing papers.
I give up easily when I fall behind.	I have twenty hours a week to devote to school.

Looking at the evidence on paper can help you determine how accurate your self-doubt really is. While you might start out believing your self-doubt 100 percent, you might only believe it 60 percent after you review the facts. Reducing your belief just a little can be key to helping you take action.

If your self-doubt is rooted in truth, take steps to increase your chances of success. Gaining more skills, practicing more, and getting more experience are just a few ways you could increase your chances of success.

Take the case of Dominique, for example. She didn't know much about business, and that was a fact. So increasing her confidence about becoming self-employed meant she had to take steps to increase her business knowledge.

If your self-doubt is mostly irrational, the best course of action is to change your thoughts. Remind yourself of the evidence that shows you can succeed each time you think you're destined to fail.

EMBRACE A LITTLE SELF-DOUBT

New York Times bestselling author Cheryl Strayed shares that she struggles with self-doubt. Despite the massive success of her books, including being picked for Oprah's Book Club and having her memoir turned into a movie starring Reese Witherspoon, she continues to doubt her writing ability. In a 2014 interview with the literary magazine *Booth,* she said, "Writing is always full of self-doubt, but the first book is *really* full of self-doubt, and it was much more of a struggle to keep the faith. By the time I wrote *Wild,* I was familiar with that feeling of doubt and self-loathing, so I just thought, 'Okay, this is how it feels to write a book.'"

Sometimes, you're better off accepting that self-doubt is part of the process. Rather than waste your energy trying to force yourself to feel confident, move forward. Use your uncertainty to fuel your effort, and you may increase your chances of success.

Keep in mind that being overconfident could be just as harmful as being filled with self-doubt. Someone who thinks, "Oh, that test will be easy," might not study. Or a person who thinks, "I'm going to rock that interview!" might not bother to prepare.

A 2006 study published in the *Journal of Applied Psychology* found that as self-confidence increased, study time and exam performance decreased. Students with a little self-doubt were more likely to succeed regardless of IQ.

Research shows a little self-doubt helps athletes perform better too. Golfers, for example, who are completely confident perform worse. Additionally, individuals who feel 100 percent confident take big risks without putting much thought into their actions. Overly confident individuals are more likely to become complacent, and as a result, they do not seek necessary preparation to succeed.

It's OK to have some self-doubt. An element of self-doubt can push you to work harder and do better. You'll put in more effort when you think there's a chance you might fail. Don't wait until you feel 100 percent confident that things will work out. Remind yourself that you can excel even when you're feeling self-doubt.

CONSIDER THE WORST-CASE SCENARIO

One of my friends does a little bit of stand-up comedy on the side. She'd wanted to do it for years, but she was paralyzed by self-doubt. She knew that she could make people laugh in social situations, but she had no idea if people would find her funny on the stage.

She finally had to ask herself, "What's the worst thing that could happen?" The worst-case scenario was the audience not laughing. That would mean a roomful of people didn't find her funny—that's it. She might experience some temporary embarrassment, but it wouldn't be the end of the world.

Once she really thought about it, the decision to move forward was easy. Now she just tells herself, "So what if they don't laugh?" and she takes the stage even when she doubts herself.

It's easy to get so caught up in self-doubt that you forget to think about why you're fearful of moving forward. Quite often, the worst-case scenario isn't that bad.

What if you started college and failed? Well, you'd be out some time and money, but that might be better than spending the rest of your life wishing you'd tried.

Here's another scenario: What if you launched a business and you failed? Same thing—you'd be out time and money. Perhaps you'd lose a lot of money. That'd be tough, but it's not the end of the world. Even if you lost your home, you might be in a rough spot for a while, but you could handle it.

Or what if you took a new job and hated it? Perhaps you could go back to your old job. Or maybe you'd quit and do something else altogether. It might not be ideal, but you'd have options.

Ironically, the emotional turmoil you put yourself through when you think you can't stand failure or making a bad choice is usually more painful than the worst-case scenario you fear. You are stronger than you think, and you can handle feeling embarrassed, being rejected, or failing to succeed.

Career

Despite her international recognition and countless awards, Maya Angelou continued to be plagued with self-doubt. She once said, "Each time I write a book, every time I face that yellow pad, the challenge is so great. I have written eleven books, but each time I think, 'Uh oh, they're going to find out now. I've run a game on everybody and they're going to find me out.'"

Despite the fact that almost everyone feels self-doubt, most people don't talk about it. So you might look around a room and think everyone else feels confident, but the truth is, no matter how confident or successful someone looks on the outside, there's a good chance they still deal with some level of self-doubt on the inside.

Thinking you're alone in your self-doubt, however, can make you feel like you don't belong. You might think every other woman at a conference has everything all figured out. Or you might assume your coworkers know more than you because they appear confident. These assumptions can lead you to compare yourself to them (like we talked about in chapter 2), and you might decide you don't belong in the same room with such confident people (we'll talk more about this in chapter 13).

Assuming everyone else is confident can also cause you to put off applying for a promotion or changing jobs. You might think you just need to wait because once you have a few more achievements or a little more experience under your belt, you'll feel confident. But you might never feel 100 percent sure of yourself. You can still take action in your career right now, even if you have some self-doubt.

When you find yourself thinking of all the reasons you are going to fail, try arguing the opposite. Ask yourself, what if this works out even better than I could imagine? When you spend a few minutes thinking about the fact that you might exceed your expectations, you can balance out your catastrophic predictions.

Family

Am I a good partner? Can I be a good-enough mother? Do I do enough for my parents? Those are good questions to ask. Reflecting on how you treat your family can grant you some insight into changes you want to make.

But sometimes, women dwell on their insecurities so much it harms their relationships. This was the case with one of my former clients. She doubted her ability to make healthy parenting choices, so she turned to her husband to help her, even over the smallest things.

She'd call him while he was on his way home from work to say things like "The kids want pizza for dinner. They just had pizza on Friday night. Is it OK to feed it to them again?" Her husband repeatedly told her that he trusted her judgment and he wanted her to make those small decisions on her own. But she was so afraid she'd mess up that she continued to seek his approval. She acted more like a teenage babysitter rather than a strong, loving mother. And it affected her relationship with her husband.

Requesting affirmation when you need it is part of being vulnerable (like we discussed in the last chapter). But needing constant reassurance taxes your relationships. It's important to trust yourself enough to make healthy decisions on your own, so you don't damage your relationships with your family members.

Social Life

The people you choose to surround yourself with may either build your confidence or fuel your self-doubt. Do your friends support your good ideas? Or are they naysayers who always point out all the reasons why you'll never succeed?

Having friends who can be honest, yet loving, is important. After all, it's good to have friends who will tell you when you have spinach in your teeth. But sometimes, people surround themselves with individuals who pick at their plans or point out their flaws (perhaps out of jealousy or their overall negative attitude about life). Friends like that can be harmful to your psychological well-being.

It's also easy to get stuck in a social rut—spending time with the same people doing the same things over and over again. And self-doubt is often at the root of that. Maybe you fear inviting someone new to spend time with you. Or maybe you worry about venturing outside your social circle because you doubt your ability to make friends.

Consider how your friends influence your confidence. While you don't want to depend on them to feel good about yourself, you also don't need pals who invoke more self-doubt than you need.

Refusing to Let Self-Doubt Stand in Your Way Makes You Stronger

How many years would you spend trying to overcome a specific problem? If your efforts failed repeatedly, would you doubt your ability to change?

Annie Glenn was an 85 percent stutterer, meaning that she couldn't get out 85 percent of the words she tried to speak. It made her daily life quite complicated.

She struggled to get her words out to the point that she wasn't able to take a taxi because she couldn't communicate the address. She couldn't answer the phone and she couldn't ask for assistance to find an item when shopping in the store.

Once, her daughter stepped on a nail and Annie had to call 911. Sadly, she wasn't able to get any words out to the dispatcher. Unable to get help, she handed the phone to a neighbor to request an ambulance.

She certainly never wanted to be in the media spotlight. But she was married to John Glenn, the U.S. senator who was the first American astronaut to orbit the Earth. Everyone from major news stations to sitting presidents wanted to speak to Annie.

Annie had tried speech therapy programs time and time again, but she couldn't stop stuttering.

In an article in the *Washington Post,* Annie recounted the days when she was in the spotlight but unable to communicate clearly. She said, "Those were difficult times for me. In times of difficulty or defeat, it's easy to think that we really have no choices. That we are trapped. I know I felt that way. Having tried, having failed so many times."

Annie didn't give up hope that she could overcome stuttering. At the age of fifty-six, she saw a doctor on TV talking about a program that helped people overcome stuttering. She signed up and spent three weeks learning how to speak again.

During her treatment, she wasn't allowed contact with her family, so by the time she called John, he was amazed at her progress. She said he cried because he couldn't believe she could talk. In his memoir, John says one of the first things Annie ever said to him was "John, I've wanted to tell you this for years. Please, pick up your socks."

Following her incredible transformation, Annie became an adjunct professor with the Speech Pathology Department in the Ohio State University Department of Speech and Hearing Science. She also became an advocate for people with disabilities, and she won many awards for her contributions to the stuttering community.

If Annie had doubted her ability to change, she would have never stopped stuttering. Fortunately, she kept getting back up every time treatment failed, and she kept trying until she found something that worked. And she did it all without any guarantees that she'd ever get better.

When you're willing to keep moving forward, even when you aren't 100 percent sure you'll reach your goals, you can accomplish incredible feats. Each time you refuse to let self-doubt hold you back, you build a little more mental muscle. And the stronger you become, the easier it is to stay confident in your abilities.

Troubleshooting and Common Traps

Sometimes women mistakenly believe that all self-doubt is bad. You should have some self-doubt. If someone suggests you invest twenty thousand dollars in a get-rich-quick idea, thinking "I'm not sure I'll get my investment back" is a sign of wisdom. So don't assume all self-doubt is a sign of low confidence.

Another common trap is believing that you should "always trust your gut." Many women think if they have a bad feeling about something, they shouldn't do it. But quite often, that bad feeling is actually fear, and their fear is filling their minds with self-doubt. That's why the gathering-evidence exercise is important. When you see the facts, you'll be able to balance the messages from your head (your thoughts) with those from your heart (your emotions).

Many women also think there's a right and a wrong choice. But that's not usually the case. Should you take a new job? There will be pros and cons to changing positions, but there isn't one right answer. If you don't love your new job, that doesn't mean you made a bad choice. Remind yourself that you can be OK, no matter what happens or which choice you make.

WHAT'S HELPFUL

- Monitoring your emotions
- Doubting your doubt
- Examining the evidence behind your self-doubt
- Considering the worst-case scenario
- Embracing a little self-doubt

WHAT'S NOT HELPFUL

- Believing everything you think
- Getting caught up in unhealthy patterns of self-doubt and inaction
- Confusing fear for intuition
- Allowing your emotions to cast more doubt on your ability to succeed
- Waiting until you feel 100 percent confident to proceed

5

They Don't
Overthink Everything

*Thinking has, many a time, made me sad, darling; but doing
never did in all my life . . . My precept is, "Do something, my
sister, do good if you can; but, at any rate, do something."*
—ELIZABETH GASKELL

When Regina called to schedule her first appointment, she said, "I need help. I think I'm unraveling." During her first appointment, she said, "I can't sleep. I can't concentrate on work. And I just can't shut off my brain."

Regina was in her mid-forties, and she'd been divorced for a couple of years. She'd recently reentered the dating scene after her friends convinced her online dating was safe and socially acceptable. And while she was happy to put herself back out there, dating in the age of social media had also sent her into a bit of a tailspin.

"We didn't have social media before I was married. I'm not used to all this texting and Facebook stuff," she explained. "It's made dating so much more complicated."

She said, "I'm Facebook friends with a man I went on a date with but there wasn't any chemistry so we never had a second date. He still likes the stuff I post on Facebook. Should I unfriend him now that I'm getting more serious with another man I'm dating?"

These were the types of questions that kept her awake at night. When she asked her friends for input, she often got conflicting advice, which made her uneasiness worse.

Her questions and concerns stemmed beyond social media etiquette, however. She spent a lot of her time researching Kurt, the man she'd been getting more serious with. She thought if she did enough digging, she'd be able to ensure that he was a good guy for her.

She searched his name in every search engine she could find. She reviewed every post he'd ever made on every social media account he had. When she was done with that, she began looking at his friend's pages to see if they said anything about him. Lately, she'd been poring over Kurt's ex-wife's social media accounts to see if she could learn more about Kurt.

I asked her if her investigation was giving her peace of mind and she said, "Well, I haven't found anything yet that would lead me to think he's dishonest, and I haven't seen any red flags. But I'm going to keep digging." She wasn't worried about her physical safety with Kurt, but she was afraid for her emotional safety. She wanted to ensure he was a nice guy who wasn't going to cheat on her.

I asked her how her investigation impacted her relationship with Kurt. She said, "I feel like I'm collecting clues. If he mentions the name of a friend or family member, I'll make a note of it so I can go look that person up later. I want to know everything I can about the people he associates with."

While doing some due diligence to keep herself safe was wise, Regina had become obsessed with researching Kurt. Analyzing every comment, piece of information, or interaction wasn't helping her feel more secure. In fact, the more time she spent thinking about everything, the more overwhelmed she felt.

She needed to accept that there's a level of uncertainty that comes with developing a new relationship. Reducing her distress meant she had to stop devoting countless hours to researching Kurt's friends and family on social media.

Regina was hesitant to let go of the "research" she conducted on Kurt. So we had to look at what it was costing her. While she had initially thought doing a little research on him would give her peace of mind, she saw now that it was backfiring. Rather than focusing on building a loving, trusting relationship, she was investing her energy into trying to find information that would discredit him. Once she agreed to stop researching him for a week, just to see what would happen, she discovered that she was able to enjoy her time with Kurt more. She had to see that overthinking wasn't resolving her fear and uncertainty—it was fueling them. Once she changed her behavior, she was able to stop overthinking everything about their relationship. This helped her be in the moment with Kurt when they were together, and she was better able to focus on healthier activities when they were apart.

Are You an Overthinker?

Self-reflection and self-awareness are healthy. Overanalyzing, dwelling, and worrying, however, can steal your joy and make it difficult to function. Do any of the following statements sound familiar?

- ❐ I often rehash conversations I had with people in my mind and think about everything I wish I'd said.
- ❐ I relive embarrassing moments in my head repeatedly.
- ❐ I worry about things that probably won't ever happen.
- ❐ I ask myself a lot of "what if . . ." questions.
- ❐ When someone says something I don't like, I replay it in my mind repeatedly.
- ❐ I spend a lot of time thinking about the hidden meaning in things people say or events that happen.
- ❐ I have trouble sleeping because there's so much stuff running through my brain.
- ❐ Sometimes I'm not aware of what's going on around me because I'm dwelling on something else.

❐ I find it hard to think about anything else once I start thinking about my failures.

❐ I relive my mistakes in my mind often.

Why We Do It

After many years of marriage, Regina had learned her husband was having intimate conversations with other women online. She never thought he would do that to her. His actions caused her to question their entire relationship and led to their divorce.

In an effort to prevent something like that from happening again, she decided she'd research everything she could about any man she dated. She never wanted to be blindsided by a man cheating on her or harboring secrets again. But the more research she conducted, the more compelled she felt to keep going.

While hurt and pain can lead to overthinking, it's not the only reason women get stuck in their heads. There are many reasons why women end up overanalyzing and second-guessing everything.

WOMEN ARE MORE INCLINED TO THINK TOO MUCH

It's likely that we've all overthought something at one time or another. Have you ever spent days thinking about how to deliver bad news and then when you finally did, it wasn't a big deal? Or have you ever spent weeks toiling over a decision as if your life depended on it, and in the end, your choice didn't really matter?

Overthinking includes one or both of these destructive thought patterns—ruminating and incessant worrying.

Ruminating involves thinking about your distress, and its possible causes and consequences. So rather than thinking about solutions, ruminating is about focusing on your problems. It often focuses on the past or things you cannot change. Rumination may include thoughts like:

- *I embarrassed myself in front of everyone. I always blurt out things without thinking. They must think I'm an idiot. They probably talked about me after I left.*
- *I should have taken that other job opportunity when I had the chance. I'd be happier there. But I was too chicken to make the move and now I've screwed up my entire life.*
- *I wish I had spoken up during that conversation, but I get so upset I can't think straight. I could have said he was putting words in my mouth. I should have reminded him of all the things he's done to mess things up.*

Persistent worrying involves negative—often catastrophic—predictions about the future. Persistent worry may include thoughts like:

- *I'll never be able to get out of debt, and I won't be able to have enough money to retire. I'll end up poor when I'm older and I'll live a miserable life.*
- *I'm going to embarrass myself at the dinner party tomorrow. Everyone else knows each other, and they'll have stuff to talk about. I'll just be the awkward person who doesn't fit in.*
- *My kids are never going to get jobs. They're going to end up living with me forever. They won't want to be independent and they'll expect me to support them.*

Studies consistently show women ruminate and worry more than men, and it may be in part due to anatomical differences in the brain. Researchers at the Amen Clinics in California analyzed data from more than forty-five thousand people. Based on brain imaging information, they concluded that women's brains are significantly more active than men's. Blood flow was higher in parts of the female brain that increase the ability to focus and empathize as well as regions that contribute to anxiety.

Scientists say this may offer insight into why women may be more susceptible to certain brain disorders, like Alzheimer's, and why men may be more likely to have other disorders, like ADHD. So neuroscience may be part of the reason why your brain works in overdrive, but it's not the only explanation.

This next possible reason is like asking which came first, the chicken or the egg. Do women tend to be given more household tasks, like managing the family's calendar, because they think more? Or do they think more because they have so many responsibilities to manage?

I have a friend who worries a lot. She always says, "My husband doesn't worry at all, so I have to worry for the both of us." Although she's joking, there is a bit of truth to this.

A 2008 study examined the roles parents play in managing a family's schedule. They found mothers devoted much more energy into organizing the family calendar and managing the behind-the-scenes legwork. So while fathers were more likely to coach sports, mothers were more likely to arrange transportation, handle the paperwork, and keep track of the schedules.

The researchers also noted that mothers' paid work hours went up when kids' activities went down, meaning that the fewer extracurricular activities a child had, the more time the mother worked—and got paid for that work. And the more piano classes a kid took, the fewer hours a mother worked. Fathers' work hours were much less likely to be affected by kids' extracurricular activities.

While this isn't the case for all families, it's a fairly common dynamic in most of the families I know. Fathers get to show up at the kids' soccer game and watch while mothers work out the carpool schedule and make sure the uniform is clean. Women tend to plan the details of a party while the men are in charge of the barbecue grill.

All of that planning and preparation can be part of the reason why women think a lot. They have a lot of things to think about if they want to keep a busy household running like a smooth-operating machine.

SELF-REFLECTION GONE AWRY

One of my former clients used to ask, "Why do you think I did that?" at least ten times during every therapy session. Whether she stayed up later than usual one night, or she called a friend she hadn't spoken to in months, she wanted clear-cut answers about why she made those decisions.

She wasn't satisfied with simple answers—like "perhaps you stayed up late one night because you weren't tired" or "maybe you called a friend from your past because you were reminded of her earlier in the day."

She insisted there had to be deeper reasons behind her behavior. She'd say, "I think the universe is trying to send me a message. And if I can just be open to that message, I'll gain better understanding."

In her quest for deeper meaning, she'd ask questions like "Do you think maybe I stayed up really late because I secretly wanted to punish myself? Or maybe my subconscious knew that the sooner I went to sleep, the sooner I'd have to wake up and face the day, and there was something going on that I didn't want to face?"

She had suggestions for why she contacted her friend too. "I think I fear abandonment. That goes back to childhood. I moved in the third grade, and of course we couldn't keep in contact at that age, because we didn't have phones or cars or anything. So I think not talking to my friend for a few years was somehow re-creating the trauma I endured in the third grade. Do you think that's possible?"

She also analyzed every move I made. One day she said, "You usually see me in the mornings, but you had said you were booked up this week in the morning. Is the real reason you want to see me in the afternoon because you needed to see how my mood is later in the day?"

When I said, "No, I actually just didn't have any morning appointments available," she nodded as if she understood. But a few minutes later she said, "Would you tell me if that was the real reason, or would you just say that so you could evaluate me in the afternoon without me knowing that's what you are doing? Because if I knew that was what was going on,

I might not act the same, and then you wouldn't get to see how I normally am in the afternoons."

Listening to her was exhausting. I can only imagine how she must have felt to be bombarded with that type of self-talk all day long.

She thought she was searching for enlightenment, and she assumed she was improving her self-awareness. In actuality, she was driving herself crazy trying to find hidden meaning in everything. It was a perfect example of self-improvement gone wrong. She confused overthinking with self-reflection.

There's value in gaining a better understanding of yourself. Yes, sometimes that means recognizing how your childhood or your unhealed emotional wounds affect the way you act. Reflection can help you learn, but rehashing the same things over and over doesn't lead to wisdom.

Why It's Bad

Regina wasn't able to enjoy her relationship because she was convinced she needed to "uncover" something about Kurt. One week she said, "I see Kurt for a total of five or six hours each week. But I spend twice as much time researching him online." When she wasn't looking up his friends and family on social media, she was asking her friends to interpret his latest text message.

And her investigative practices were hurting their relationship more than they were helping. She said, "One time, I gave Kurt the cold shoulder for a while because another woman said he looked good in one of his Facebook pictures. I assumed he was cheating but I found out later it was just his cousin."

Although deep down she knew her practices weren't helpful, she was afraid to stop. She thought that she might miss something important, so she kept analyzing every little bit of information—and often, her assumptions and conclusions were wrong. Her relationship might have potential, but questioning it constantly was going to ruin her chances of forming a trusting, meaningful connection.

Thinking too much won't solve your problems. In fact, it's likely to create some new ones.

OVERTHINKING MAKES LIFE HARDER

Thinking too much isn't just an annoying habit. It can take a serious toll on your well-being. Here are just a few ways overthinking will diminish your quality of life:

- **It increases your risk of mental health problems.** A 2013 study published in the *Journal of Abnormal Psychology* found that dwelling on your shortcomings, mistakes, and problems may lead to depression and anxiety. Rumination sets you up for a cycle that is hard to break; overthinking creates mental health problems, and as your mental health declines, your tendency to ruminate increases.

- **It exacerbates existing mental health problems.** Negative thoughts intensify psychological distress and worsen mood. If you already have a mental health condition, dwelling on your distress increases the symptoms and the duration.

- **It makes it harder to bounce back.** When something bad happens—whether it's a minor inconvenience or a major hardship—reliving it over and over again reduces your resilience.

- **Overthinking leads to analysis paralysis.** Overthinkers believe they're helping themselves by reviewing their problems repeatedly. But rumination actually interferes with problem-solving. You can't develop a solution when you're dwelling on the problem.

- **It may lead to unhealthy behavior.** A 2008 study published in *Perspectives on Psychological Science* linked rumination to unhealthy coping strategies, like binge eating, binge drinking, and self-harm.

- **It interferes with sleep.** It may come as no surprise to hear that you can't sleep when you feel like your mind won't shut off.

Many studies, including one from 2003 published in *Personality and Individual Differences,* have confirmed that rumination and worry lead to fewer hours of sleep. And sleeping in later doesn't necessarily help. Overthinking impairs the quality of sleep too. It's hard to fall into a deep slumber when your brain is working overtime.

THINKING TOO MUCH TAKES A TOLL ON YOUR RELATIONSHIPS

When I was in college, there was a student who lived in my dorm who regularly surveyed other students about which outfit she should wear. Sometimes, she would go door-to-door soliciting opinions. Although most people were polite enough to tell her which outfit looked better, in reality, no one cared what she wore to calculus class or the gym.

At one point, she bought three winter jackets and kept the tags on them. Then she surveyed everyone in the dorm. When she was done, she returned the two jackets that received the fewest votes.

I suspect she thought wearing clothes people liked would help her win friends. But the ironic thing was, people were annoyed by her indecision.

While overthinkers don't mean to drive everyone crazy, they often do. They ask for advice they refuse to take. Or they rehash situations with anyone kind enough to listen. Offering constant reassurance or frequent cajoling exhausts their friends and family.

What to Do Instead

Regina had to stop indulging her desire to overthink her relationship. That meant she needed to resist the urge to research Kurt online all the time. And she had to stop asking her friends to help her analyze their relationship. The more she talked about it, the more she investigated him.

And the more she investigated him, the more she kept overanalyzing everything.

Whenever Regina felt anxious, she'd turn to social media to learn more information about Kurt and everyone he associated with. Rather than help her feel better, her investigations fueled her anxiety even more. Putting an end to her overthinking meant she had to find something else to do when she felt anxious.

She began asking herself, "What can I do to improve our relationship?" Then she might send Kurt a quick text message to tell him she was thinking about their relationship. Or she might plan a special date with him. And while that was hard for her at first, she found that it helped put her nervous energy into something that helped their relationship, rather than damaged it.

Developing a healthy relationship also meant talking to Kurt directly when she had questions or concerns. It required her to be vulnerable (like we discussed in chapter 4) and to conquer some of her self-doubt (like we discussed in chapter 3).

DIFFERENTIATE BETWEEN OVERTHINKING AND PROBLEM-SOLVING

Preparation and planning are solid strategies for dealing with problems. You might identify a creative way to deal with a challenge, or you may develop a plan to prevent you from repeating a mistake. Whether you're dealing with relationship issues, work-related problems, or financial dilemmas, devoting your mental energy to the obstacle can help you develop effective solutions.

If, however, you spend hours analyzing your problems, you might be creating more distress for yourself. When you're in a bad mood and you focus on the things that cause you to feel awful, you'll feel worse. When you're anxious, imagining bad things happening to you will keep you stuck in a state of perpetual anxiety.

The difference between overthinking and problem-solving isn't about the time you invest—it's about the way you think. When you find yourself thinking about a problem or a distressing event, ask yourself these questions:

- **_Is there a solution to this problem?_** Some problems can't be solved. You can't make a loved one's illness disappear, and you can't undo a traumatic event that already happened. Dwelling on things in an unproductive way could be detrimental for your psychological well-being.
- **_Am I focusing on the problem or searching for a solution?_** If you're faced with a financial issue, looking for strategies to earn more money or pay off your debt is helpful. However, imagining yourself becoming homeless or thinking about how unfair your financial situation is will keep you stuck.
- **_What am I accomplishing by thinking about this?_** If you're proactively trying to gain a new perspective, you might find thinking about an issue is helpful. If, however, you're repetitively thinking about how you wish things were different or imagining all the things that could go wrong (without identifying actions that will help you be successful), you're overthinking.

Asking yourself these questions can help you begin to identify when you're overthinking things. When you decide your thoughts aren't productive, you might switch to a problem-solving approach. Or you might decide there's nothing you can do and thinking any more about the issue isn't going to be helpful. The following exercises can help when you struggle to stop overthinking.

SCHEDULE TIME TO WORRY

If your goal is to reduce worrying, scheduling time to worry seems absurd. But it really works. If you contain your worry to a specific time frame, you won't fret all day.

It's a theory that has been around for a while, and Dutch researchers finally put it to the test. They found that people who scheduled time to worry reduced their anxiety and depression significantly more than people who relied on more traditional treatments for anxiety.

Researchers discovered that containing worry to a specific part of the day required a four-step process:

1. Identify when you are worrying.
2. Set aside a specific time and place to think about worries.
3. When you catch yourself worrying, postpone worrying and stay focused on the task at hand.
4. Use your "worry time" to problem-solve the issues you are concerned about.

Let's say you decide that you'll worry from 8:00 to 8:30 P.M. every night. When you find yourself worrying at any other time throughout the day, remind yourself that it isn't time to worry. You might tell yourself, "I'll worry about that tonight, but right now my job is to focus on getting this report done." Then, when 8:00 P.M. rolls around, think about those things you worried about over the course of the day and see if you can solve any problems, reduce your risk, or create a plan for positive action.

You might decide to write down your worries during your worrying time. Or you might just sit down and think.

It's a strategy I've recommended to many therapy clients over the years, and most of them find it very effective. Rather than allowing their worrisome thoughts to affect every waking hour, they find they're sufficiently able to contain their worrying to a specific portion of the day.

CHANGE THE CHANNEL

Whether you can't stop thinking about that mean comment someone made or you keep replaying that embarrassing moment that happened last week, it can be hard to get your brain "unstuck." But telling yourself

"Don't think about it" won't work (unless you have a "worry time" set aside to return to it).

Distraction can be a good way to get your brain to move on to something more productive. In therapy, we often refer to this as "changing the channel."

So instead of sitting on the couch thinking about that problem at work, get up and get moving. Turn on some music and sweep the floor. Or call a friend to talk about a completely different subject.

You might need a change of scenery—go outside or into a different room. Or you might need to get your body moving—turn on some music and dance around the room, but find something that will help you change the channel in your brain. When you begin doing something else, your brain will think about other things. And that will help you feel better.

Changing the channel works well when you're simply rehashing things that already happened or worrying about things in the future that might never happen. But what about the things you do have control over?

Shouldn't you invest a lot of time into thinking about whether to buy that house? Shouldn't you spend more time thinking about the career move you're considering? Well, thinking longer and harder may not necessarily lead to an epiphany. In fact, research shows changing the channel can help you solve complex problems.

In a 2010 study published in *Psychological Science*, researchers examined how an incubation period affected choices. In the first experiment, participants were asked to evaluate potential roommates. Then one group was asked for their decision immediately following their evaluation. The other group was given an anagram to complete for several minutes before they were asked about their decision. The participants who were given the unrelated task to work on for a few minutes made better decisions.

In a second experiment, participants were asked to evaluate potential job candidates. The results were the same—those who had a brief incubation period before making the decision made wiser choices.

Many other studies have yielded similar results—taking time to *not* think about a problem can lead to the best decisions. Your unconscious mind is surprisingly astute, and giving your brain a chance to develop solutions in the background can help you make the best decisions.

So when you're tempted to stay up late and work through a problem, you might be better off sleeping on it. Your brain might solve the problem for you. Or, the next time you're tempted to talk through all your options with your partner for the fifth time, go do something else. A flash of inspiration may come to you while you're weeding the garden or cleaning the closets.

PRACTICE MINDFULNESS SKILLS

I once had a client who came into my office saying, "I can't sleep at night. My mind won't shut off." She said she tossed and turned for hours because she couldn't stop thinking about all the things that happened earlier in the day or all the things she had to do tomorrow.

Her solution was to turn on the TV. If she could hear a show playing in the background, it quieted all the chatter in her brain enough to help her fall asleep. But the TV prevented her husband from being able to sleep, and he'd started retreating to the couch every night.

She had initially sought sleeping medication from her physician, but her physician referred her to therapy. When she came in to her first appointment, she said, "My doctor seems to think talking about the fact I can't sleep will help. That doesn't even make sense."

She was partially right—we didn't need to keep talking about the fact she was struggling to sleep. That might make her even more anxious. (Often, people who can't sleep worry about not sleeping, and that anxiety makes it even harder to sleep.)

She needed to learn relaxation skills that would help reduce the thoughts that were overwhelming her every night. So I began talking to her about mindfulness. She agreed to give it a try, and within a few weeks, she reported she no longer needed to sleep with the TV on, because her brain was quieter.

Mindfulness involves being present in the moment. When you're fully aware of what's going on right now—the sights, sounds, smells, and tastes—your mind won't be worried about anything else. The benefits extend beyond the time that you're actively practicing mindfulness—practicing the skills reduces your tendency to ruminate.

The goal of mindfulness is to pay attention to the present moment without judgment. There are many ways to become more mindful. Here are a few basic steps:

1. **Observe what is happening right now.** No matter where you are, pause and pay attention to what's going on. What do you hear? What do you see? What do you taste? What do you smell? What do you feel?

2. **Let the judgments pass through.** Make note of the judgments you have, but don't pay too much attention to them. Imagine them simply floating through your brain. Don't fight them, and don't judge yourself for being judgmental.

3. **Return to observing the present.** Your mind will want to wander, or you may get caught up in some of your judgments. Simply return your focus to the present moment.

4. **Treat yourself with kindness.** Mindfulness is a skill that requires your practice. Your mind will wander. Don't judge yourself for it. Simply return your attention to the present over and over again.

If you need more structure to practice mindfulness regularly, there are many apps, books, videos, and audio products available. There are even mindfulness groups cropping up where you can learn and practice the skills in a group setting.

Career

In the case of Regina, her quest to study Kurt's friends and family began to impact more than just her relationship. She was having trouble focusing on other tasks because it was all-consuming.

She found herself using her work time to conduct searches sometimes, and she admitted it affected her productivity. She felt distracted on days when she'd received a new tidbit of information or times when she had more things she wanted to investigate.

Despite her decline in productivity, Regina didn't really worry about work. In fact, she was so worried about researching her boyfriend that she wasn't worried enough about her job.

For some overthinkers, however, career concerns cause their brains to work on overdrive. They constantly worry about whether to take a promotion, accept a new position, or switch jobs altogether. Or they rehash business meetings in their heads over and over again late into the evenings.

If you find yourself convinced you made a mistake that killed your career or you feel you're in a dead-end job, remind yourself you have options. And don't start thinking it's too late or you're too old. Plenty of successful women have changed careers later in life.

If you struggle to stop thinking about work in your spare time, try setting aside time to worry about work specifically. Contain your worrying to your commute or to your lunch break, and you'll free yourself up to focus on your personal life outside the office.

Family

Family can be a rich source of ruminating. Why did my parents favor my brother? Why did my mother stay with my stepfather? Why can't my family accept me for who I am?

Family can also lead to lots of worries. Will my sister quit drinking? Will my mother-in-law belittle me at this family gathering? Will my parents ever be the grandparents I want them to be?

Healing old wounds that stem from family issues can be the key to letting go of overthinking. And quite often that means going through a grief process—even for family members who are still living.

Perhaps you need to grieve that your childhood was less than idyllic.

Or maybe you need to come to terms with the fact that your mother doesn't accept you for who you are.

Healing doesn't involve rehashing your childhood or wishing things were different, however. If you have unresolved family issues that are causing you pain, you have two choices: change the situation or change the way you think.

Changing the situation could include anything from limiting contact with a family member to spending time with a family member only when that individual is sober. Changing the way you think might involve changing the channel each time you start to rehash your childhood or owning your story (like we discussed in chapter 3).

Social Life

A woman once came into my office saying, "I feel like a loser. I have no friends." Since becoming a stay-at-home mom, she found it increasingly difficult to socialize. She had lost touch with most of the people she used to work with, and she had little in common with her friends from college anymore.

"I talk to other moms when I'm waiting for my kids at swim lessons or soccer games, but I don't see any of them outside of those activities. I can't ask, 'Do you want to be friends?' because that sounds stupid, but I don't know how else to say, 'Let's hang out sometime.' I don't want to sound desperate even though I feel desperate."

She went on to explain that she went to great lengths to try to make conversation with the other moms. "Sometimes, I write down several talking points before I go to an activity where I know I'll see a few moms that I'm acquainted with, just to make sure I'll have stuff to say, but nothing ever comes of it. I still don't have anyone that I'd call a friend," she said.

She shared more things she did to prepare for these encounters with other moms—she kept track of the things they liked and tried to bring up subjects she knew they'd be interested in. She invested a lot of time in trying to figure out how to make these other moms want to be friends with her.

Despite all of her effort, she'd never once invited another mom for coffee or suggested they bring their kids on a playdate together. She was so nervous that she wouldn't be able to make friends that she forgot to simply ask someone to spend time with her. As soon as she extended a few simple invitations, she found other mothers were eager to get to know her better.

Your social life can be as simple or as complicated as you make it. Overanalyzing your friend's actions, holding grudges, or allowing others to violate your boundaries makes it much more complicated than it needs to be.

The simple advice we give to kids—the best way to make a friend is to be one—holds true in adulthood. Sticking to simple advice can prevent you from overthinking all of your friendships.

Being Present in the Moment Makes You Stronger

Oprah has a lot of things to think about. She's been dubbed the "richest African-American" and the "Queen of All Media." Even though *The Oprah Winfrey Show* has been off the air for years, she's still reaching millions of people each week through her TV network and magazine.

She's never been shy about sharing her personal struggles either. From her history of being sexually abused to growing up in poverty, she's overcome a lot of adversity.

She freely shares that much of her inner strength comes from meditation. In an article for *O, The Oprah Magazine,* she writes, "The outside world is constantly trying to convince you you're not enough. But you don't have to take the bait. Meditation helps you resist." She acknowledges that she's a fan of formal meditation, but she's practicing mindfulness throughout the day so she can be present in the moment all the time. She says, "It's a heightened state of being that lets whatever you're doing be your best life, from moment to astonishing moment."

If Oprah wasted her energy constantly rehashing things that happened or if she replayed every interview or conversation she's ever had in her mind, she wouldn't be able to accomplish nearly as much as she does. Similarly, if she wasted all of her time and energy worrying about all the bad things that could happen in the future, she'd struggle to make the necessary decisions that helped her get to where she is today. Her desire to be in the moment helps her enjoy life to the fullest while also inspiring millions of people to become their best.

Overthinking causes you to miss out on the things going on in front of you right now. You can't be in the moment when you're replaying what happened yesterday or when you're worrying about what might happen tomorrow. You'll grow stronger when you refuse to waste your time and energy overthinking everything.

Troubleshooting and Common Traps

If you have a mental illness, like depression or anxiety, you will be more likely to ruminate and worry. That doesn't mean you're not strong, however. It does mean you should seek professional help. Talk to your physician and ask about seeing a mental health professional. Treatment may be necessary to help you stop—and without treatment your symptoms may get worse.

If you've been through traumatic experiences, you may have PTSD. PTSD alters your brain, leads to flashbacks, and may cause you to dwell on your distress. That doesn't mean you're not strong either—but it also means you may benefit from professional help.

Another common trap involves journaling. Writing in a journal offers many benefits, but for overthinkers, journaling may backfire. If you write about bad things that happen, things you worry about, or uncomfortable emotions you experience, your journal may reinforce your negative thoughts.

If you enjoy writing in a journal, but you often get caught up in the emotional aspects of life, try sticking to the facts. Recount events by describing what happened, not the emotion you felt. Exposing yourself to the facts surrounding an event can help take some of the sting out of it, which is a good thing.

WHAT'S HELPFUL

- Scheduling time to worry
- Changing the channel in your brain
- Practicing mindfulness
- Taking a break from thinking about something to give your brain a chance to work on the problem in the background

WHAT'S NOT HELPFUL

- Drawing your friends into your tendency to overthink
- Allowing overthinking to overtake your entire day
- Getting caught up in analysis paralysis
- Believing that devoting more time to thinking will help you resolve everything

6

They Don't Avoid
Tough Challenges

A strong woman looks a challenge dead in the eye
and gives it a wink.
—UNKNOWN

Sharon sought counseling because she was feeling depressed. She had been living with her father since her mother passed away twenty years earlier, because she didn't want her father to live alone.

While she was happy to help with the cooking and cleaning, living in her childhood bedroom wasn't good for her social life—or her romantic life. Sharon didn't feel like she fit in anywhere. Most people her age were married and had children. And those who were single seemed to have bustling careers that kept them busy.

Sharon had a college degree, but she never pursued a job within her major. Instead, she worked a low-paying job as a customer service representative for a call center.

Her work schedule consisted of four ten-hour days each week. She didn't love her job—and she also didn't love having three days off without anything to do. She felt stuck.

I asked her about any goals she had for herself, and she said, "I just want to keep helping my dad, I guess." I asked specifically about her career aspirations, and she said, "Usually, employees get promoted to team leader after they've worked there awhile. I always decline when they approach me about that."

She didn't want to become a team leader because she thought that would add more stress to her life. "Most of my coworkers don't stick around long. For most of them, this is their first big job. It would be too stressful to supervise first-time employees who need to be reminded to show up for work on time," she said.

Avoiding stress seemed to be a common theme in Sharon's stories. There was a concert she wanted to go to, but the venue was three hours away. She worried her car might break down or that she'd get stuck in traffic, so she decided not to go.

She'd also declined to join a hiking group because she thought taking part might be too much of a hassle. She'd heard they held meetings to plan future hikes and to talk about safety issues. "I just want to hike. It sounds like they're making things overly complicated by holding meetings," she said.

Sharon offered a lengthy list of things she passed up because she thought participating would create unnecessary problems in her life. Although she thought she was just "keeping life simple," she was actually avoiding the things that could help her experience happiness. It was no wonder she was depressed.

Depression wasn't actually her main issue, however—anxiety was. But she didn't recognize that. When I asked her if she felt anxious very often, she said no. That made sense, because she avoided everything that might be even the slightest bit anxiety-provoking—like changes in job responsibilities, new social settings, and everything in between.

She'd created a really small, safe life for herself. And while her lifestyle reduced her anxiety, it also fueled her depression.

If Sharon really wanted to address her depression, she needed to challenge herself to try new things and to get out into the world. That meant facing some of her fears and tolerating some anxiety.

When I presented this to her, she resisted at first. She said, "My dad needs me to stick around," and "My work schedule is too inconsistent for me to join any activities. I'd never be able to attend everything because I may have to work weekends and evenings."

But the truth was, her father didn't need her to be home all the time—he was in great health. And while her work schedule varied, there was no reason she couldn't join the hiking club. It was an informal group of people who were going to walk in the woods together. If she missed a meeting, they weren't going to expel her from the group.

To feel better, Sharon had to seek more challenges. And while that meant she'd experience more stress in the short term, it would improve her mood and the quality of her life in the long term.

Over the course of several weeks, Sharon agreed to take a few steps toward living a fuller life. She joined a church group who visited elderly and disabled individuals who were homebound. To her surprise, she enjoyed doing it. In fact, she found that it gave her a sense of purpose.

Then she joined the hiking group, and she found their outings to be a much-needed social outlet. She also made it a goal to schedule one big activity each month, like going to a concert or watching a play.

Even though taking small steps toward her new future was stressful, each new activity she tackled helped her make a mental shift. She began to see herself as someone who could handle new challenges, and her depression lifted. During one of our last appointments together, Sharon said, "I guess I can handle more than I gave myself credit for. Stress isn't the worst thing in the world."

Do You Avoid Tough Challenges?

Tough challenges can teach you a lot about life—perhaps even show you that you're stronger than you think. But, when given the choice, it can be tempting to dodge anything that feels hard. Do any of the following points sound like you?

❏ I have trouble recalling the last time I did something really hard.

❏ I turn down invitations to do things that would cause me to feel anxious.

❏ I avoid new opportunities if I fear I'm going to fail.

❏ Other people encourage me to do things, but I don't dare try.

❏ I want to stay inside my comfort zone rather than test my limits.

❏ I go to great lengths to avoid feeling uncomfortable.

❏ I can't handle much stress.

❏ I often decline opportunities because I fear the stress would be too tough for me to handle.

❏ I prefer to play things safe rather than take risks.

❏ I want to tackle tough challenges but I struggle to make myself take action.

Why We Do It

One week, as Sharon and I were talking about why she avoided challenging herself, she told me a story that explained where her belief that she shouldn't try new things came from. She had always received above-average grades in school. In high school, her guidance counselor invited her to join the honors program. There were only a few select students who were invited, and Sharon was excited to be included.

But the program was far more taxing and the work was more demanding than she had expected. Her grades slipped and it seemed like the harder she tried, the further behind she fell. After one semester and several failed classes, she was placed back in the regular academic program.

Being demoted back to the regular program felt terrible. Sharon was angry she'd wasted her time and effort. She was upset her guidance counselor invited her to join the program in the first place, because her GPA plummeted and her transcripts looked terrible. And it was all for no real reason.

That experience taught Sharon to play it safe. She concluded that challenging herself offered no real payoff—and adding unnecessary stress would only hurt her in the end.

Perhaps you can relate to Sharon's experience. Maybe you've decided living far beneath your potential feels most comfortable. Or maybe you've decided playing it safe is the best way to preserve your self-esteem. If you never fail, make mistakes, get rejected, or feel overwhelmed, you might assume you'll feel better about yourself. But no one feels confident when they're hiding deep inside their comfort zone.

WOMEN APPROACH RISK DIFFERENTLY

Some people naturally enjoy challenges more than others—and biology may be part of the reason why. Some people are genetically predisposed to be giant risk-takers. Others are born worrywarts.

Your upbringing also matters, because childhood is when you first learned about challenges. Did your parents encourage you to go for it when you were given a big opportunity? Or did they send a message that you shouldn't bother trying or that you'd probably fail?

Being a woman also plays a role in how you approach obstacles and opportunities. Studies consistently show that men and women perceive risk differently.

When faced with a new opportunity, women are more likely to hesitate while men tend to jump right in. Katty Kay and Claire Shipman, the authors of *The Confidence Code: The Science and Art of Self-Assurance— What Women Should Know,* say confidence is the core issue. The authors argue, "The natural result of low confidence is inaction. When women hesitate because we aren't sure, we hold ourselves back."

In the book, Kay and Shipman cite a fascinating study that depicts how women are more likely to shy away from tough challenges. The study was conducted by Zachary Estes, a research psychologist who gave five hundred students a series of tests that involved reorganizing 3-D images on a computer.

When the students were given spatial puzzles, the women scored far worse than the men. But, upon closer examination, Estes discovered that women performed poorly because they hadn't attempted to answer many of the questions.

He repeated the experiment again. But this time, he told students they had to attempt all of the puzzles. The women's scores then matched the men's scores.

In another experiment, Estes asked students to answer every question on the test. The men and women scored equally—with 80 percent of the answers correct. He then tested the students again, and after each question, he asked them how confident they felt that they got the correct answer. The women's scores dipped to 75 percent while the men's scores skyrocketed to 93 percent.

Isn't that incredible? When women reflect on their performance, they're more likely to experience debilitating self-doubt and underestimate themselves to the extent that they perform worse. Meanwhile, men perform even better after they reflect on their confidence.

It's likely that self-doubt (like we talked about in chapter 4) is a factor in why women avoid challenges. Overthinking (like we talked about in 5) and the quest for perfection (that we addressed in chapter 2) also play a role. Women are more likely to get stuck inside their heads—which prevents them from moving their feet.

Of course, there's a chance men might take more risks because the world is less risky when you're a man—especially a white man. Women are more likely to become victims of intimate partner violence, sexual assault, and sexual harassment. They're also more likely to live in poverty and less likely to be given a raise. The risks and problems women face could go on and on, so it might be natural for women to avoid tough challenges.

OUR COMFORT ZONES ARE COMFORTABLE

One day, I created a Facebook post that talked about the importance of letting yourself experience uncomfortable emotions like fear, anxiety, embarrassment, and sadness so you can build confidence in your ability to tolerate discomfort. A woman responded to that post by asking, "Why on earth would I want to let myself be uncomfortable? I spend all my time and energy trying to feel *more* comfortable. I'm uncomfortable almost all the time!"

I've received similar comments from therapy clients. Shouldn't we be working toward a more comfortable life for ourselves where there are fewer distressing emotions?

A more comfortable life in the long term means you have to tolerate discomfort in the short term. Losing weight, paying off debt, improving your relationships, or sharpening your skills isn't easy. You'll feel uncomfortable along the way when you're working toward big goals. But the payoff is that you'll be more comfortable in the end.

But I often see women who have spent decades chasing happiness. They do what feels good right now so they can feel happy, but that instant gratification backfires and they suffer the consequences.

We all do this in some areas of our lives. Perhaps you scroll through social media when you're writing a boring report for work. You gain a few minutes of temporary entertainment, but it ends up taking longer to get your work done.

Or perhaps there's an acquaintance whom you're interested in. But rather than strike up a conversation and risk embarrassing yourself, you choose to play it cool. You avoid the anxiety that comes with taking the risk, but in the long term, you might regret never putting yourself out there and taking a chance.

Your brain will tell you that you can't handle uncomfortable emotions. It will push you to play it safe and tell you to avoid things you find most challenging. But the cruel ironic twist is that your desire to stay comfortable creates more distress in the long term.

Why It's Bad

During one of her therapy appointments, as we discussed her desire to avoid stress, Sharon said, "One of my coworkers asked me to help plan a retirement party for one of our colleagues. I said no because I've never been to a retirement party and I wasn't sure how much work it would entail. A retirement party seems pretty important."

Sharon had grown so accustomed to saying no to everything that she declined even the simplest of tasks. She was capable of helping someone throw a little retirement party at the office, but she feared it would be too anxiety-provoking for her to do it.

She didn't recognize that she needed more challenges in life—boredom is stressful. She was living so far within her comfort zone that she created an environment that fostered depression.

But even if you don't avoid tough challenges to the extent that Sharon did, you might find you avoid some opportunities that could enhance your life.

YOU WILL MISS OUT ON THINGS

Avoiding challenges isn't always a bad thing. Just because you *could* double your business revenue by taking on a new challenge doesn't mean you should take the leap. Taking on more work in that way may require you to give up more hours with your family or make other tradeoffs in your life—and perhaps that's not in line with your values.

And of course, there are many risks you're better off not taking. The fact that men are more likely to accept challenges means they're also more likely to die doing stupid things. Men are more likely to be admitted to the emergency room after accidental injuries or with sports injuries. They're also more likely to die in traffic accidents. One of the reasons men typically die at a younger age may be in part due to the fact that they accept challenges they shouldn't. So avoiding *some* challenges is actually an advantage. It's important to tackle the right kind of challenges head-on, and make decisions to avoid other ones.

A 2006 study published by *Judgment and Decision Making* found that women accept different kinds of challenges than men. So while you're more likely to see men engaging in riskier physical and recreational behavior (which explains why car insurance rates are higher for them), women are more likely to donate a kidney (even though they are less likely than men to be recipients of organs).

But women are dodging some of the challenges that could help them succeed. Women are grossly underrepresented in leadership positions—even though companies with women in leadership perform better. This may be in part because women are less likely to apply for promotions.

Research shows that, on average, women negotiate lower starting salaries than men. Of course, there are many possible reasons why men outearn women (in the next chapter we'll address the fact that some women may be punished for negotiating too strongly). But one study found that a major factor that prevents women from negotiating is that they don't feel as though they're being invited to ask for more money.

In 2014, researchers from Harvard examined how applicants negotiated salaries based on job advertisements. They discovered that when ads mentioned that wages were negotiable, women were just as likely to negotiate as men. But when the ad didn't specifically mention that wage was negotiable, women were far less likely to negotiate their starting salaries than men.

Imagine how much money women might be leaving on the table because they don't dare to broach the subject. It could be hundreds of thousands of dollars or more over the course of their careers. And that's just one example. Think of all the other things women might miss out on simply because they don't dare try.

Most hiring managers aren't going to come out and tell you that you can ask for more money if you aren't satisfied with your pay. It's to their advantage to cause you to think their first offer is the only offer you're going to get. But when women don't negotiate, it perpetuates the idea that women shy away from tough challenges. And the more entrenched that belief becomes, the more difficult it is to be assertive. It's a difficult cycle to break.

YOU WON'T PERFORM AS WELL

You're actually at your best when you're experiencing a little bit of anxiety. When you're given a tough challenge, you'll try to rise to meet that expectation. But in the absence of tough challenges, you won't grow and stretch.

Researchers have found that people perform at their peak when they're under a little bit of stress. Perhaps you've experienced this for yourself. Maybe you've gotten more done than you imagined you could when you had to meet a tight deadline—and in the absence of that deadline, you might have procrastinated. Or maybe when you pushed yourself to head a committee, you discovered that you are better at organizing fund-raisers than you thought possible. But you only learned that because you stepped outside of your comfort zone.

There's a psychological principle known as the Yerkes-Dodson law. According to the law, performance improves with physiological or mental arousal—but only up to a point. When stress becomes too high, performance decreases.

For years, psychologists have studied the "optimal zone of functioning." It was initially studied in terms of athletes. Some stress and anxiety helps elite athletes perform better. But over the years, researchers have been discovering that we all have an optimal zone of functioning in everyday life.

Finding your zone—and staying in it—proves a little tricky. Let's say you take one step outside your comfort zone. Within a few weeks, your comfort zone will have shifted. So to stay in the optimal zone of functioning, you'll need to take another step. You have to keep moving to keep your stress at just the right level. And it's easy to let your foot off the gas and allow yourself to grow complacent.

But as you get used to stepping outside of your comfort zone, tolerating a little bit of anxiety isn't so scary anymore, and you'll feel confident in your ability to take another step.

A 2013 study published in *Psychological Science* examined how staying inside one's comfort zone affects the aging mind. Researchers found that activities, like listening to classical music or completing word puzzles, weren't sufficient in helping keep older individuals' minds sharp.

Instead, people received the most benefits when they challenged themselves to step outside their comfort zones. Learning new skills, like photography or quilting, or attending social activities in new places, was vital in preventing cognitive decline. Lead researcher Denise Park from the University of Texas at Dallas said, "It seems it is not enough to just get out there and do something—it is important to get out and do something that is unfamiliar and mentally challenging, and that provides broad stimulation mentally and socially. When you are inside your comfort zone, you may be outside of the enhancement zone."

Perhaps you've seen that firsthand. Someone retires and begins spending time in their recliner in front of the TV and within a year or two, that person doesn't seem to be as sharp as they used to be.

It's not just an issue for older adults. All of us likely perform at our physical and mental peak when we're regularly challenging ourselves to do our best.

What to Do Instead

Sharon had to take a leap of faith—step outside her comfort zone in hopes it would help her in the long term. Once she started putting herself out there, she felt motivated and confident about her ability to keep going.

But she had to go at her own pace and do things on her terms. For her, that meant identifying one small thing she could do each week that was outside of her comfort zone—like introduce herself to someone new or venture into a new coffee shop. She also identified one big goal each month—like approaching her boss about taking on more responsibilities in the office. She thought a systematic approach would help her feel as though she was in control, and it would help her to see some progress one step at a time.

Sometimes, tough challenges will find you whether you want them to or not. But there will be other times when you can proactively challenge yourself to become better. Learning a new skill, practicing an old skill, and doing something that feels a little uncomfortable are just a few activities that can help you grow stronger.

DRUM UP POSITIVE EMOTIONS

At twenty-three, Lindsay Avner became, at the time, the youngest woman in the United States to undergo a risk-reducing double mastectomy.

She had a lengthy family history of cancer. She lost her grandmother and great-grandmother to breast cancer before she was born. When she was just twelve years old, she watched her mother battle both breast and ovarian cancer.

At age twenty-two, Lindsay underwent genetic testing to learn more about her chances of developing cancer. The test revealed she carried a mutation on the BRCA1 gene, which meant she had an 87 percent lifetime risk of developing breast cancer and up to a 54 percent chance of developing ovarian cancer.

Upon hearing that news, Lindsay chose to be proactive. She opted to get a double mastectomy.

The experience showed Lindsay there were few resources for women who wanted to take a proactive approach to their health before being diagnosed with cancer. It led her to launch Bright Pink, a nonprofit organization that offers programs, resources, and strategic partnerships that help young women become proactive advocates for their health.

When asked how she found the courage to face such a tough challenge, Lindsay said, "In the movie *We Bought a Zoo*, one of the characters says, 'Sometimes all you need is twenty seconds of insane courage—just, literally, twenty seconds of just embarrassing bravery—and I promise you, something great will come of it.' Whenever I'm scared, whenever I need that extra boost of confidence, I remind myself that anyone can do anything for twenty seconds. It works every time, I promise!"

It's fun to learn that such a brave woman found courage in a line from a fictional movie. But the advice is spot-on.

So often, when we're faced with a difficult challenge, we invest our energy into trying to decrease uncomfortable emotions, like fear, dread, and anxiety. But the key to taking the leap may be found in increasing positive emotions, rather than decreasing negative ones.

If you're thinking about whether to say yes to an opportunity that you're a little apprehensive about, you might be tempted to sit and stew about it. But as long as you're still feeling a little nervous, you'll likely focus on all the potential drawbacks. If you want to see the situation in a more positive light, go do something that makes you feel good.

Go for a walk, work in the garden, or enjoy coffee with a friend. Boosting your mood can also boost your confidence. When you're happy, you'll be more likely to think of the positive aspects of moving forward—and that just might give you those twenty seconds of insane courage you need to accept a challenge.

ACT BRAVE TO BECOME BRAVE

It's funny how small challenges can sometimes seem like insurmountable obstacles. Even silly little things like introducing yourself to someone new, or scheduling a doctor's appointment to talk about an issue that you are scared to address, can feel overwhelming sometimes.

Those things feel really scary when we lose perspective. Two minutes of awkwardness isn't a big deal when you consider it might pay off big. Or facing your fear at the doctor's office might be the key to putting your mind at ease for the rest of the year.

Often, we do things in the wrong order. We want to wait until we feel a sudden boost of courage before taking action. But if you want to feel brave, you have to act brave. Change your behavior first and the emotions will follow.

Of course, that's easier said than done. How do you take that first step when you feel paralyzed by fear?

Well, one thing that will help you move forward is to remind yourself of challenges you've accepted in the past. There's a good chance you've done something way more challenging than the current challenge you're facing. Think of the hardest things you've ever had to do and how you managed to do them.

Recalling the times you've been courageous before might help you put things in perspective. Perhaps you had to endure the death of a parent. That was likely way more challenging than applying for a promotion. Or maybe you struggled to learn how to read as a child. Surely, going through that was a bigger challenge than asking for a raise.

Take the first step even if you're terrified. Act as if you feel brave and keep moving.

DEVELOP A NETWORK OF PEOPLE WHO ACCEPT CHALLENGES

Throughout college I worked at a homeless shelter for teenagers. Some of the kids who stayed there had been kicked out of their homes, for anything ranging from substance abuse to their sexual orientation. Others had chosen to run away from home for one reason or another.

The vast majority of the teens who regularly stayed at the shelter didn't attend school. Instead, they spent their days wandering the streets. Some of them stood outside the bus station asking people for money. Others made money by selling drugs or their bodies. But every evening, most of them trickled back into the shelter to eat a warm meal, take a shower, and find a safe place to sleep. Most of them lacked hope for a brighter future.

There was one girl who regularly stayed at the shelter who was different. Her name was Anna and she loved to style the other girls' hair. She talked about wanting to become a hairstylist someday.

One of the support workers at the shelter took her to tour a cosmetology school. Anna loved everything about it, and the staff assisted her in getting the financial aid she needed to attend. Within a few weeks, she started attending classes.

She'd bring the mannequin heads back to the shelter with her in the evenings, and she'd style their hair while the other kids watched. And she talked about how excited she was to learn how to apply makeup.

Her excitement was short-lived, however. Within two weeks, Anna said cosmetology school was boring and the other students were annoying. She soon stopped attending class altogether and dropped out of school.

When the other teens were out of earshot, Anna explained that she had felt like she was straddling two worlds. By day, she was surrounded by people who wanted to gain new skills and improve their lives. But every evening she was surrounded by teens who lacked any long-term goals. She felt like she didn't fit in anywhere and ultimately, the teens at the homeless shelter influenced her more than the students at the school.

What happened to Anna was sad but not particularly surprising. Who you hang around with matters. Spend time with go-getters and you'll feel inspired to tackle tough challenges.

Research consistently shows that courage is contagious—and it's likely the inverse is true as well. Surround yourself with anxious people who don't dare step outside their comfort zones, and you'll likely lose your motivation. Create an inner circle filled with brave people who strive to better themselves, and you'll begin to see yourself as someone capable of tackling tough challenges too.

Think about the people who surround you. Do they inspire you to keep reaching for new heights? Do they give you courage to tackle tough challenges? Or do they help you become complacent, tucked safely inside your comfort zone?

Seek out like-minded people who aren't afraid to look a challenge square in the eye. You may need to join a group to meet others who are looking for new opportunities. Or you might find taking a class or signing up for a new activity exposes you to people who are challenging themselves in a way that inspires you to keep going too.

KNOW YOUR PURPOSE AND YOUR VALUES

There's a big difference between tackling a tough challenge simply for the thrill of it versus challenging yourself to fulfill your mission in life. When your goals have purpose, you'll put your heart and soul into your effort. That's just what Billie Jean King did.

Billie Jean King played softball as a young girl, but at age eleven, her parents encouraged her to try tennis because it was a more "ladylike sport." She excelled in tennis, and at just seventeen, she made sports headlines when she and Karen Hantze Susman became the youngest pair to win the Wimbledon women's doubles title in 1961.

In 1972, she won the US Open, the French Open, and Wimbledon to claim three Grand Slam titles in one year. And she was named the top female tennis player in the world. Her winning streak continued, and she became the first woman athlete to earn over $100,000 in prize money.

Despite her success, she couldn't let go of the fact that she wasn't earning as much as her male counterparts. When she won the US Open in 1972, she received $15,000 less than the men's champion.

So at the height of her career, in 1973, she leveraged her status to form the Women's Tennis Association. She lobbied for equal prize money for men and women at the US Open, and as a result of her work, it became the first major tournament to offer equal prize money to both sexes.

But not everyone was happy with the change. Former champion Bobby Riggs claimed women's tennis was inferior, and he challenged Billie Jean to a tennis match. Billie Jean accepted his invitation, and their much-anticipated match was televised to an estimated ninety million viewers. And Billie Jean won.

After beating Bobby, Billie Jean launched the Women's Sports Foundation to provide equal access to sports for girls. She continued to fight for equal pay and equal rights for women.

In 1981, she was outed as a lesbian. As the news story broke, her publicist and advisors urged her to deny the claim. But Billie Jean insisted on telling the truth. When she acknowledged she'd had a relationship with another female, she lost all of her endorsement deals.

But she didn't quit tennis or shy away from the spotlight. She continued to be a fierce advocate for women. And her efforts have been fruitful.

She was inducted into the International Tennis Hall of Fame in 1987 and became the first women to have a major sports arena named after her. The USTA National Tennis Center, home of the US Open Grand Slam tennis tournament, is now known as the USTA Billie Jean King National Tennis Center. In 2009, she was awarded the Presidential Medal of Freedom by President Barack Obama, for her advocacy work on behalf of women and the LGBTQ community.

Then, in 2014, she even founded the Billie Jean King Leadership Initiative, a nonprofit dedicated to addressing the critical issues required to achieve diverse, inclusive leadership in the workforce.

Billie Jean wasn't simply interested in playing tennis only to gain fame or fortune. She had a bigger purpose. She wanted to make a difference in the world. Her purpose led her to tackle many tough challenges—from agreeing to play against Bobby Riggs to speaking up about the gender pay gap and being honest when she was outed as a lesbian. Through it all, she stayed true to her values.

It's important to know what your purpose is. Why do you get out of bed every day? You need a reason behind "going to work" or "earning money." What's the purpose of having a job or earning a paycheck?

Think about the bigger picture. What could you accomplish if you reached your greatest potential? What kind of contributions could you make?

You don't necessarily need to change the whole world. But you are capable of changing someone else's world. And when you keep that bigger purpose in mind, you'll be more willing to tackle the tough challenges that come your way.

Career

One of my former clients began therapy because she was overwhelmed by the demands of her job. She often said things like "My boss expects way too much from me" or "It's nearly impossible to meet all my deadlines."

We talked about her two options: change her situation or change how she thought about the situation. Changing the situation could involve anything from approaching her boss about her concerns to quitting her job and getting a new one. But she didn't really want to do either of those things. There were a lot of things she liked about her job—such as her coworkers and the type of work she did. And she didn't think talking to her boss was a good idea.

So we decided to tackle the way she thought about work. Instead of thinking, "I can't stand this," and "This is impossible," she began to remind herself, "My boss expects a lot from me because I'm capable and dependable," and "I can do more than I think when I really put my mind to it."

Of course, that wasn't the only thing we did to address her stress level—we also worked on finding healthy ways to manage her life, like eating a healthier diet and engaging in leisure activities outside the office.

But changing the way she thought about challenges was instrumental to helping her cope. She realized that having an ambitious job and a demanding boss gave her opportunities to tackle tough challenges on a regular basis. That didn't mean she had to passively agree to whatever was thrown her way. Sometimes, the tough challenges she chose to tackle were speaking up for herself and pushing back. Once she was equipped with a new mind-set, she felt empowered.

Think about the tough challenges you avoid in your career. What could you do to face some of those challenges head-on? Are their situations where you need to change the way you act or should you focus on changing the way you think? Reflect on your work life and think about the overall picture of what you'd like to achieve. That can help you avoid getting stuck in a career rut.

Family

When it comes to family relationships, it can be tempting to sweep problems under the rug and stuff painful emotions so far down you feel numb.

But ignoring relationship problems doesn't make them go away. They usually grow worse over time.

Family challenges can feel like the toughest ones to tackle, because we're so tempted to avoid them. They often seem like "little problems" that are easy to ignore. But in the back of our minds, we often know they could turn into bigger problems if we don't address them.

Perhaps you are feeling neglected by your spouse lately but you don't want to stir things up by mentioning it. Or maybe your child seems to be struggling academically more than you think he should, but you put off talking to the school because you fear he may have a learning disability.

It can feel easier to let those things slide while you tackle "tougher challenges," like completing a work project on time or battling your insurance company after they denied your claim. But if family is most important to you, don't ignore the problems going on right under your roof.

Social Life

I once worked with a young woman who had high hopes for her career. But a lucrative career wasn't available to her in the rural area in which she lived. She'd need to move at least three hours away to find a job in her field.

She was excited about future job opportunities and the things she thought she could accomplish. But the one thing that kept her from making the move was her friends.

She'd had the same group of girlfriends since kindergarten and they felt like sisters. But every time she mentioned moving, they said things like "You'd be miserable if you went somewhere else" or "Do you think you're too good for us now?"

She knew her friends were discouraging her from leaving because they'd miss her if she left. At times, she felt guilty for even thinking about moving away. She said, "I don't want to break up the gang. We've been together our whole lives." But she also wanted to advance her career.

After a few weeks of therapy and a bit of soul searching, she came to the conclusion that she didn't have to choose between her career and her friends. She had an honest conversation with her friends about her desire to build a better career and how it would mean a lot to her if they could support her efforts. Fortunately, she was able to get her friends on board with her move. If they refused to support her, she was prepared to acknowledge that they weren't really good friends after all.

A strong support system can be key to reaching your greatest potential—but friends can also keep you stuck. Do your pals encourage you to do your best, or might they discourage you from tackling tough challenges? Consider how your support network influences your decisions.

Facing Tough Challenges Head-On Makes You Stronger

Anita Mann had been a dancer her whole life. So when the chance to be an extra in an Elvis movie came up, she jumped at the opportunity. The scene Anita appeared in was recorded over and over again. So, just for fun, Anita began to choreograph her own routine—something the extras weren't supposed to do.

In between takes, she was told, "Mr. Presley would like to speak with you." She thought she was in trouble. But to her delight, Elvis said he'd been watching her dance and he was impressed. He invited her to help choreograph his next film!

Anita said yes right away. But she didn't actually know how to choreograph for a movie. While she had experience choreographing live performances, camera angles for a movie were very different. She wasn't about to pass up the opportunity, however. She knew she could learn, and she began going to the library every day to study camera techniques.

Her hard work paid off. Not only was her work with the Elvis movie successful, but it also landed her an invitation to work with Lucille Ball. And Lucille Ball became her mentor.

You've likely seen Anita's work somewhere. Her impressive career includes choreographing Dick Clark's *American Bandstand Live,* the *Academy Awards,* the *Golden Globe Awards, Sesame Street Live, The Cher Show,* and *Solid Gold*—just to name a few. She's also the producer and director of *Fantasy* at the Luxor in Las Vegas.

I had the opportunity to speak with Anita, and I asked her about her experience as one of the female pioneers in choreography. She said wearing dance clothes in a male-dominated industry wasn't easy. But she said, "I never blamed not getting a job on being a woman. I felt accountable and was never going to blame someone else."

I asked her how she became so successful, and she said, "I always gambled on myself. I wasn't frightened. I would just tell myself this is how I'm going to move forward."

It's no wonder she was named one of America's top five contemporary choreographers, and it's clear why she's been nominated for five Emmy Awards—including one win. She describes herself as a lifelong learner but she acknowledges that she makes mistakes. She said, "If you don't make mistakes you don't make anything."

While you may never be invited to take part in an opportunity in such a grand way, there will be times that you'll be presented with big opportunities. If you're willing to accept those challenges, it could change the entire course of your life.

Tackling tough challenges will also help you learn and grow. You'll build confidence in your abilities. And even when you fail, you'll gain wisdom that will help you reach your greatest potential.

Troubleshooting and Common Traps

You can't always control the outcome when you accept a challenge. If you apply for a job, you can't control whether the hiring manager picks you. Or when you ask someone out on a date, you can't control whether that individual will accept.

Too often, people look at failed ventures as proof they shouldn't accept new challenges in the future. But that's not a helpful way to look at the situation. Just because you were rejected or you failed to meet your goal, that doesn't mean you shouldn't have tried.

At the end of the day, ask yourself, "Did my willingness to accept a new challenge sharpen my skills?" Perhaps you learned more about courage, or maybe you sharpened your social skills.

Another common trap is when people declare themselves "brave" or "not brave." Bravery doesn't cross all facets of an individual's life.

Just because you choose to engage in physical challenges, that doesn't mean you'll battle moral issues with gusto. And just because you can give a presentation to your colleagues, that doesn't mean you'll dare to prepare a complicated meal for your neighbors. We all have things that come easy to us as well as things that feel a lot more challenging.

WHAT'S HELPFUL

- Proactively boosting your mood so you'll look at the positive aspects of a challenge
- Acting as if you feel brave
- Surrounding yourself with people who choose to challenge themselves
- Knowing your values and your purpose
- Thinking about challenges as opportunities, not obstacles

WHAT'S NOT HELPFUL

- Avoiding anything that feels stressful
- Passively waiting to feel courageous
- Looking at past failures or rejections as proof you shouldn't try again
- Letting other people discourage you from trying to reach your goals

7

They Don't Fear
Breaking the Rules

Well-behaved women seldom make history.
—LAUREL THATCHER ULRICH

Amber was seven and a half months pregnant with twins when she began therapy. She was tearful when she entered my office and she said, "I don't even know if you can help me. But I don't know what else to do."

Throughout her pregnancy, she'd planned to become a stay-at-home mom once the babies were born. But the closer she got to her due date, the more uneasy she felt about giving her notice at work.

It was important to her that she or her husband be a stay-at-home parent for at least the first year of the babies' lives. And she'd always imagined that she'd be the one to stay home.

Her husband, Doug, was a software engineer. He worked long hours and his job required him to be away from home a few nights each week.

Given his schedule, Amber worried about caring for the twins without much help from Doug. She didn't have any family close by to assist her, and she kept picturing herself being stressed out and overwhelmed with a baby on each hip.

"I'm starting to think Doug should be the stay-at-home parent. I earn almost as much money as he does, so financially we'd be fine. I'm home by five o'clock every day so I could help him. But I'm worried about what people would think if he didn't work and I did," she said.

She thought other people might think Doug was lazy if he became a stay-at-home dad. She also worried about how their marriage might be affected. "He's always been a hard worker. I don't know how he'll feel about himself if he's not earning money," she said.

"Have you talked to Doug about this yet?" I asked. She said, "Yes, I have brought it up a couple of times. He says he'll do whatever makes the most sense for us. But I worry that he's just saying that now because I'm pregnant and stressed out. I don't know if he'll really be happy as a stay-at-home dad."

Since the babies were due soon, there wasn't a lot of time to make the decision. So at the end of her appointment, I gave her a homework assignment: sit down with Doug and create a list of the pros and cons of Doug staying home as well as the pros and cons of her staying home, and then we'd talk about it the following week. I wanted her to really look at the logic behind their decision, not just the emotions she was experiencing.

She returned to her next appointment with her lists in hand. She said, "We talked about it and I don't think Doug shares my fears that people will think he's a loser for not working. He takes a more practical approach and says it looks like that makes the most sense for our family."

But Amber still wasn't convinced it was the best idea. She said, "Both options still look sort of scary."

So I asked, "Is your goal to choose the one that will create the least amount of anxiety for you, or is it to do what's best for your family?" She said, "Oh, that's a good question. I wonder if I was thinking if I picked the 'right choice' it wouldn't feel scary."

We talked about how fear can mean you're making a bad choice, but it can also mean you're doing something brave. And I asked her about her beliefs about the roles men and women should play in the family.

She said, "I think I probably used to assume women made better stay-at-home parents, but I guess that's not necessarily true. I think moms usually stay home because we think we're better at being loving and nurturing to kids. But I'm not sure that's a fact. I'll need to think more about where that belief came from."

I encouraged her to spend the next week thinking about how many of her fears were based on fact and how much of her anxiety stemmed from breaking traditional gender roles.

I didn't see Amber the following week, however, because she gave birth to the twins just a couple of days after her appointment. It was two months later before I saw her again. When she came to her appointment, she announced, "I am going back to work next month when my maternity leave ends, and Doug is going to be a stay-at-home dad."

She said she was confident in their decision but some people didn't agree. "Everyone asks me, 'Are you going back to work?' When I say yes, they usually assume the babies are going to daycare. No one ever thinks to ask if Doug is going to stay home," she said.

She went on to say, "At first, it was awkward telling people and I felt like I had to launch into a lengthy explanation of all the reasons why. But Doug just says, 'We decided it's what works best for our family.' And I think that's the best way to explain it."

I saw Amber about once a month over the course of the next year. Her treatment involved the same issues many other new moms deal with—feeling exhausted, experiencing guilt about going back to work, and struggling to find quality time to spend with her husband.

She acknowledged that going against the grain was scary. But ultimately, she decided it didn't matter what everyone else thought of their choices. She cared more about the well-being of her family.

During her last session she said, "Choosing to make Doug a stay-at-home dad was unconventional, but we made the right choice for us and the babies."

Do You Follow the Rules to Your Own Detriment?

Maybe you were raised to be a "good girl." Or maybe you just aren't the type of person who likes to create waves. Being a rule-follower can serve you well in many ways. But there are times when breaking the rules might be the key to living a better life. Do you answer affirmatively to any of the following points?

- ❒ I fear that somehow I'll "get into trouble" if I break a rule.
- ❒ I'd rather blend in than stand out.
- ❒ I feel really guilty when I break a rule, even if it's something minor and even if it doesn't hurt anyone else.
- ❒ I'm often the first one to speak up and say, "But that's not allowed," or "I don't think we're supposed to do that," if someone suggests breaking a rule.
- ❒ I worry about offending people.
- ❒ Doing things differently feels like too much effort to me.
- ❒ I don't think I have the power to make much of a difference so I don't bother trying.
- ❒ I don't like to stir up trouble.
- ❒ I'm a "go with the flow" kind of person.
- ❒ I don't spend much time questioning the reasons behind why we do things the way we do.

Why We Do It

As Amber grappled with whether she should go back to work or stay at home, she described how she was raised by parents who ascribed to traditional gender roles. Her father was a hardworking construction foreman, and her mother stayed home to raise Amber and her brother until Amber was in the fourth grade. At that point, her mother found work at a grocery store, but she continued to do all the cooking, cleaning, and child-rearing after she returned to work.

While she could say she thought fathers could be good stay-at-home parents, she wrestled with the idea. She'd seen comedic movies that depicted dads attempting to care for their babies, but she didn't know any actual stay-at-home dads. She'd also say things like "There are Mommy and Me groups for a reason, right? No one offers play groups for stay-at-home dads."

Amber's decision involved a lot of factors: taking Doug's feelings into consideration, thinking about how it would affect their marriage, determining what would be best for her babies, evaluating their finances, and imagining what it would be like for her to return to work. But, most important, she had to evaluate her core values.

There are many "unwritten" rules that we follow in life. Some of them are a good idea—like not to reply to text messages during a job interview. But some of the social guidelines we subscribe to don't serve much of a purpose in today's world.

Men tend to drive when couples go somewhere. Women are more likely to do the cleaning. We buy fire trucks for boys and dolls for girls.

Some unwritten rules stem from fear, such as "don't say anything if you're being harassed at work." Speaking up might end the problem, but you also might face backlash that could end your career. Even though there are laws in place to protect women who speak up, many have been taught not to create any waves.

GIRLS ARE TAUGHT TO FOLLOW THE RULES

There are many different types of rules in life. Employers have rules about expense reports and vacation time. Homeowners' associations have rules that dictate the color of houses or type of landscaping allowed in a neighborhood. From speed limits to taxes, there are consequences for breaking the rules.

But there are also those unofficial rules that dictate our behavior. Some involve basic etiquette, like waiting for your turn in line at the grocery store. It's not illegal to jump to the front of the line, but it's rude, so most people would never think to do it (at least not on purpose).

These unofficial rules often involve social norms. For example, you probably wouldn't hold a conversation with someone with your eyes closed. Depending on your culture, you may have learned to make eye contact with people who are speaking to you. If you kept your eyes shut while people were talking to you, they'd likely think you were strange.

When it comes to breaking rules—especially the written ones—studies show boys break more rules than girls do. Starting at a young age, boys are more likely to act aggressively or be defiant in school. Of course, following the rules can have advantages for girls. It may be part of the reason why girls tend to do better academically overall. But many women hold on to that childhood belief that rules need to be followed so tightly that it becomes detrimental.

There's a popular statistic that shows that men apply for jobs when they're 60 percent qualified, but women only apply when they're 100 percent qualified. The statistic apparently came from an interview that the global management consulting firm McKinsey did with an executive at Hewlett-Packard (as opposed to a peer-reviewed study). But many journalists and authors who cite the statistic draw the conclusion that women aren't applying for jobs that require qualified candidates because women lack confidence.

Even though that statistic probably isn't accurate, it's opened the door to some interesting conversation. Tara Mohr, the author of *Playing Big: Practical Wisdom for Women Who Want to Speak Up, Create, and Lead*, says the real reason women don't apply for jobs that are just outside their qualifications is because they don't want to break the rules. She surveyed more than a thousand men and women, predominantly American professionals, and asked them why they didn't apply for jobs if they didn't meet all the qualifications.

The survey revealed that 22 percent of women said they didn't apply because they were afraid to fail (compared to 13 percent of men). But 15 percent of the women said, "I was following the guidelines about who should apply," as compared to 9 percent of men.

If the job advertisement said fifteen years of experience were necessary, it appears women with fourteen or fewer years weren't applying. Or, if the ad said applicants should have a degree in marketing or a related field, women with a psychology degree weren't likely to send in their résumés.

Men, on the other hand, were more likely to view the advertisements as "guides" or "suggestions." They weren't afraid to argue their case if they weren't 100 percent qualified.

Some women's desire to follow the rules could be holding them back. They may be so invested in doing everything right that they struggle to see how social norms and unofficial rules can be broken.

WOMEN HAVE A LOWER THRESHOLD FOR WRONGDOING

A few years ago I worked in a medical office with a receptionist who apologized multiple times a day. She'd say sorry for asking a question or she'd apologize for sending too many emails—even though they were all vital to keeping the operations running smoothly.

Even when I was standing behind the photocopier waiting for my documents, or when I was in the kitchen waiting for the Keurig machine to spit out my coffee, she'd apologize for interrupting me if she had something important to tell me. She often apologized for things that weren't within her control—like when a blizzard forced us to close the office early.

Everyone reassured her that her updates were important and her interruptions were welcome. But she continued apologizing. It was almost as if she felt like she was sorry she existed.

Unfortunately, excessive apologies aren't that unusual. Research shows that, on average, women apologize more than men. And an interesting study sheds some light on why that might be.

A 2010 study published in *Psychological Science* found that men and women have different thresholds for perceiving offensive behavior. In the first study, both men and women were asked to log all of the offenses they committed or experienced and whether an apology had been offered. Women reported offering more apologies and committing more offenses.

In a second experiment, participants were asked to evaluate both imaginary and recalled offenses. For example, they were asked how serious an offense it would be if they called a friend late at night and woke him up, causing him to perform poorly on an interview the following day because he was overtired. Women rated those types of offenses as far more serious than men.

The authors concluded that women have a lower threshold for wrongdoing. While men may see their behavior as perfectly acceptable, women who engage in the same behavior think they've broken the rules or violated a social norm.

That's not to say that men are right and women are wrong. But it does explain why it may be harder for women to take bolder steps—they view small boundary crossings as serious offenses. Interestingly, the authors also found that women tend to be more forgiving of others when boundaries are crossed.

I suspect these differences in beliefs about boundary violations begin in childhood. The "boys will be boys" notion excuses little boys when they're talking about gross things or when they're holding burping contests with their friends. That same behavior that gets a chuckle when boys do it may result in little girls being reprimanded for being impolite or unladylike to those around them.

WOMEN RULE-BREAKERS AREN'T HELD IN HIGH ESTEEM

When it comes to violating behavioral norms, men are also more likely to be given a free pass than women. It's a double standard that's seen often in the workplace: women who cross the line will be less likable than men.

A 2008 study published in *Psychological Science* found that men receive a boost in their perceived status after expressing anger. Women, on the other hand, were seen as less competent if they expressed anger. Similar to what we discussed in chapter 3, women are punished for showing anger.

The study found that male leaders gain respect when they raise their voices or express displeasure. Female leaders who yell, however, are considered "bossy" or "emotionally unstable."

Other studies have found that violating gender norms can cause others to exert "social control" in an attempt to get women "back in line."

Women who violate social norms are likely to be met with angry looks, less money, fewer promotions, negative comments, or ostracism.

Take negotiating, for example. Women are often told the reason they make less money is because they don't negotiate enough. But there's evidence that women might be punished for negotiating because they're not being "nice" or "appreciative" when they're asking for more.

Of course, it's not just workplace social norm violations that could lead to backlash. You might be penalized for violating social norms outside the office too. What if you're a plumber and you show up to your kids' soccer games wearing your work outfit? Perhaps the other parents won't include you in the conversations about the carpool. Or what if you're a serious online gamer? Telling people you love to play *Call of Duty* in your spare time might cause you to get some sideways glances. There can be social consequences for being a little out of the ordinary when it comes to societal gender norms.

Why It's Bad

Amber's concerns about breaking out of traditional gender roles created a lot of unnecessary stress for her during the final months of her pregnancy. At one point, she avoided her parents' phone calls for three days. She didn't want to tell them Doug was going to be the stay-at-home parent, because she feared they'd tell her that was a big mistake.

When she finally did tell them, her parents were confused. In fact, after she got off the phone with them, her father called Doug's cell phone and asked, "Is this just the pregnancy hormones causing her to think like this?" Doug assured him that it was a well-thought-out decision they'd made together.

Once her parents came to terms with it, they were a little more supportive than Amber expected. Her father occasionally made comments about Doug running "Daddy daycare," and he sometimes expressed concern about the stress being the sole breadwinner put on Amber. But Amber knew if she'd stayed home, she would have satisfied her parents, not herself.

When there's something you want to do but you avoid doing it because you're afraid it's against the rules, you might be tempted to concede. Societal norms and expectations might get in the way of making a choice that's best for you. Remind yourself that conformity has consequences too.

FOLLOWING THE RULES KEEPS THE STATUS QUO

In 1872, Susan B. Anthony cast an illegal ballot in the presidential election. She was arrested because women did not have voting rights at the time. She fought the charges, but her fight was unsuccessful. She was fined a hundred dollars—but she never paid it.

She was considered a criminal during her time. But she opened many people's eyes to the fact that women deserved to vote. And more than seventy years after the government told her she couldn't cast a vote, she was honored with her portrait being placed on the dollar coin. She became the first woman to be given that honor.

Unfortunately, she never got to see the fruits of her labor. It wasn't until fourteen years after her death that the 19th Amendment to the U.S. Constitution gave women the right to vote. But her willingness to break the rules paved the way for all women.

No one wants to be the first to speak up, often for good reason—early trailblazers receive the most backlash, just as Susan B. Anthony did. When one or two brave women step forward to try to create change, they usually aren't supported by many allies. Instead, the first movers and shakers usually aren't taken seriously.

This is the case with sexual harassment in the workplace. Who wants to be the first woman to reveal being sexually harassed by a boss? The first person to bravely break the silence risks the most.

A 2016 study by the U.S. Equal Employment Opportunity Commission found that anywhere from 25 to 85 percent of women experience sexual harassment in the workplace (since it goes underreported, it's hard to know the real numbers). But even according to the most conservative estimate, one in four women is sexually harassed at work.

Speaking up against the men in charge goes against the unwritten rules. And while I don't blame any individual who decides the risk is too great to step forward, the fact that women aren't backing one another up allows this harmful behavior to continue. Sometimes, you have to break the rules to open the doors to change.

The good news is, once we break the status quo, there's often enough momentum to keep things moving. Take the U.S. secretary of state position, for example.

This position was created in 1789. The person who holds the office is considered an extremely important person in the president's cabinet. Up until 1997, presidents had only appointed men to the position. That changed when Madeleine Albright became the first female secretary of state. While it took over two hundred years for a female to hold the office, once the first woman was appointed it didn't take long for things to change. Condoleezza Rice was appointed in 2005 and Hillary Clinton held the position beginning in 2009. Once we open the door to change, it's easier to continue the trend. But someone has to be the first woman to bravely step forward and say, "I know this isn't the way things are usually done. I'd like to change that."

THINGS NEED TO BE SHAKEN UP TO CREATE CHANGE

Everyone has biases about gender, whether we recognize them or not. And those gender biases can hold women back.

A 2014 study by Columbia University found that men were twice as likely to be hired for a mathematical task, even when women showed superior math acumen. The hiring managers felt men were better candidates for the jobs, even when they had evidence to the contrary.

In the study, 150 participants were asked to complete a math assignment that involved adding as many two-digit numbers as possible in four minutes. After the task was completed, candidates were given their scores.

Some participants were randomly paired together as "job candidates" while the rest of the group acted as "employers." The employers were presented with pairs of candidates and were instructed to "hire" one of them to perform a second math-related task. Employers could earn a bonus prize for correctly hiring the job candidate who performed the best on the next task—so it was in their interest to hire the individual with the superior math ability.

When hiring managers had to hire candidates based on photos alone—without any information about their skills—they were twice as likely to hire a man over a woman.

In another experiment, managers were given hard data on the candidates' performance on the math task. Even when women had a concrete record of superior performance, men were still more likely to be hired.

In another variation, researchers gave job applicants an opportunity to communicate their math skills. They found that men exaggerated their math skills while women understated theirs. Consequently, men were chosen more often than women. As long as people continue to believe men are better at math and science, men will still hold the majority of the positions.

One of the women I interviewed for this book is a teacher. She said, "Ninety percent of the teachers at my school are female, and almost all of the administrators are male. I think that has a trickle-down effect. The kids learn that men have more power than women." Unfortunately, the notion that men are bosses and women are assistants is widely held, and it will take a long time for that notion to change. Otherwise, the status quo will continue.

What to Do Instead

Amber said one of the things that helped her make the final decision about returning to work was thinking about what life lessons she wanted her babies to learn. Did she want to raise them thinking about gender roles the same way she did? Or did she want them to know that it was OK for them to do whatever they wanted? Answering that question helped her find the courage she needed to do what was best for her family.

But not everyone agreed with her decision. Her grandfather told her "a real man would support his family." And she felt uncomfortable at times when people asked her what she was doing for daycare.

Over time, she grew more comfortable with the idea that not everyone had to agree with their decision—and she realized it wasn't her job to make them agree. Instead, she could choose to do what was best for her family and perhaps inspire others to do what was best for theirs.

Stepping up to break the rules—whether they're official regulations or unwritten norms—is tough. But taking that first step can be the key to bettering your life and the lives of those around you.

RECOGNIZE THE UNWRITTEN RULES

Eleanor Roosevelt wasn't thrilled about becoming the first lady. She didn't want to give up her job as a teacher, and she didn't want to abandon the social reform she'd started. But after her husband, Franklin Roosevelt, was sworn into office in 1933, she stepped up to the plate.

All of the previous first ladies spent their time acting as hostesses in the White House, but Eleanor wanted to be more than an entertainer. She wanted to use her position to create social change.

She became an early champion for civil rights and an advocate for women. She encouraged her husband to appoint more women to political offices. And she held women-only press conferences during a time when female reporters were typically barred from attending White House press conferences.

She traveled the country during the Great Depression so she could gain firsthand knowledge of what was going on. She reported back to the president about what was working and what wasn't.

For almost thirty years she wrote a syndicated newspaper column where she explored topics such as women and work, women in war, and equal rights.

Before she could do all that, she had to recognize that there was an unwritten rule that said first ladies should be socialites, not game-changers. Acknowledging that idea was the first step in deciding whether that was something she wanted to do. When she realized it wasn't, she chose to do things differently.

It's easy to fall into the trap of thinking, "This is how we do things because it's the way it's always been done." Even when the current way things are done serves no real purpose, you might get swept up into doing things the same way.

Before you can break the rules, you have to recognize the unwritten rules that already exist. Otherwise, research says you'll just go along with the crowd.

A 2014 study published in the *Journal of Consumer Research* highlights this principle. Researchers put two people in a room together and asked each individual—one at a time—to choose a type of tea. The description of the tea was written in Korean, and the participants didn't speak Korean, so they weren't able to base their decisions on the descriptions.

The study found that the person who chose a tea bag second was very likely to copy the first person's choice. Either they assumed the other person knew better or they wanted to fit in.

It's an idea that has been studied time and time again. Social influence plays a big role in how people behave in regard to things like littering, donating to charity, and purchasing items. We mimic the behavior of those around us when we don't have our own opinion.

The key to escaping the herd mentality is to form your opinion. So before you make decisions, pause and think about why you're making them. Giving yourself a little bit of time, even if it's just a minute or two, to develop an opinion could help you catch yourself when you're simply going along with the crowd.

JUSTIFY YOUR CHOICES

Whether you choose to go with the flow or you opt to go against the grain, be prepared to justify your choices. To be clear, you don't owe that explanation to anyone but yourself. You need to understand why you're doing what you're doing.

By default, we're more likely to do what takes less effort. Usually, that means going along with our default options.

Take things like 401(k) contributions, extra health-insurance benefits, and organ donation, for example. If your company wants employees to donate to their retirement program, they'll get more participants by sending around a form that says, "Check here if you want to opt out." If they sent a form around saying, "Check here to opt in," fewer people would sign up.

That's the case with organ donation as well. Countries who have an "opt-in" plan get fewer organ donors than countries who make it the automatic default to become an organ donor.

Isn't that incredible to think about? Major life decisions—ones that may mean life or death for someone else—hinge on whether you have to sign an extra form or check an extra box.

Studies consistently show people are less likely to mimic the behaviors of others when they know they're going to have to explain their choices. So simply asking yourself why you're doing something—or why not— can help you escape the herd mentality.

That's not to say you need to take a stand about everything. You might decide the risk is too big for you or the consequences might be too great. And you might be right.

Perhaps you decide to follow the usual career track for women in your office because you don't actually want to be in a leadership position. You're happy where you are now and aren't interested in taking on the stress of becoming a manager.

But maybe you aren't OK with the fact that your daughter's school spends more on boys' sports than girls' sports, and you decide that's an issue you want to address. So you begin speaking out against the fact that the girls wear worn-out uniforms, play on fields and courts that are barely functional, and have fewer opportunities to play.

You might imagine having to explain to your daughter someday why you were OK sending her to a school where boys' sports were heavily funded and girls' sports were neglected. Thinking about how you'd answer that question might inspire you to take action—because you can't justify staying silent.

Whatever decision you make, justify your answer inside your own head. Then you'll at least know you made a conscious decision and didn't simply opt in because it was simpler.

SHOW, DON'T TELL

When it comes to breaking the rules, there isn't a "rule" about how to do it and how to do it well. Asking for permission and waiting to get the green light to proceed, however, might not be particularly productive. Sometimes, you just have to dive in headfirst, knowing there will be consequences for your actions.

One of my favorite examples of a fierce rule-breaker is Kathrine Switzer. She was the first woman to run the Boston Marathon, in 1967.

Kathrine was a sophomore at Syracuse University who'd been training hard with a running coach. At that time, there was a widely held belief that women didn't have the physical capabilities to run 26.2 miles. No one stopped her when she signed up for the marathon, however, so she stepped up to the starting line next to the men and began running the race alongside her coach and her boyfriend.

Around the two-mile mark, an official ran toward her and tried to force her to leave the race. Her coach told the official to leave her alone, but when he persisted, Kathrine's boyfriend blocked the official and knocked him off course.

The entire incident was caught on camera by the nearby press truck. So as Kathrine kept running, journalists and photographers followed to ask her questions like "What are you trying to prove?" or "When are you going to quit?" Kathrine said she wasn't trying to prove anything. She simply wanted to run the race she'd been training for.

Kathrine finished the race in four hours and twenty minutes, and her picture appeared all over the newspapers the next day. Not long after the story made headlines, she received hate mail from people who didn't appreciate her efforts. The negative outcry lasted for years—including many angry letters from other women.

The Boston Athletic Association's director, Will Cloney, was asked what he thought about a woman competing in the race. He said, "Women can't run in the marathon because the rules forbid it. Unless we have rules, society will be in chaos. I don't make the rules, but I try to carry them out. We have no space in the marathon for any unauthorized person, even a man. If that girl were my daughter, I would spank her."

Following that experience, Kathrine became an advocate for positive social change. And finally, in 1972, women were officially invited to run the Boston Marathon.

In 2011, Kathrine was inducted into the National Women's Hall of Fame for creating a social revolution by empowering women around the world through running. In 2017, on the fiftieth anniversary of her first marathon, she ran the Boston Marathon again. She was given bib number 261, the same number she'd been assigned in 1967. And later that year, the Boston Athletic Association retired her number forever.

Now it's absurd to imagine anyone believing that women couldn't run a marathon. But not that long ago, that belief was the norm.

Sometimes, talking will only get you so far. Telling someone you're capable or asking them to reconsider might not be enough. If you really want to change things, you have to take action. Show people that you're competent if you want them to truly believe in you.

OPEN DOORS TO HELP OTHERS

There are many ways to create positive change in the world. Certainly, one way is to lead by example. But you can also open the door to help other people create positive change.

By all accounts, Reshma Saujani has an impressive résumé. After receiving her master's in public policy from Harvard, she attended Yale Law School. From there, she worked on Wall Street. Soon, she entered the political arena in New York City and became the first Indian-American woman and the first South Asian–American woman to run for Congress. She was even named to *Fortune* magazine's 40 Under 40 list.

It was important to Reshma to help young women, and she decided the best way to do that was by teaching girls about computers.

She founded Girls Who Code, a nonprofit organization dedicated to closing the gender gap in technology by changing the image of what a programmer looks like and does. Girls Who Code offers seven-week summer immersion programs, two-week specialized campus programs, and after-school clubs to teach girls computing skills like programming, robotics, and web design. The organization's goal is to teach one million girls to code by 2020.

While you might not be able to start a national program that reaches over a million people, you might find one woman to help. If you work in a career where women are underrepresented, mentor another woman. You could also volunteer to be a speaker at a career day at your local school.

Talk to your daughters, granddaughters, nieces, and friends' children about what they want to do when they grow up. Make sure they know that girls can enjoy the same careers as boys. They don't have to be the nurses while the boys are the doctors. And they don't have to be the teachers while the boys are the principals.

Career

Bending—or breaking—a few rules might actually be good for your career. Take Lori Greiner, for example. Not only is she one of the cast members on *Shark Tank,* but she's also known as "the Queen of QVC." She's an inventor and entrepreneur with an estimated net worth of $50 million.

But she certainly doesn't follow all the rules. Take sleep, for example. You don't have to look very hard to find books or articles that will tell you the secret to success is waking up early and getting a head start on the day. And you'll likely hear Tim Cook wakes up at 3:45 A.M. and Richard

Branson gets up at 5:00 A.M. because they both want to start the day before sunrise.

Not Lori, however. She told *Parade* magazine she usually goes to sleep at 1:00 or 2:00 A.M. And what does she do right before she goes to bed? She exercises. I doubt you'll find too many health gurus or productivity specialists who will recommend a robust workout right before you hit the hay. But Lori says she's a night owl and that schedule works for her.

There's evidence that says breaking the rules can contribute to success—especially when those rule violations date back to childhood. A forty-year study published in *Developmental Psychology* found that kids who broke the rules were most likely to earn more money as adults. The study began examining twelve-year-olds in 1968.

Researchers noted their characteristics, behavior, and intelligence, and their parents' socioeconomic status. Then they followed them through adulthood. To their surprise, the "naughty kids" were the highest income earners. While they didn't necessarily have the most prestigious job titles, they were making more money than the kids who had been labeled "studious."

The authors of the study offered several possible reasons for this outcome. Perhaps the kids who broke the rules weren't afraid to ask for raises more often. Or maybe they were more likely to become entrepreneurs and innovators who blazed their own trails.

So, despite the articles that will tell you what you should do to be most productive or successful, keep in mind that you need to do what works best for you. That doesn't mean you shouldn't learn about people who are doing great things, but you don't have to copy them. You might find breaking a few rules helps you create your own path to success.

Family

Families often have a lot of unwritten rules. Parents who go to college usually expect their kids to go to college—and quite often, they expect their kids to earn more money. Or entrepreneurial parents may expect their kids to go into the family business. But sometimes, you have to defy those expectations to reach your goals.

We should be thankful that many people throughout history took a chance and broke their parents' rules. Take Florence Nightingale, for example. Her parents were wealthy landowners. When Florence told her parents she wanted to be a nurse, they forbade her from doing so. They expected her to marry a man who would ensure her class standing, not train for a job that was viewed as menial labor.

But Florence refused several marriage proposals and remained determined to pursue nursing, despite her family's objections. She went on to do great things for health care, such as improving the sanitary conditions in hospitals. Her work attracted attention and awards from the British government, including an engraved brooch from Queen Victoria.

But she was only able to create such positive change because she went against her parents' rules. You might have to do that in your own life at one time or another.

I see many young people in my therapy office who are struggling to decide whether to follow their passions or follow their parents' advice. And I see a lot of people later in life who are experiencing a midlife crisis because they did what their parents wanted and they regret their decisions.

There can definitely be consequences for breaking the family rules. Perhaps your parents won't pay for your education. Or maybe you don't fit in at family functions. But it's important to consider the consequences you'll face for following the rules too.

Social Life

A few years ago I came across a book that belonged to my husband Steve's ninety-six-year-old grandmother. It was a book about social etiquette that had been written in the fifties. Each page offered tips on how women could be polite entertainers and good hostesses for their guests. It emphasized the importance of acting ladylike regardless of how your guests behaved. It was filled with tips about how to be the picture of elegance and grace while entertaining guests and serving food.

Thankfully, we've come a long way from the era when women were viewed as domestic goddesses. But there are still a variety of social norms women are expected to follow—from the way you dress to the choices you make on a daily basis.

But of course, you don't have to. And just recognizing that you get to make those choices on a regular basis can be freeing.

You don't have to paint your kids' rooms blue or pink based on gender. You don't have to wait for a man to propose marriage to you. And you don't have to order wine if you prefer to drink beer. Although we've come a long way in making it socially acceptable for women to break some of the rules, we've got a long way to go. So keep in mind that your willingness to break a rule here and there might help others be more willing to follow suit.

Breaking a Few Rules Makes You Stronger

From *Are You There God? It's Me, Margaret* to *Blubber,* Judy Blume has been writing about female adolescence since the 1960s. Her books have sold over eighty-two million copies and been translated into thirty-two languages. She didn't become that popular by writing the same stuff as everyone else, however.

She was the first author to write frank commentary about the tumultuous times of adolescence. Not everyone has appreciated her candid approach to topics like puberty, masturbation, and birth control. Some places banned her books for being "sexually offensive." She's received hate mail and death threats over the years from people who were outraged by her work. There was a point in time when she even needed a bodyguard.

But Blume kept writing. And her books helped millions of young fans get through some of the most awkward stages of their lives. She received so much fan mail that she even published a book of the letters. She's been dubbed "the author who understood," because so many young girls have been able to relate to the characters in her books.

Singer Amanda Palmer even wrote a song about Judy Blume's books. She said the characters opened up emotional doors and windows she'd started to lock off.

And while millions of girls and women all over the world loved what Blume had to say, she admits that writing all those stories about girls struggling through adolescence also helped her. She told *The Guardian,* "Writing saved my life. It saved me, it gave me everything, it took away all my illnesses." But she had to break the rules to do that. During a time when books like *Charlie and the Chocolate Factory* and *A Wrinkle in Time* were popular, she dared to talk about girls and sex.

When you break a few rules in life, you'll have the satisfaction of knowing that you lived your life according to your terms. And even though you might encounter some people who aren't happy with your decisions, you can find strength in knowing you stayed true to your values and acted according to your beliefs.

Troubleshooting and Common Traps

There's a difference between breaking the rules because you're taking a stand and simply being disrespectful. I hear a lot of people say things like "Well, they're just going to have to deal with it" when they're violating policies because they're lazy or disinterested, not because they're actually taking a stand. So before you declare yourself a rebel, take a minute to think about your purpose.

When it comes to breaking the rules, it can be tempting to wait for other people to go first. It's much easier to join a movement that someone else already started than to be the first person to step forward. If you're thinking about doing something different, there's a good chance other people are thinking about it too. You just might need to be the one to take the first step.

It's easy to overlook the "rules" because we get used to them. Take time to consider the rules and procedures that you follow. Just because you've been doing something for a long time doesn't mean it's a good idea.

Finally, you might be tempted to think past generations were too tolerant or that they should have created change. After all, it was only a few short decades ago that we thought women were too fragile to run marathons. But there's a good chance future generations will raise an eyebrow about some of the things we do too. It seems logical now to divide sports teams up by sex, but is it really? Might kids a few generations from now ask, "What on earth made that OK?" At this point, it seems like that makes things fair, but perhaps we'll think differently about things like that down the road.

WHAT'S HELPFUL

- Identifying the unwritten rules you follow
- Justifying your choices to yourself
- Showing, rather than telling, people what you're capable of doing
- Helping others see their potential
- Considering the consequences of following the rules

WHAT'S NOT HELPFUL

- Violating rules out of laziness or disrespect
- Waiting for everyone else to take action first
- Following the rules without considering whether they're helpful
- Going with the flow even when you don't want to

8

They Don't Put Others Down to Lift Themselves Up

Be the woman who fixes another woman's crown
without telling the world it was crooked.
—UNKNOWN

Meredith looked frazzled when she walked into my office for her first therapy appointment. "I barely made it on time, because my coworkers kept asking stupid questions while I was trying to get out of the office," she said.

Most of her concerns—and sources of stress—centered on her "stupid coworkers." She was a team leader for a busy company that hired a lot of recent college graduates. And Meredith disliked almost every new hire who walked through the door.

"Have you seen kids these days?" she asked. "They have no work ethic. They're lazy and entitled and completely clueless!"

Meredith had grown disheartened about her work over the last few years. "I'm afraid to think what young people are going to be like five years from now. I've got to get out of there before then. I mean, how can it get worse than these snowflakes we're currently catering to?"

Meredith's stress about work spilled over into her personal life too. Every evening she complained to her husband about all the stress she'd encountered over the course of the day. "I tell him who won the 'stupidest person of the day' award," she said.

I asked Meredith why she stayed at her job and she said, "I like the work I do. It's just the people I can't stand." She went on to explain that she didn't dislike *everyone* at work—just the people who worked under her.

"When I get together with the other team leaders, we have some good conversations about the idiots they expect us to lead," she said. "If it wasn't for those conversations, I might think I was crazy. But the other team leaders are just as disgusted as I am with the caliber of employees they're hiring these days."

Given that Meredith had already concluded the people on her team were the problem, I asked her what she hoped to gain by coming to therapy. "I know I can't make my bosses hire better people, but I'm hoping there might be something I can do to feel less stressed," she said.

Meredith was right—there were some things she could do to feel better. But I wasn't sure she was going to go for any of them. Changing the way she thought about the other employees, reducing the amount of time she invested in talking negatively about them, and staying focused on her own career were just a few ideas that came to mind.

But I knew I had to tread lightly. Meredith wasn't likely to make those changes as long as she viewed herself as a shepherd who was leading a flock of lazy, pea-brained sheep.

So the first issue we tackled was the amount of time she spent complaining to her husband about her employees. Initially, she thought she was using humor to reduce her stress by telling her husband who won the "daily award." As an experiment, she agreed to stop doing it just to see if she felt better or worse.

After a few weeks of therapy, I asked her, "Have you considered that all the energy you put into thinking about, talking about, and disliking the people on your team is the reason you're stressed out? Maybe it's not the people themselves, but the way you're thinking about them and how much time you're putting into thinking about them."

"Well, if you worked with stupid people all day you'd see you have to think about them all the time. If you don't stay on top of them, they'll mess everything up," she said.

Even though I could tell she was frustrated, I asked, "Does talking to your husband about your employees prevent them from messing up? Is talking to the other team leaders about them productive?"

She acknowledged that making fun of the employees behind their backs didn't keep the employees in line, but she thought it helped reduce her stress. "I have to blow off some steam somehow. You don't want to keep that stuff all bottled up, you know," she said.

That statement opened up an opportunity for me. I showed her the research behind the common misconception that venting helps you feel better. Studies show venting adds fuel to the fire and increases frustration and anger.

With a little bit of evidence, Meredith became a little more open to changing her behavior. We spent the next several sessions looking at other things she could do differently—like invest fewer hours in complaining about the people on her team.

Then we examined her thoughts. It was one thing to spend less time talking negatively about people, but she also needed to change her inner dialogue. We began talking about how she might reframe the way she viewed the people on her team.

Instead of thinking of them as "stupid" she could remind herself that new employees need guidance. And that was why she was the leader—to offer advice and feedback, not insults.

Over the course of several therapy sessions, Meredith began shifting her mind-set. Rather than focus on her frustration over the employees on her team, she concentrated on her skills as a leader. And once she began focusing on something she had control over—how she responded to people—she began to make progress. While her stress level didn't magically disappear overnight, changing her attitude helped her take some steps in the right direction.

Do You Put Others Down?

We learned not to call people names when we were kids. But, for some, putting others down is a hard habit to break. In fact, adults have subtler but more harmful ways of hurling insults. And sometimes, people aren't even aware that they're putting others down. Do any of the following statements ring true to you?

- ❏ I'm quick to point out other people's flaws.
- ❏ If someone says something mean about someone who isn't present, I don't feel compelled to speak up.
- ❏ I like listening to gossip and I've been known to spread it too.
- ❏ When I decide someone isn't a nice person, I want to make sure that other people know why.
- ❏ I say some not-so-flattering things about my friends when they aren't around.
- ❏ I get a bit of a rush when I'm sitting with a group who points out others' flaws.
- ❏ Putting other people down seems like a good way to bond with people around me.
- ❏ I point out another individual's mistakes because I want everyone to see that person has flaws.
- ❏ I call people names in my head regularly.
- ❏ Putting other people down makes me feel better about myself.

Why We Do It

I asked Meredith what she gained by insisting her employees were stupid. She said it served two purposes: it made her feel smart, and she thought laughing about the "common sense" things her employees didn't know provided comic relief that reduced her stress.

She said, "If they're going to put me in charge of incompetent people I might as well have fun with it." But, clearly, she wasn't having fun. The more she complained about work, the less satisfied she felt with her job. She'd gotten caught up in a negative cycle and she was having trouble breaking it on her own.

If we're honest, we could all probably pinpoint some times in our lives when we've put others down in one way or another. Perhaps it helped us feel good for a few minutes. Or maybe it was our way of coping when we felt put down by others.

SAYING MEAN THINGS PUTS YOU AT THE TOP OF THE PECKING ORDER

Putting others down in an "adult" fashion is called relational aggression in clinical terms. It refers to rumor-mongering, sabotage, exclusion, public ridicule, and gossip. I suspect most people would say they don't do those things. But the sad truth is that a lot of people do.

Modern-day society isn't exactly conducive to cheering one another on and pointing out one another's strong suits. Instead, we seem to love tearing each other down.

From *Fashion Police* to *The Real Housewives,* insults have become entertainment. We live in a world where bloggers can make a living pointing out people's flaws and celebrity gossip magazines line the checkout aisles in grocery stores.

Not only are put-downs entertainment, but they can also help you gain status. The easiest way to prevent yourself from being on the bottom of the pecking order is to make fun of someone else—then at least people will think you're above that individual.

University of Texas psychologist David Buss says women aim to knock those above them in the pecking order down a peg or two. According to Buss, women are especially threatened by attractive women. So they gossip or tear those women down as a way to try to even the playing field. In his book *The Evolution of Desire: Strategies of Human Mating*, he says women who appear willing to have casual sex are an especially high threat to women who want long-term relationships. So women are more likely to shame those they view as promiscuous by gossiping or making disparaging remarks like "She has fat thighs."

In a study that took place at McMaster University in Ontario, researchers examined how women react to individuals who dress provocatively. The participants were all women between the ages of twenty and twenty-five. Women who took part in the study were paired with either a friend or a stranger and were told they were going to talk about female friendships.

During the experiment, the pairs were interrupted by a blond actress. She wore khaki pants and a T-shirt when she interrupted some groups and a short skirt, boots, and a low-cut blouse when she interrupted the others.

The pairs of women who observed the actress when she was dressed conservatively barely noticed her. No one made any derogatory comments about her.

But the pairs who were interrupted by her when she was wearing the short skirt and low-cut blouse had plenty to say. They made negative comments about her appearance and whispered to one another about the way she dressed. This was especially true in the women who were paired with a friend, as compared to those who were paired with a stranger.

In an interview with *The Atlantic*, the author of the study, Tracy Vaillancourt, was asked about indirect aggression. In contrast to men, who tend to throw punches or get in heated verbal altercations, she said women "tend to do it such that you won't be detected. Or you make an excuse for your behavior, like 'I was only joking.'"

Of course, it's not just women's appearances that lead to snarky comments, however. The "mommy wars" are another way women often try to make themselves look and feel superior. Whether they're snubbing a neighbor who chooses not to breast-feed or they're making snarky comments about stay-at-home moms, many women are engaging in a battle over whose parenting habits are superior.

It's as if reprimanding another mother about pacifiers, vaccinations, or sleeping habits somehow gives them a leg up in the parenting realm. Insults about another woman's parenting choices are often backed up by "science." Saying "All the studies say you shouldn't do that" somehow makes a rude comment justifiable. Clearly, most of these belittling comments aren't meant to ensure children are cared for better—they're meant to put other moms down so the critic can feel elevated.

GOSSIP CAN FEEL GOOD

Whether you tell your coworkers you heard the boss is having an affair, or you and your girlfriends talk about the one friend who wasn't able to attend your gathering, gossiping can be fun. And studies show that it can even make you feel good.

A 2012 study conducted by researchers at the University of California, Berkeley, found that spreading gossip can actually decrease your stress level—but only when it's "prosocial gossip."

The study examined what happened when participants witnessed someone cheating during an economic game. Those who discovered the cheater experienced a spike in heart rate. But as soon as they told someone else what they'd witnessed, their heart rates returned to normal.

The authors concluded that people felt better when they were warning others about the cheater. They thought telling someone could prevent that individual from being taken advantage of.

So, warning someone about a potential scammer could be good for you and good for the listener. But sometimes, it's easy to convince yourself that sharing damaging information about others is somehow making the world a better place, even if that's not quite the case.

Warning a woman that her boyfriend (who happens to be your ex) is a loser might not exactly have a prosocial purpose. And being the first to tell your friends about the latest rumor you heard might not actually be a humanitarian effort.

Instead, your willingness to spread gossip might be about giving a temporary boost to your status. You might feel powerful when you're the first one to have a bit of juicy news. You might also feel as if spreading some not-so-nice news about others might boost your status in the eyes of the group.

Gossip can also be a way to bond. Perhaps you have a core group of co-workers who love to share the latest workplace rumors. It might make you feel like a select group and help separate you from the rest of the workers.

Why It's Bad

During one of Meredith's therapy appointments I asked her about her effectiveness as a team leader. She said, "I'm probably as effective as I can be, given the caliber of people they gave me to lead."

I shared a famous study with her that showed that students tend to perform to the teacher's expectations of them. When teachers thought their students were gifted, the students performed better on standardized testing.

After lengthy conversations—and after Meredith reviewed the studies for herself—she was able to see that concluding she worked with inept people was harmful. Not only were the people on her team less likely to succeed, but she was also less likely to be an effective leader. Feeling ineffective was probably a big contributor to her high stress levels.

But limiting other people's opportunities is just one reason why putting others down is bad. It can be damaging in many other ways.

TEARING PEOPLE DOWN CREATES
LONG-LASTING EMOTIONAL SCARS

We used to tell kids to say, "Sticks and stones may break my bones, but names will never hurt me." But clearly, that isn't true. The way people speak to one another—and act toward each other—has the potential to do a lot of damage.

One of the women I interviewed was a graduate student who said that she was sexually assaulted by a well-known male student. She chose not to report the incident because she knew if she did, everyone would find out, and she was afraid of the gossip that would be spread about her on campus. So she stayed silent and continued attending classes alongside the male student who had assaulted her. She said doing so was painful, but she thought the cruelty she might endure from others might be even more painful.

Unfortunately, her fears about the rumor mill weren't exaggerated or distorted. It reminded me of the story of Kelly Valen. Valen had joined a sorority in college, and when a handsome man invited her to a frat party during her first semester of school, she happily accepted. But after they drank heavily, he led her upstairs, where she passed out. He raped her while some of his frat brothers watched. Some of them tried to discourage him, but no one stopped him.

Valen felt a burden of responsibility for getting drunk and losing control. She wrote an article for the *New York Times* in which she said, "There was never any talk of criminality; for whatever reason, we simply didn't think of it that way." She went on to say she wasn't prepared for the burden her sorority sisters would place on her.

In the weeks that followed the rape, her sorority sisters gossiped. Some of them confronted her and said she brought shame upon the sorority and the rape was her fault. Then they distanced themselves from her. Eventually, she was expelled from the sorority after her sorority sisters held a meeting where they declared she wasn't "sorority material."

In talking about her sorority sisters, Valen says, "They not only failed to support me in a crisis, they collectively kicked me as I lay in the gutter, judged me from under a veil of hypocrisy, then cast me out leper-style. Their betrayal cut so deep that it has left me anxious and cowering to this day."

After her article appeared in print, she received backlash from other women. But she said the women who expressed outrage at her were simply proving her point—women judge one another and betray each other ruthlessly even when they're supposed to be friends.

The experience sparked her book, *Twisted Sisterhood,* in which she explores the "dark side of female friendship." As part of her research, she surveyed three thousand women about how they relate to one another. She discovered that 76 percent of them reported feeling hurt by jealousy or competition from other women.

But that's what women often do, because we're socialized to put other women down. Women want to be part of a group. Ostracism and bullying exclude women who appear to be threats. If you feel like you're in constant competition for scarce resources, like good jobs or suitable mates, you'll be more likely to do whatever it takes to get ahead.

We've woken up to the idea that bullying has a major impact on other people's lives—their psychological well-being, their health, and their experiences in life. When we think of bullies, we tend to refer to the mean kid on the playground. But bullies come in all forms, and the worst kind of bully is the one who pretends to be your friend.

PUTTING WOMEN DOWN KEEPS THEM FROM SUCCEEDING

The idea that making someone else look bad will make you look good is misguided. Never does anyone raise themselves up by hurling insults or being mean.

But there's this notion that women have a "crab mentality." It's the idea that if you put crabs in a bucket you don't need to put a lid on the top, because as one crab starts to make its way out of the bucket, the other crabs will pull it back down.

There may be some truth to the crab mentality. Women are underrepresented in local, state, and federal government positions. The 2018 Fortune 500 list only included twenty-four female CEOs—that's less than 5 percent of the total list. And only 30 percent of college presidents are women, according to a 2016 study conducted by the American Council of Education.

It could be tempting to blame men for those statistics. But women likely play a role in holding other women back too.

Since there are fewer positions at the top available to women, it's natural for women to feel threatened by others who may be good candidates for those positions. It may be to a woman's advantage to speak ill of her rivals in an effort to try to keep those around her from succeeding.

And what about the ones who do succeed? Once they make it to the top, shouldn't they help other women find their way up? Well, women who advocate for other women might pay a price. A study of more than three hundred executives found that men who promote diversity received higher performance ratings. They looked like nice guys trying to break down the good old boys' network. But when women executives promoted diversity, they received lower performance ratings. Their superiors thought they were giving women an advantage.

Of course, that's not a phenomenon unique to women. Research shows any minority leader who tries to hire diverse candidates is likely to be viewed as less effective. But the issue highlights how difficult it is for women leaders to help other women. They take a big risk if they try to help other women climb the ranks.

But distancing yourself from other women only perpetuates the problem. Saying things like "I'm not like other women," or "I fit in better with men," can be a subtler way of saying, "Include me among the ranks of the men but don't include them."

It's understandable why many women feel compelled to do this—they want to secure their own position. But sadly, the more we continue to do that, the less likely we are to move forward.

What to Do Instead

In the case of Meredith and her frustration with the people on her team, reducing her stress meant changing her thoughts and changing her behavior. But it also required a little bit of soul-searching.

One week I asked her what she gained from putting down the people on her team, because undoubtedly, she was getting something out of it. She acknowledged that making fun of the other employees made her feel a little better about herself. It helped her feel as though she was separate from them, like she was drawing a line in the sand between "us" and "them" with the other team leaders on her side and the new employees on the other.

Part of her treatment involved finding strategies that could help meet her needs without making fun of others. For example, she could find ways to bond with the other team leaders that didn't involve insulting the employees. And she could mentor the other people on her team and help them learn.

That didn't mean she needed to look at people through rose-colored glasses. She could acknowledge that some of them made mistakes or weren't fast learners. But she didn't need to label them all incompetent.

If you're not used to lifting others up, it can be tough to do at first. But over time, you'll see what a difference it can make in other people's lives—as well as your own.

CATCH YOURSELF WHEN YOU'RE TEMPTED TO PUT OTHERS DOWN

It can be tempting to blame everyone else for being the mean ones. But if we're honest, we can all likely identify plenty of times when we've put others down in one way or another. One of the women I interviewed for this book, Susan, hosts a podcast called *Estrogen Bombs*. One of the things she's talked about on her show is how people are quick to tear one another down—and she's willing to acknowledge that it's something she's personally working on as well. She said, "I think that there are so many things that have contributed to that. I'm certainly guilty of it myself, and it's the thing that I continually want to sharpen the saw on. It just shines on our own insecurities when we come from a place of judgment. It's not just women who are doing it to one another. It's everybody. We need to find common ground and show respect for each other."

The 2017 Civility in America Survey (the fact we survey people about this is telling) found that three-quarters of Americans believe that incivility has risen to crisis levels. The surveyors, who defined civility as "polite and respectful conduct and expression," found that on average, Americans experience 6.7 uncivil encounters each week.

When asked who is most likely to experience incivility, 73 percent of people said women. Only 53 percent of people said men.

Despite those startling statistics, a whopping 94 percent of Americans say they are always polite and respectful to others. Is it possible that only 6 percent of the population is wreaking havoc on the rest? It's far more likely that people who behave with insensitivity don't even realize they're doing it.

It's easy to convince yourself you'll never be the person who says mean things to others. But you might want to be wary of saying you'd never stoop so low.

I recently had a conversation with Sue Scheff, the author of *Shame Nation,* about how the internet gives all of us more opportunities to be unkind, and for many women, social media can become a nightmare. She said, "Not only are women quick to attack, but they are also being attacked. Women who don't feel empowered offline believe they can rip each other apart online."

Sue knows a thing or two about how the internet can be used as a tool to put others down. She was the victim of a vicious cyberattack where her reputation was damaged and her company was ruined. But she fought back and won. In 2006, she was awarded $11.3 million by a jury who heard her story of internet defamation.

Rather than call the individual who started slandering her online an "evil lunatic" or a "malicious psycho," Sue said, "I don't believe she was a bully, so to speak. She was a wife, a mother, had a very good job at a bank—and didn't like me. Not every person that is unkind to each other is morally bankrupt or mentally ill, as we assume trolls are. Hurt people will hurt people."

I've seen that many times in my therapy office. People who feel small or insignificant feel powerful when they hurt other people. And the internet can be an easy way for people to get swept up into treating others with disrespect.

So before you declare that you would never say or do mean things, remember that all of us are unkind sometimes. Putting others down isn't always about things that you do—sometimes it's the things you don't do as well. Perhaps you exclude a coworker you don't like, or maybe you offer a backhanded compliment to a friend when you're feeling a little jealous. Those things can be hurtful too.

When you're tempted to put others down, ask yourself a few questions:

- ***What am I feeling?*** Are you feeling jealous? Do you feel anxious? Are you angry? Take a minute to really understand the emotions driving your temptation to be insensitive or spiteful.
- ***What am I trying to accomplish?*** Do you hope the other person will feel bad? Do you want to harm someone's reputation? Are you hoping other people will side with you? Consider what you hope to gain by putting someone down.
- ***What does this say about me?*** Do you feel threatened by someone else's success? Do you have low self-esteem? Are you struggling to deal with personality differences in a healthy way? It can be a difficult question to answer, but it's very important to help you learn more about yourself.

If you've already been cruel or nasty toward someone, ask yourself those questions anyway. It could help you find ways to get your needs met without putting someone down next time.

BUILD YOUR SELF-WORTH ON A HEALTHY FOUNDATION

When you are struggling to feel good about yourself, you'll be tempted to put others down to gain a temporary boost in status. But the more you put others down, the worse you'll feel. It's a vicious cycle.

Examine how you're measuring your worth as a person. If you've built your self-worth on an unhealthy foundation, you will be more likely to put others down.

Here are five common but unhealthy things that shouldn't dictate your self-worth:

- **Your appearance**—Maybe it's the number on the scale that determines your happiness for the day. Or perhaps it's the number of romantic partners you attract that determines how you feel about yourself. Since there will always be women who look more attractive than you, basing your self-worth on your looks may compel you to point out others' flaws to temporarily feel better about yourself.

- **Your net worth**—If you measure your self-worth by your net worth, you'll never feel "valuable enough." There are always more toys to buy, bigger houses to be bought, and more luxurious vacations to take. You'll never feel like you have enough to be content, because there's always going to be someone who has something that you want.

- **Who you know**—While one person may only feel good about herself when she's in a relationship, someone else may feel as though name-dropping well-known people will gain the admiration from others she needs to feel good. But depending on other people to make you feel good is like chasing a moving target.

- **What you do**—Rather than say, "I program computers," most people introduce themselves by saying, "I *am* a computer programmer." For many, a job isn't what they *do*—it's who they *are*. Their career reinforces to them that they're "somebody," but an economic downturn, an unexpected shift in the job market, a major health problem, or even a planned retirement will destroy your self-worth if your identity is wrapped up in your job title.

- **What you achieve**—Sometimes people want to be known solely for their achievements. You'll need to experience constant success to feel good about yourself—and that means you'll likely avoid doing things where you could fail.

If you base your self-worth on an unsteady foundation, you'll feel bad every time you meet someone who is smarter, prettier, wealthier, faster, or more successful than you, and you'll be tempted to put them down to feel better.

Instead of chasing things that temporarily boost your self-esteem, measure your self-worth by who you are at your *core*. Behave according to your values and create a life of meaning and purpose. Then you'll be less threatened by those around you.

REFRAME YOUR THOUGHTS

It's easy to make sweeping judgments about other people, like "She's annoying," or "He's a jerk." But those are your opinions, not facts. When you draw those conclusions about people, however, your mind isn't likely to change.

Once you begin to view someone through a certain lens, it's hard to see them differently. If you conclude your coworker is annoying, you'll be on the lookout for behavior that reinforces this belief. Every time you look at her, you'll criticize her body language in your head. Or each *click clack* you hear as she walks down the hall will feel like she's tap-dancing on your last nerve.

So what if instead of telling yourself, "She's annoying," you reframed your thoughts? You might think, "She talks more than I do," or "She enjoys being the center of attention." It's OK to acknowledge, "I feel annoyed by those things," but it doesn't mean someone is an annoying person. Perhaps it means you have a low tolerance for people with certain characteristics. Or maybe it means you simply have different personalities. Stick to the facts without the judgment.

The people you are most tempted to put down may have the most to teach you about life. The person who annoys you most might be able to teach patience. Or that coworker who is really tough on you might be able to help you learn how to speak up for yourself in an assertive manner.

There are lessons to be learned everywhere in life, and figuring out how to treat others with kindness, even when we don't feel like it, is a skill. That's not to say you need to bend over backward for people who treat you poorly, but getting through a difficult encounter without hurling unkind words could be an opportunity for growth.

MAKE A CONSCIOUS EFFORT TO BUILD PEOPLE UP

I recently watched a wonderful example of female comradery unfold on Facebook. My friend Lisa wrote a post stating that her back felt better when she walked for twenty minutes. But her back hurts a lot, especially at the beginning of the walk. So she posted again on Facebook and bravely asked, "Would someone be willing to post every day and ask me if I have gone for a walk yet? I need the accountability until it becomes a habit." Our mutual friend Jodi immediately stepped up to the plate.

Over the next few weeks, Jodi became Lisa's biggest cheerleader and encourager. She began asking her, "Did you get your walk in today?" If Lisa confirmed she had, Jodi was quick to say, "Great job!" Or on the days when Lisa beat Jodi to the punch by announcing she'd already been on a walk, Jodi cheered her on by saying things like "Go, Lisa, go!"

Imagine what life could be like if we all did that sort of thing for each other? What could you accomplish if you had your own cheering squad who genuinely wanted you to achieve great things?

It can be tempting to think, "Yeah, but I don't have that. I don't have friends who would hold me accountable in a kind way, and I don't work with people who actually want me to succeed." I suspect many women feel that way. But, even if that's true, one thing you can do is become a cheerleader for others.

There's a great quote by Nishan Panwar: "The world is full of nice people. If you can't find one, be one." The same can be said for being a cheerleader. If you don't have anyone cheering you on in life, become that person for someone else.

But be a genuine cheerleader. Generic platitudes and empty compliments aren't necessarily helpful. Find someone with a goal and make it your personal mission to cheer on their efforts. It could be as simple as spurring on a friend with her exercise goals, or it might be as big as supporting a friend who is trying to put her life back together after a divorce. But treating others with kindness and support will help you feel better about yourself. And the more you do it, the more you'll want to do it.

Career

Only one woman won a major award at the 2017 Grammys—Alessia Cara was named Best New Artist. Men racked up the rest of the awards. After the awards were given, Recording Academy president Neil Portnow responded by saying women "who have the creativity in their hearts and souls" need to "step up."

Pink, who performed during the ceremony, responded on Twitter by saying, "Women in music don't need to 'step up'—women have been stepping up since the beginning of time. Stepping up, and also stepping aside. Women owned music this year. They've been killing it. And every year before this."

She went on to say, "When we celebrate and honor the talent and accomplishments of women, and how much women step up every year, against all odds, we show the next generation of women and girls and boys and men what it means to be equal, and what it means to be fair."

Pink could have easily separated herself from other women by pointing out that she'd performed at the Grammys or by telling other women to step up—as a way to show she's different from most female recording artists. But she didn't. She chose to speak up for women in the recording industry.

There may be times in your career when you'll be faced with a choice—do you declare you're different from other women as a way to separate yourself from the pack? Or do you speak up for those who are being marginalized?

Even if you can't speak up in a big way like Pink did, you can still extend a hand to other women. Help a new graduate find her place in your industry, or devote time to helping other women figure out how to succeed in your business. Becoming a mentor could give another woman the support she needs to keep going.

Family

Although the people closest to you should be the ones you treat the best, for many people, that's not the case. They feel comfortable with their spouse, their kids, or even their parents and lash out at them in the harshest manner.

Hearing unkind words from the people who are supposed to love you the most can cut the deepest. So if you're guilty of being unkind to your loved ones, commit to ending that habit. Your words have a lasting effect on your relationships. Make sure you're treating your loved ones better than you'd treat a stranger or an acquaintance.

If you have children, your kids will learn how to interact with others by watching how you communicate. If you're rude, insulting, and unpleasant, your kids will grow up thinking that type of behavior is OK, and they may develop a warped sense of love and family.

Decide that you're going to build up your family members both inside and outside your home. Offer genuine praise, kind words, and lots of love. And when others are around, speak positively about your family too. Your friends don't need to hear about your spouse's mistakes, shortcomings, and failures.

Social Life

My late husband's grandmother "Gram" has had the same group of girl-friends for nearly ninety years. Now in their early nineties, Gram's squad formed in the first grade (apparently they didn't have kindergarten in 1930).

All four girls played on the basketball team throughout school. They spent nights at each other's houses, went swimming, and worked on their schoolwork together. In 1941, after they had graduated, three of the friends moved to New York to become airplane mechanics during World War II. They shared a one-bedroom apartment and when they weren't working, they were out enjoying the city together.

From health problems to being widowed, they've gone through many hardships over the years. But there have been many celebrations too—marriages, children, and grandchildren, to name a few. And the four of them have stuck together through thick and thin.

Gram speaks about her friends with high regard. And I suspect their respect for one another has been the secret to their ability to create such enduring friendships.

One of Gram's sayings is "You shouldn't speak ill of your mother-in-law because someday you might be one." I suspect that's a philosophy she's applied to friendships too. I've never heard her so much as hint about anything bad when it comes to her friends. Instead, she shares their triumphs and joys as if they were her own.

So while you might not have friendships that last for ninety years, you can create trusting, enduring relationships that can still stand the test of time. And one of the best ways to do that is by deciding that you'll never put your friends down.

It also means sticking up for your friends. When one friend excuses herself to go to the restroom, and another friend says, "Can you believe she wore that dress?" that's your opportunity to be a good friend. Set a precedent that shows you're not going to put other people down—especially your friends.

Lifting Others up Makes You Stronger

If anyone should get a free pass to put others down, it might be Lizzie Velasquez. She's been on the receiving end of cruelty a time or two.

Lizzie has a rare genetic disorder that prevents her from being able to gain weight. Despite consuming thousands of calories each day, she's never weighed more than sixty-four pounds.

When she was seventeen, she discovered a YouTube video called "The World's Ugliest Woman." Upon closer inspection, she realized the video was about her. By the time she watched it, the eight-second clip had already been viewed more than four million times.

After seeing the video, Lizzie scrolled down to see what people were saying. There were thousands of comments and not a single one was kind. Instead, they said things like, "Do everyone a favor and kill yourself," and "If people see her face in public, they will go blind."

Lizzie says that was the worst moment of her life. But she chose not to retaliate. Instead, she decided to become an anti-bullying activist. She wrote books, she gave a TEDx talk that became one of the most popular talks of all time, and she started her own YouTube channel. There's even a documentary about her that appeared on Lifetime. Her work has educated countless people on kindness and strategies for putting a stop to bullying.

In her book *Dare to Be Kind,* Lizzie says she tries to practice feeling compassion for others, even when they're spewing hate. When someone commented on her YouTube channel, "Why is everyone lying to Lizzie, telling her she's pretty? We all know she isn't pretty. SHE knows she isn't pretty. I may be rude, but at least I'm not a liar," she demonstrated her ability to be kind in the face of cruelty. Lizzie replied by saying, "We each have our own perspective and that's great. I respect your opinion. But there's a way to voice it that isn't so blunt. Thanks for your comment. I hope you have a great day!"

To Lizzie's surprise, the person responded within minutes by saying, "Wow, it's really you!! I'm a huge supporter of yours!!" Lizzie acknowledges that it's tough to show compassion and respect sometimes, but she says, "We are here to help each other. That, in my mind, is our purpose as a species. It's the whole point of being human: to love ourselves and each other and do it better every day if possible."

No one ever made themselves stronger by putting others down. But by lifting people up—even the people who you might think don't deserve your kindness—you can make a difference in the world. Challenging yourself to be better and do better, even when it's hard, can also help you develop your mental muscles. Putting others down is easy. It takes true strength of character to be kind and respectful in all circumstances.

Troubleshooting and Common Traps

Deciding that you're not going to put people down doesn't mean you have to tolerate unhealthy behavior. It's important to set limits with people who aren't good for you. That may mean physically distancing yourself or speaking up for yourself. But you can do all that without blaming the other person or putting them down.

Use "I" messages to communicate your intentions. Instead of saying, "You're a jerk," say, "I'm feeling disrespected." That small change in the way you communicate can make a big difference in how effective you'll be in creating change.

It can also be hard to treat others with respect if your inner dialogue is overly self-critical. If you're calling yourself names all day, you'll be much more likely to call other people names. Take a hard look at the way you speak to yourself. You won't be doing anyone any favors—especially yourself—if you're constantly finding fault in yourself.

Developing compassionate self-talk, forgiving yourself for mistakes, and not taking yourself so seriously could help you stop putting others down. When you feel good about who you are, you'll be able to appreciate others for who they are—flaws and all.

WHAT'S HELPFUL

- Recognizing when you're tempted to put someone down
- Uncovering the thoughts and feelings behind your desire to lash out
- Building your self-worth on who you are at your core, not factors you can't control
- Reframing the thoughts you have about other people to acknowledge that it's your opinion, not a fact
- Proactively building other people up

WHAT'S NOT HELPFUL

- Lashing out when you feel threatened by someone else's success
- Separating yourself from other women to gain a competitive edge
- Pointing out other people's flaws to ensure that they see them
- Venting or complaining because you think you are reducing your stress
- Convincing yourself you are "warning" others when you speak ill of someone

9

They Don't Let Others Limit Their Potential

No one can make you feel inferior without your consent.
—ELEANOR ROOSEVELT

Marcia wanted therapy because she felt "stuck in a rut." The first thing she said when she stepped into my office was, "I feel like I'm going nowhere in life."

Marcia and her boyfriend lived with two roommates because they couldn't afford their own place. She worked part-time as a cashier at a gift shop. Her boyfriend also worked part-time, in a store in the same strip mall.

She and her boyfriend had the same goal—to work as little as possible so they could fully enjoy life. "I want to work to live, not live to work," she said. But she was starting to feel the effects of those choices.

Marcia wanted to have kids someday, but she wasn't sure how they'd ever be able to afford children. "We don't have any benefits. We can't afford to fix our car either. I like riding my bike sometimes, but when it's cold or when I don't feel well, I wish our car worked."

She agreed to begin treatment to address some of the turmoil she was experiencing and to find strategies to help her feel "unstuck." I spent the next few weeks getting to know Marcia better. She said her relationship with her boyfriend was good. And although she liked her roommates, she wanted to get her own place with her boyfriend.

One of the most interesting things I learned about Marcia had to do with the family dynamics when she was growing up. She had two older siblings, and her parents referred to her sister as the "athlete" and called her brother the "mathlete," since he was so good in math. But they always called Marcia their "free spirit."

"I'd always wished they'd called me the musician, because I loved to play the guitar and sing. But nope, they just thought of me as a tree hugger because I was different," she said.

Although her parents were loving—and they probably assumed their label was harmless—calling Marcia a "free spirit" affected her deeply. "I always felt different and not necessarily in a good way," she said.

Her parents' label likely turned into a self-fulfilling prophecy. Unlike her siblings, Marcia didn't go to college. Rather than seek a higher-paying job, she opted for a part-time retail position in an independent store.

And while there was nothing wrong with any of that, Marcia felt like she needed to fully embrace being a "free spirit," even when it didn't serve her well. To her, that meant not valuing money and not caring about material items. But she feared she wouldn't be able to raise children in a stable environment if she continued.

Marcia was essentially experiencing a quarter-life crisis. Her entire identity had become wrapped up in the idea that she was a free spirit, and now she wasn't sure that was really who she wanted to be. She had to decide what she really valued and needed to think about what type of changes she might want to make.

Over the course of several months, we discussed what it would mean for Marcia if she got a more traditional job—one that would help her feel more financially secure. Marcia wrestled with the idea for quite some time. She feared being a "boring, regular person," but at the same time, she craved more stability in her life.

So one week I asked her, "What would happen to your relationships if you had a full-time job and a home?" Marcia said, "Well, I dread hearing my family say, 'I told you so.' They'd think I finally came to my senses and gave up that phase of my life."

She also worried her friends might think she'd changed for the worse or that she was giving up her identity to become like everyone else. She wasn't sure they'd like her.

Marcia's treatment focused on helping her identify her values—and live according to them. She could create any type of life she wanted, and she was free to change her lifestyle as often as she wanted. But she was allowing others' beliefs about who she thought she *should* be to limit her potential.

We uncovered who she actually wanted to be. And then we identified the steps she could take to become that person.

She eventually decided to get a full-time job—as did her boyfriend. They moved into their own place and got their car repaired. And slowly, Marcia's view of herself began to expand. Rather than pigeonhole herself into a specific type of person, she began to see herself as multifaceted. She could still be a free spirit with a full-time job.

Do You Let Other People Limit Your Potential?

There are some obvious ways someone might limit your potential—like giving up when someone says you won't succeed. But there are also subtler ways you might be allowing other people to hold you back from becoming your best self. Do any of the following points describe you?

- ❏ If I get rejected, I'm not likely to try again.
- ❏ I believe the criticism I hear about myself, regardless of the source.
- ❏ When someone discourages me from doing something, I don't do it.
- ❏ While I might live up to other people's expectations, I don't exceed them.
- ❏ I feel like I've fallen into specific roles and it's hard to break free.
- ❏ There are certain things I'd never try because I fear people might make fun of me.

❏ Other people's opinions matter greatly.

❏ I need a lot of support or encouragement to branch out.

❏ I listen to other people's advice (even when it's bad) because I don't trust my own opinion.

Why We Do It

In one of her therapy sessions, Marcia said that in a strange way, she felt like being a "free spirit" gave her parents something to brag about. When they talked to people about her sister, they told people about the basketball team she coached. When they told people about her brother, they talked about his work as an engineer. And when they talked about Marcia, they said things like "Well, Marcia lives by her own rules!" From upcycling other people's discarded items to growing organic vegetables, her activities gave her family something to talk about.

She feared that if she gave up some of those things, they'd stop talking about her altogether. She'd lose some of the things that made her unique. Growing up in a successful family made it hard to stand out. Since she wasn't the smartest or the most athletic kid in the family, being a free spirit seemed to be the best way to garner attention.

But she'd never really spent any time thinking about this. It was just something that subconsciously happened. She grew into the label more and more over time without considering whether it was something she actually wanted to do.

While you might not have been given a clear label as a kid, there may be some ways you've allowed your family of origin, your boss, your friends, or even strangers to limit your potential.

GIRLS BECOME NURSES; BOYS BECOME DOCTORS

There's an old riddle about a father and son who are in a terrible car crash. The father dies. The son is rushed to the hospital. The surgeon takes one look and says, "I can't operate on this patient. This boy is my son." How do you explain that?

Researchers posed that question to 197 students at Boston University, many of whom were self-described feminists. Only 14 percent of them said the surgeon was the boy's mother. Other students suggested the surgeon might be the stepdad or the boy's gay second father. Even female participants who had mothers who were physicians weren't likely to guess the surgeon was the boy's mother.

Participants were also given an alternative version of the riddle: a mother is killed in a crash, the daughter goes to the hospital, and a nurse says, "I can't care for that patient because that girl is my daughter." The results were almost identical—very few people guessed the nurse was the patient's father.

Researchers ran the riddle past children, between the ages of seven and seventeen, and 15 percent of them guessed the surgeon was the boy's mother. The rest of the kids offered other creative ideas, such as the surgeon being a robot or a ghost. Some of them even thought that officials must have made a mistake when they thought the father died.

The idea that men are doctors and women are nurses stems from our gender schemas—generalizations that help us explain our complex world. Schemas are shortcuts that help us navigate the world quickly and more efficiently by placing things in categories. We form these schemas early in life and we tend to hold on to them, even when we're faced with evidence to the contrary.

So even though you know on the surface that a woman can be a doctor and a man can be a nurse, you are still likely to possess some subconscious gender bias based on the schemas you've developed.

Researchers from Harvard studied just how deeply ingrained our notion is about gender stereotypes in a study that examined implicit-association tasks. The researchers told participants that Jonathan is a nurse and Elizabeth is a doctor. Then they were shown a pair of words and asked to press a button if the words were related.

When shown the words "Elizabeth" and "doctor," participants were much slower at pressing the button. When they were told Elizabeth was a nurse and Jonathan was a doctor, they were able to associate the two words much faster. Researchers concluded that no matter what participants were told, they still subconsciously saw Jonathan as a doctor and Elizabeth as a nurse.

Studies show we don't view women as leaders either. In fact, studies repeatedly show when people are asked to draw a picture of a leader, both men and women almost always draw a man.

It's quite probable that these deeply ingrained stereotypes limit our potential. How many girls became nurses because they didn't think it was an option to be a doctor? Or how many girls decided to be receptionists because the bosses are men?

Even if someone told you that you could be a firefighter, construction worker, or astronaut, did you truly believe that you could do it? Perhaps you had a gender schema that gave you a bit of doubt about whether girls really could do those things.

Amber, one of the women I interviewed for this book, was raised as a Mormon in Utah. From a young age, it was instilled in her that as a woman, her job was to become a mother and take care of the home.

She said her parents encouraged her to go to college, not to get an education, but to meet a husband. They never wanted her to be a "career woman." She met her husband in college and got married just as she was finishing up her bachelor's degree. Together, they had three children, and Amber was a stay-at-home mom.

At some point, her husband began to question their faith, which made Amber think more about her religion and her beliefs. She said much of what she was doing felt like a façade. Together, she and her husband decided to step away from their Mormon beliefs.

But she says many of her husband's behaviors and expectations remained the same even after they left the church. He continued to expect her to be subservient. Amber wanted more for herself, but she wasn't sure how to gain independence.

She lacked confidence too. And that caused her to make some mistakes—like having an extramarital affair. She had hoped a man would help her feel good about herself. But it didn't work. She did, however, find the strength to become more self-reliant, and she chose to divorce her husband.

She got her master's degree in education and she became a teacher. And for the first time ever, she lived on her own. She said, "My husband had always done all the finances. I didn't even have the password to our online bank. I had no clue how to pay the mortgage or the car loan." She figured it out on her own and gained confidence that she could keep going.

She said her goal is to teach her children and her students that they have a lot of choices about what they want to be when they grow up. She said her daughter used to say, "I want to be a mom when I grow up." So she responded by saying, "That's fine, but what career do you want?," which is something she never heard when she was young.

WOMEN ARE MORE SENSITIVE TO CRITICISM

No one wants to hear, "You're off pitch," or "You're not as fast as the other employees." Those words sting. And if you're not careful, criticism can knock you off course. You might decide you're a bad singer or you're a bad worker based on the words you hear. In fact, there's a good chance that as a woman, you might be more likely to allow those words to hold you back from reaching your greatest potential.

A company called PsychTests created a "Sensitivity to Criticism" test. They administered the test to 3,600 participants and concluded that women are more likely to take criticism personally. In addition, they found that women are more likely to be hard on themselves for not doing something well.

Men, on the other hand, are more likely to convince themselves the critic is wrong and they're more likely to argue with the critic.

While there are definitely pros and cons to both approaches, taking criticism too personally could certainly affect your performance and your choices in a negative way.

So while men may be more likely to think, "My supervisors have no idea what they're talking about," women may be more apt to respond to the exact same criticism by thinking, "I am bad at my job."

A 2014 study conducted by researchers at the University of Texas at Austin and the University of Southern Mississippi found that women respond to criticism and rejection in the same way. Men, however, treat criticism and rejection like separate entities.

Researchers discovered the difference in the way men and women respond to criticism when they examined positive face—things that could threaten an individual's identity—on social media. The participants were told they were testing out a new social-networking site for college students. Then they were told to ask to join certain groups, such as a group for people who loved animals or one for people who loved Apple products.

Sometimes, individuals were rejected and told things like "We don't want you in our group." At other times, they were accepted into the group but received criticism, such as "No offense, but when we saw your profile, we laughed."

After being rejected or criticized, participants could respond with a virtual gift—either a smiley face or a ticking time bomb. Men sent more ticking time bombs when they were rejected, as compared to when they were criticized. But the women responded to both rejection and criticism in an identical manner. Even when they were accepted to the group, women reacted as though they'd been rejected if they were given criticism.

The study demonstrates an interesting point. If women equate criticism with rejection, feedback of all kinds could seriously limit their potential. Instead of ignoring unhelpful criticism or growing from negative feedback, women might give up if they feel rejected by someone else's evaluation.

Criticism is another person's opinion—it doesn't make it fact. Listening to someone else's opinion can provide you with valuable information that could help you improve. But automatically believing negative feedback might also stop you in your tracks.

If you produce something (like blog posts) or you provide a service (like cutting people's hair), not everyone will appreciate your work. And some of those people may become very vocal about how much they dislike your products or services—especially on review sites or in comment sections online. But that doesn't mean you are bad at what you do. It just means someone wasn't a fan.

SOMETIMES MEN ABUSE THEIR POWER

Of course, it's easy to say, "I'm not going to let anyone else hold me back." But, in practice, things can get quite complicated.

We've seen countless examples in the media of men abusing their authority in a way that made women feel powerless to proceed. Take Heather Graham's reports of what happened to her in Hollywood.

In an article for *Variety,* she said she met with Harvey Weinstein to talk about acting opportunities. Weinstein told her he had an agreement with his wife that he could sleep with whoever he wanted when she was out of town. Graham said, "There was no explicit mention that to star in one of those films I had to sleep with him, but the subtext was there."

Graham had another meeting scheduled with Weinstein at his hotel. She canceled at the last minute when a friend who was going to accompany her wasn't able to make it. Weinstein told her that her friend was already at his hotel and they were waiting for her together—but Graham knew that wasn't true and she refused to meet him.

Graham said she never met with Weinstein again. And she never got picked to star in any of his films.

We know now that Weinstein did the same thing to many other women. He offered many women work in exchange for sex. How do you not let that limit your potential?

Unfortunately, many other women have found themselves in situations where advancement—or even maintaining their current status—meant compromising their morals or doing something they didn't want to do.

If you were subjected to someone who abused his power—whether it was a domestic violence situation or a workplace issue—you may have felt you had few options. That doesn't mean you're weak. It does mean we need to create changes on a societal level that put an end to men abusing their power.

Why It's Bad

Ironically, Marcia thought that becoming a "regular person" would mean she was giving people the power to limit her potential. She said, "I don't want to work a full-time job just so I can buy more stuff. I'm not materialistic." But, at some point, she realized that her desire to live up to the "free spirit" label was actually allowing her parents' expectations to limit her potential.

During one of her appointments she said, "I sometimes catch myself dreaming of living in a little house with the white picket fence and a couple of children playing in the yard. Then I remember that's not who I am and it's not what I want." But after a while she admitted to herself that the image of the house with a fence *was* what she wanted. It just didn't line up with the image of herself she was clinging on to.

Reaching your greatest potential doesn't mean you need to earn more money, accept a more prestigious position, or accomplish more. In some cases, it may mean passing up a promotion so you can spend more time with your kids. Or it may mean accepting a career that is less lucrative yet provides a service that helps you feel more fulfilled. Only you can really know if you're reaching your greatest potential. But if you're not careful, it's easy to let others hold you back from becoming your best.

REJECTION STOPS WOMEN FROM TRYING AGAIN

After college, I applied to two different graduate schools. My first-choice school rejected me. Reading the letter that said, "We're sorry to inform you . . ." felt terrible. I held my breath as I waited for the other letter. I wondered if I wasn't graduate school material. Fortunately, my second-choice school accepted me.

While the rejection letter stung at the time, I sort of forgot about it as the years passed. Then, last year, I was speaking at an event and a member of the audience came up to me afterward. She said, "Your book is on my college's list of recommended readings." I asked her where she went to school, and she named the college that rejected me for graduate school. It took me a minute to realize that the same college that thought I wasn't good enough to pay them for an education was now recommending their students read my book.

I'm glad I applied to two graduate schools at the same time. I would like to think I would have applied to another school after I received my rejection letter if I hadn't already done so. But I'll never know for sure. What if I would have given up?

Studies show most women do give up after they're rejected. A study of more than ten thousand senior executives in the U.K. found that women were less likely to apply for a job if they had already been rejected for a similar position. Men were also less likely to apply after being rejected, but the effect was more than 1.5 times stronger for women.

Women begin their careers with just as much ambition to climb the ranks as men. But their enthusiasm subsides over time. There may be many reasons for that. Getting married, having children, or simply growing older may shift their goals. But giving up after rejection may also play a role.

Employees who eventually succeed have typically been turned down for assignments and rejected for promotions several times. They don't give up after feeling disappointed or turned away. Giving up after being rejected lets other people limit your potential. Just because one person didn't think you had enough skills or talent doesn't mean you don't have talent or that you can't improve yourself.

CRITICS' COMMENTS ARE MORE LIKELY TO BE REFLECTIONS OF THEMSELVES, NOT YOU

I once worked with a client who was raised by an abusive, alcoholic father. All throughout her childhood, he told her she was useless and worthless and she'd never amount to anything. Those words replayed in her head throughout her adult life. She said, "As I'm walking into a job interview I can hear my father telling me, 'You'll never amount to anything,' or when I'm on a date I recall him saying, 'No one will ever want you.'"

I asked her how she thought her father felt about himself. We made a list of all the words and phrases she thought described his self-esteem. When we were done, I read back over the list of things she had said: "He hated himself. He knew he was a bad father. He felt worthless. He felt unsuccessful . . ."

The words she used to describe her father's self-esteem were almost identical to all the things he said to her. That exercise helped her see that his comments were never about her. He was actually talking about himself all those years.

Of course, that may not seem like much of a surprising revelation—an abusive individual lashes out because he doesn't feel good about himself. But there's evidence that says much of the criticism people give is likely a reflection of the critic rather than the individual being criticized.

A 2010 study conducted by researchers at Wake Forest University tested this theory. They asked college students to rate their friends, other students who lived in their dormitories, or others within their sorority or fraternity. They found that the level of negativity someone used to describe others actually reflected how unhappy, disagreeable, or neurotic the rater was.

Researchers followed up with the raters one year later. They discovered not much had changed. The raters' views of others remained highly stable—as did their perception of themselves.

This is why it's so dangerous to believe what others say about you. That stranger online who called you a loser actually feels like a loser. Or that coworker who complains that you are a poor communicator might actually feel like no one ever listens to her. It may have nothing to do with you or how others perceive you.

What to Do Instead

Marcia had to expand her thinking in order to expand her life. She could still think of herself as a free spirit while also embracing some aspects of a more traditional lifestyle. But she worried what other people would think if she gave up some of the things that made her different.

She decided that if anyone questioned her decisions, she would simply say, "We all grow and change, and I've decided this is what best suits the current phase of my life." She also reminded herself that she could always do things differently down the road.

Perhaps she'd homeschool her kids and live on a farm. Or maybe she'd travel the country in an RV. Reminding herself that she didn't need to work a full-time job and live in the same house forever gave her some peace.

You can't go back in time and change the choices you made. If you allowed someone to limit your potential in the past, you might not be able to chase those dreams you gave up. But you can move forward with confidence that you're going to create the type of life you want to live.

THINK ABOUT THE LIMITATIONS
YOU MAY HAVE ACCEPTED

I once worked with an entrepreneur who felt guilty she was earning a lot of money. She said, "I am finally living the dream but it doesn't feel as good as I thought." We explored her beliefs about money and where those beliefs came from.

She grew up in a hardworking middle-class family. One day, when she was about seven years old, she overheard a woman in the store talking about her lottery ticket. So she asked her father why they never purchased lottery tickets. He said, "I'd never play the lottery because I'd be afraid I'd win. Money corrupts people." That one comment from her father had instilled a deep-rooted core belief that money was bad. It was such a small thing that made such a big impact on her life.

She felt selfish about making more money than she needed and she worried that her wealth would turn her into a bad person. She also felt guilty she wasn't enjoying her money. She knew a lot of struggling people who would love to have "too much money." She said, "It's like I just can't be happy no matter what."

The things you learned about yourself, other people, and the world as a child shaped the person you became as an adult. That's not to say you need to go back and "remold your inner child" or anything too hokey like that. But it can be helpful to think about some of the lessons you learned as a child that affected how you viewed yourself and what you were capable of becoming.

Here are some examples:

Situation #1—A girl is at the community pool and she overhears a stranger say, "Wow, look at the size of that kid's foot. She's going to be a big girl."

> **Self-limiting belief:** The girl grows up thinking she's big-boned. She wears baggy clothes and steers clear of activities like cheerleading because she worries that she's fat. Her body image issues continue into adulthood.

Situation #2—A girl tells her mother she wants to dress like a teacher for career day at school. Her mother responds by saying, "People like us don't get good jobs. You have to go to college to become a teacher, and we don't have the money to send you there."

Self-limiting belief: The girl assumes she'll never be able to go to college, so school becomes less important to her. She thinks she is destined to work in a low-paying job so she never bothers applying to college.

Situation #3—A teenager asks her father to edit her English essay before she passes it in. After reading it he jokingly says, "Good thing you're pretty, honey, because no one is ever going to marry you for your mind."

Self-limiting belief: She thinks she is unintelligent and she believes boys are only going to like her for her body. She sometimes "plays dumb" around boys to get even more attention as the "cute dumb blonde." As an adult, she gets into relationships with men whom she has chemistry with, but none who are truly compatible with her, because her relationships are all based on superficial things.

It's not helpful to blame anyone who may have led you astray as a child. But connecting some of the dots between your beliefs and their origin can give you some insight into how and why you may have allowed others to limit your potential. Can you think of any examples of times when someone's comments about you may have shaped your beliefs and perhaps limited your potential?

PAY ATTENTION TO YOUR SELF-TALK

Regardless of how you first developed beliefs about yourself that limit your potential, the conversations you have with yourself either reinforce or refute those beliefs. You likely don't pay much attention to your thinking patterns, however. After all, who thinks about thinking?

Start paying attention to your self-talk. You might even keep a thought journal to really track your inner dialogue. You'll likely notice some clear patterns in the way you think.

Identifying the unhealthy thinking patterns you've developed is the first step in changing the way you think. Psychologists refer to maladaptive and irrational thoughts as cognitive distortions. And while there are many types of cognitive distortions, here are the thinking errors that are most likely to let others limit your potential:

1. **All-or-Nothing Thinking**

   Sometimes, it's easy to assume you are good or bad at certain things. You might think, "I'm bad at math," or "I'm a terrible communicator." In reality, you aren't a total success or a complete failure at anything. You have skills, talents, and abilities that lie somewhere in between.

2. **Overgeneralizing**

   Overgeneralizing involves taking a specific situation and applying it to the bigger picture of your life. If you fail to close one deal, you may decide, "I'm a terrible salesperson." Or if you are treated poorly by one family member, you might think, "Everyone in my family is rude to me."

3. **Filtering Out the Positive**

   It can be tempting to dwell on the negative and ignore the positive. You might declare your job interview a "complete disaster" because you made a mistake, or you might decide all of the leaders in your company don't like you just because one supervisor gave you negative feedback.

4. **Mind-Reading**

   You never know what someone else is actually thinking. But you likely guess by saying, "She thinks I'm stupid," or "He has never liked me." Those statements are nothing more than guesses, and believing that you know what others think affects your relationships and the choices you make.

5. **Catastrophizing**

   Imagining worst-case scenarios and exaggerating your misfortune can prevent you from taking positive action. Thinking, "If my boyfriend finds out about my past he'll leave. I'll never find anyone else to love me," may cause you to invest your energy into hiding your past, rather than building a healthy relationship.

6. **Fortune-telling**

   Although you never know what might happen in the future, you might waste a lot of energy predicting what you think will happen. Telling yourself, "I'm going to embarrass myself during my presentation," or "I'm going to mess my child up for life," isn't helpful. In fact, those types of thoughts can turn into self-fulfilling prophecies.

7. **Personalization**

   As easy as it is to say you know the world doesn't revolve around you, it can be easy to personalize everything. When a friend doesn't call you back, you might think, "She must be mad at me," or if a coworker acts grumpy, you might conclude, "He doesn't like me." Thinking other people's choices are somehow related to you will affect your behavior.

Becoming aware of your cognitive distortions can help you think more realistically. Thinking realistically can empower you to become your best, despite times when others may try to limit your potential.

When you catch yourself catastrophizing, and you can remind yourself, "OK, I'm catastrophizing and this isn't helpful. It likely isn't as bad as I think," you'll see that your thoughts aren't necessarily facts. Or when you recognize that you're mind-reading, you can remind yourself that your thoughts are just guesses and are likely inaccurate. That can help you dial it back and develop a more realistic outlook.

KEEP GOING EVEN WHEN PEOPLE DON'T BELIEVE IN YOU

When Shakira was a child, her music teacher said she couldn't sing well enough to join the school choir. Her classmates laughed at her and told her she sounded like a goat. But she didn't stop singing.

Her first records were launched in the early 1990s—but they weren't well received. She kept working on her voice and kept singing until her hard work paid off. Between 2000 and 2009, Shakira had four of the twenty top-selling hits. That was more than any other artist. She's won five MTV Video Music Awards and three Grammy Awards, and was nominated for a Golden Globe. She has sold over 125 million records worldwide and has a star on the Hollywood Walk of Fame. Not bad for someone who was told she sounded like a goat.

She's a shining example of someone who didn't give up even when other people told her to do so. But that's not to say you should never listen to other people's feedback.

If you ignore everyone who says you can't sing, you might be at risk of the *"American Idol* Effect." The show gained fame by showcasing young people who were trying to become the best singer in America. While many of these young people were extremely talented, others seemed oblivious about their lack of skill. That lack of self-awareness isn't likely to serve you well (unless you happen to be William Hung, who gave an off-key performance so bad he gained a cult following for a brief period of time).

Studies show we tend to be pretty bad at gauging our own creativity. We rate our abilities very differently from the way professionals or critics might rate us. So while you don't need to believe every bit of advice you hear, you might want to listen up if there's a general consensus.

But the point is, you don't have to let criticism change your behavior. You can choose to keep trying even when you don't get picked or even when other people tell you that you'll never make it. Keep going and don't let one person's opinion limit you from reaching your greatest potential.

SET BOUNDARIES WHEN YOU RECEIVE UNHELPFUL CRITICISM AND UNWANTED ADVICE

Vocal fry refers to the low-pitched rough creaking sound that often comes near the end of a sentence. It's something that is often associated with women (Kim Kardashian is known for it), but researchers have found that men may use vocal fry just as often as women. Women, however, are far more likely to be criticized for it. In fact, women's voices in general receive a lot more criticism than men's.

A podcast called *99% Invisible* grew tired of fielding emails from listeners who complained about their female reporters' voices. So they created a special folder that sent an automated reply to anyone writing in to complain. Their response read:

"Hello. You've written in to voice your dislike of one of our female reporters' voices. You're not alone. We have a filter set up that automatically sends these types of emails into a folder labeled zero priority. We'll review this folder and consider the complaints within, well, never. Amazingly, we don't even have a folder for our complaints about the male voices on our show because we've never gotten one. Isn't that strange? We think so. Anyway, hope you can continue to enjoy our free podcast somehow. And if you can't, there are plenty of shows that don't feature women's voices at all."

They aren't wasting their time arguing with people who complain. And they aren't trying to justify why they choose to have women on their show. Instead, they've automated a reply that shows they just aren't interested in addressing those issues.

Far too often, there seems to be a notion that if you don't speak up, you must be a doormat, or that you're allowing someone to bully you. But sometimes, silence (or an automated reply) speaks volumes. Refusing to put your time and energy into arguing, and ignoring someone completely, could be a better use of your resources.

So while you may not want to create a folder that automatically responds to complaints, filter out the stuff that isn't helpful. The more time you invest in trying to change someone's mind or to prove your worthiness, the less time you'll be working on your goals.

It can be easy to ignore criticism or unwanted advice from strangers. But when it comes from friends, coworkers, or family members, you may need to set some clear boundaries. Here are some things you might try:

- **Express the pain.** If it's a loved one expressing their concern that you might "burn out" or that you're chasing a dream that won't ever happen, acknowledge that those words are tough to hear. Say something like, "It's painful to hear that." You don't have to argue or justify yourself beyond that.
- **Acknowledge what you heard.** Whether your mother-in-law criticizes your parenting or your cousin says you should change your eating habits, try saying, "Interesting idea. I'll consider if that's right for me." That makes it clear that there isn't a one-size-fits-all solution to life.
- **Make it clear you aren't interested.** When someone weighs in on how you could be doing things better, but you don't value their input, say something like, "I'm actually not looking for any advice right now."

Career

Researchers at Stanford found that women are given vague feedback at work and it may be hurting their careers. In a 2016 article in *Harvard Business Review,* Shelley Correll and Caroline Simard say that when they analyzed over two hundred performance reviews with a large technology company, they found that women's reviews were more likely to include statements like "You had a great year," while men's performance reviews pinpointed exactly what they did that was great.

Feedback about what participants could do better was also vaguer for women. Comments such as "Her speaking style and approach can be off-putting to some people at times" were common. The comments on what men could do better were more likely to offer clear-cut strategies of how they could improve, such as "You need to deepen your domain knowledge in X space—once you have that understanding, you will be able to contribute to the design decisions that impact the customer."

Clearly, comments like "You're doing great," or "You should communicate better," aren't helpful. Those types of ambiguous comments are likely to leave you feeling frustrated.

So while it isn't your job to tell your manager how to communicate better (ironic, isn't it?), you might ask questions that pinpoint specific things you can do to improve your job. Ask for examples or clear strategies you might employ.

Your goal shouldn't be to avoid all criticism. Although it can be uncomfortable to hear, criticism can be key to helping you improve and get better. And your supervisors are the ones who can tell you what you need to do better to improve your performance at work.

Family

Your family of origin plays several interesting roles in your ability to reach your potential. Like we talked about earlier, your parents shaped some of your core beliefs. But when it comes to your family, there's another interesting dynamic at play—they established beliefs about you when you were a kid. And it can be hard to break free from their expectations.

It's not just your parents who see you as that same kid you used to be. Your older siblings may still refer to you as the "baby of the family" and treat you as such. Your aunt might still call you by your ridiculous childhood nickname. Your grandmother might still remind you of that embarrassing thing you did at age ten every time you see her.

No matter how much you've grown and changed over the years, your family's view of you might not have shifted. Even if you're raising your third child, your mother might still offer you advice on how to get a baby to sleep through the night. Or perhaps you earn a six-figure salary and your grandfather scolds you for spending too much money on that new car you just bought.

It can actually be tougher to be your authentic self around people who have known you your whole life. If you've ever found yourself confiding something in a complete stranger—like that person next to you on the airplane or that new hairdresser you found—it's because that individual doesn't have any preconceived notions about you. They don't know that you were bullied as a kid because you were bad at math, or they don't know that you wet the bed until you were twenty-two. Strangers don't expect you to fulfill a certain role or to be a certain way.

So it's important to think about how your family's expectations of you play into your potential. Do you shrink yourself to fit their beliefs about you? Or are you able to be you even if the "adult you" doesn't quite match the version of you they have in their heads?

Social Life

I once worked with a young woman who was deep in college loan debt. She made the decision to take on an extra job on the weekends to help her pay off her loans as fast as she could. But, rather than support her efforts, her friends told her she was crazy. Some of them told her she was going to kill herself working so many hours, and others told her she was wasting the best years of her life working extra hours. One of her friends even reminded her, "No one ever says I wish I would have worked more when they're on their deathbed."

But my client was motivated to get her loans paid off as fast as she could. She liked her weekend job and she felt good about herself for getting her loans paid down. She couldn't understand why her friends couldn't be happy for her.

Unfortunately, not everyone will want you to succeed in life. Even some of your so-called friends and family members may try to talk you out of bettering yourself. There could be lots of reasons for that. You doing awesome things might be threatening to them—what if you outgrow them? Or your success might remind them of their lack of success.

There's also the possibility that they're truly worried about your well-being. They may have the best of intentions when they warn you or try to convince you to change your behavior. So it's important to consider their comments, but you aren't obligated to do as they please. Set healthy boundaries that will keep them from holding you back or dragging you down.

Refusing to Let Others Limit Your Life Makes You Stronger

While real estate mogul Barbara Corcoran has attracted some criticism from other women for admitting she's worn high skirts to get attention in meetings—and she's encouraged other women to do the same—she's also been vocal about the nonphysical attributes women can bring to the table.

And she's proven that you don't have to let rejection hold you back. She's used to fighting for what she wants even when she's told no.

In 2008, she landed one of the highly coveted spots as a shark on the ABC series *Shark Tank*. But shortly after she signed the contract accepting the position, she received a call from producers saying they'd changed their minds. They'd decided to cast another woman in the role.

Rather than walk away with her head down, Barbara fought back. She wrote an email to the show's producer, Mark Burnett. She didn't demand the job, though. Instead, she asked for a chance to prove herself. She also didn't complain or play the role of a victim. She painted herself as someone who was able to bounce back and beat the odds. And she outlined the reasons why she was the best person for the job.

In the message, she gave him three reasons why he should consider inviting her and the other woman to audition:

1. I do my best when my back is against the wall.
2. If you have both ladies in L.A., you can mix it up a bit and see which personalities make the best combination for your show.
3. Last, I've known from the get-go the shark role is a perfect fit for me.

Barbara went on to say she'd booked her ticket to L.A. already, and she hoped to be headed to an audition.

Her email worked. She was given an opportunity to prove herself, and she landed the job. She's gone on to become a fan favorite.

While begging for an opportunity will make you come across as desperate, telling someone you'd like a chance to prove yourself shows you feel confident. Of course, you might want to think twice about calling someone who rejected you for a job or someone who rejected you for a date. But there may be times in life where it's worth saying, "Even though you don't believe in me now, I'd like a chance to show you I'm up for the job."

It's important to have supportive people on your side in life. But not everyone will back your efforts—and that's OK. You can choose to put in your best effort when someone is trying to limit your potential.

Troubleshooting and Common Traps

It can be tempting to become overly defensive when someone doubts you or says you can't do something. But, depending on the source, that information could be helpful to hear. So keep an open mind and be willing to at least hear why someone may be concerned.

It's also important to note that not everyone is purposely trying to limit your life. It won't be helpful to you or anyone else if you begin believing the whole world is against you. Someone may simply be expressing their opinion to explain why you didn't land the part or offering advice on how you might improve.

Another common trap is trying to prove someone wrong when you don't need that person's approval. Saying "I'll show them" might feel empowering for a moment, but ultimately, it could cause you to lose sight of what's important. You don't need to prove to your parents that you're better than they think, and you don't need to show that old boyfriend that you're smarter than he ever gave you credit for. In fact, no matter how successful you are, you might never gain their approval. So make it a priority to work on your goals for yourself, not to try to gain status with anyone else.

Also, don't blame anyone for holding you back. You're in control of the type of life you create. So even if other people have hurt you, you have the power to move forward and live your best life.

WHAT'S HELPFUL

- Examining the self-limiting beliefs you may have accepted as truth
- Recognizing thinking errors
- Working toward your goals despite other people's doubt
- Establishing clear boundaries
- Seeking helpful feedback

WHAT'S NOT HELPFUL

- Giving up because you were rejected
- Living up to your labels
- Staying stuck in unhealthy thinking patterns
- Letting other people's doubt prevent you from trying
- Allowing unwanted advice to hold you back

10

They Don't Blame Themselves When Something Goes Wrong

Don't be too hard on yourself. There are plenty of people willing to do that for you.
—SUSAN GALE

It had been three years since Erin's younger brother died of a drug over-dose. But the more time passed, the deeper her grief felt. When she walked into my office she said, "Every day that passes means I'm growing further away from the days I spent with my brother. I just don't know how much more I can take."

Erin and her brother had grown up in a happy household with two loving parents. And while Erin immersed herself in sports during her teenage years, her brother grew a bit lost during adolescence. "He started hanging around with the wrong crowd, and some so-called friends intro-duced him to drugs," Erin explained.

By the time Erin left for college, her brother was abusing pain medica-tion and experimenting with hardcore drugs. But her parents looked the other way when her brother came home high, as if they couldn't bear to acknowledge what was actually going on under their own roof.

Halfway through her first semester of college, Erin got a phone call from her father saying she needed to come home immediately. Her brother had died of a drug overdose.

Erin went home to be with her family. She fully intended to return to school after the funeral, but never went back.

She said, "I was so focused on college and my friends and my life that I hadn't even talked to my brother for months. I feel so guilty about that now. Maybe I could have talked some sense into him. I knew what he was doing and I didn't say anything."

It was clear why Erin felt stuck in her grief—she blamed herself for her brother's overdose. She thought she should have been able to prevent him from his own self-destruction.

Like many family members who are dealing with a loved one with an addiction, Erin's treatment focused on letting go of her self-blame. Erin had to see that she didn't cause her brother's addiction, she couldn't control it, and she couldn't cure it.

"I feel so sad that my brother wasn't able to create a life for himself that didn't involve drugs. He could have been anything he wanted. But the drugs took over and he never found his way back out," she said.

It took a long time for Erin to accept she wasn't responsible for her brother's choices and she couldn't have talked him out of using drugs. She had to let go of all of the anger, guilt, and self-blame she held on to surrounding her brother's death.

Healing required her to learn more about addiction. She began to see that withdrawing from her brother while he was actively abusing drugs was her way of coping with his addiction. And it was a healthy way to handle it.

Once she began to think about addiction differently, she began to let go of some of her self-blame. Then she was finally able to begin the grieving process and start down the path toward healing.

Do You Blame Yourself Too Much?

It's important to accept responsibility for your behavior. Guilt is a healthy response to wrongdoing. But excessive self-blame is a problem. Do you answer affirmatively to any of the following statements?

- ❑ When people treat me poorly, I think I deserve it or that I caused it.
- ❑ Other people tell me I shouldn't apologize so much.
- ❑ When things go wrong, I always think I'm at fault.
- ❑ When my team loses or fails, I assume it was me who messed up.
- ❑ When something bad happens, I look back and think of all the things I should have done to prevent it.
- ❑ I struggle to be kind to myself because I don't think I deserve it.
- ❑ When someone around me is unhappy or uncomfortable, I feel responsible for their feelings.
- ❑ I feel guilty almost all the time.
- ❑ When I make a mistake, I don't think I made a bad choice—I think I'm a bad person.
- ❑ Sometimes I feel like I can't do anything right.

Why We Do It

Erin thought drug addicts only grew up in abusive homes in bad neighborhoods. She couldn't wrap her brain around the fact that her brother could turn to heroin when he came from a loving, middle-class family with supportive parents. She said, "We had the same upbringing. There has to be a reason why he chose to go down the wrong path and I didn't." The only possible conclusion she could draw was that she didn't give her brother enough support and guidance. As the older sister, Erin felt like it was her job to guide her brother down the right path in life. And since he didn't make good choices, she felt she failed.

She said, "As a woman, I feel like I'm supposed to be nurturing and caring and a good communicator. Instead of caring for my brother when he needed me, though, I ditched him. How could I ever be a good wife or a good mother if I don't lend a helping hand to the people I love when they need me the most?"

Erin had to see that her brother's death wasn't her fault. But before she could do that, she had to change her beliefs. She had to acknowledge that good people can get addicted to drugs even when they have loving families. And she had to recognize that her job wasn't to save her brother from himself. No matter how much she loved him, she couldn't have talked him out of his substance abuse problems.

Even if you've never blamed yourself for the death of a loved one, you might have felt like you weren't doing enough or that you just weren't good enough. Maybe you blame yourself for not being able to save your marriage. Or maybe you blame yourself for not being able to care for an elderly parent at home. Or maybe you feel responsible for your child's diagnosis. Whatever it is you feel guilty about, you're not alone.

BOYS ARE TAUGHT TO BLAME OTHERS; GIRLS ARE TOLD TO BLAME THEMSELVES

Many girls grow up hearing things like "Don't make your brother mad!" Comments like that instill in little girls that they're somehow responsible for boys' behavior. If your brother hits you, it is because you provoked him. It's your fault.

For some children, the message runs even deeper. I've worked with many women whose abusive parents insisted the physical, sexual, or emotional abuse was their fault. They began believing, "I'm bad," and started blaming themselves for everything that went wrong.

Studies show women experience more guilt than men—at least in individualistic cultures where personal achievement is valued above all else. In collectivist cultures, men tend to report similar levels of self-blame as women.

In a 2009 study published in the *Spanish Journal of Psychology*, researchers asked men and women of all ages what situations most often caused them to feel the most guilt. They found that habitual guilt was significantly higher for women in all age groups.

That's not to say women are wrong for blaming themselves more. In fact, many researchers suggest men need to take more responsibility for their behavior, meaning they don't feel guilty enough. But there's a big difference between accepting appropriate responsibility and engaging in toxic self-blame. One of the reasons women feel excessive guilt could be because of all the victim-blaming we tend to do. Society blames victims of sexual assault for dressing too provocatively or for putting themselves in harm's way. Women in abusive relationships are blamed for not leaving their partners when they get hit.

We're just starting to recognize how wrong it is that we put so much blame on victims for being in the wrong place at the wrong time or for not fending off their attackers. Fortunately, the #MeToo movement has opened some people's eyes to the problem.

One way we're seeing this change is in the way women are interviewed by the media. For years, anyone who was ever raped, assaulted, or harassed underwent a character assassination. While many victims are still questioned about their choices, we're slowly recognizing that many of the media's questions still place blame on the victim.

Talk show host Megyn Kelly has shared a bit about her own experience with this issue. In her book, *Settle for More,* she shared that she was sexually harassed while working at Fox News. She said she was targeted by Roger Ailes, who promised to help her career in exchange for sexual favors.

Kelly says news anchors often asked her why she didn't report the sexual harassment at the time. She said, "I finally found the right response, which was, 'You don't get to ask me that question anymore until you first ask me whether there was a safe avenue for reporting in my company. And only if the answer to that is yes do you get to ask question number two.'"

As a society, we like to place blame on someone when something goes wrong. When a couple gets divorced, people talk about which partner messed up. Or when there's an accident, we want to know whose fault it was. Our desire to point the finger makes sense. Knowing what went wrong could prevent us from making the same mistake.

When we see someone get violated in some way, we feel a sense of relief when we learn that the victim broke the rules. It puts our minds at ease to learn a woman's husband cheated "because she was a workaholic" or a woman was sexually harassed by her boss only after she had an affair with another coworker. It reassures us that if we follow the rules, nothing bad will happen to us. Of course, this sense of security is nefarious much of the time.

WHEN AN INCIDENT GOES AGAINST YOUR BELIEFS, YOU MIGHT BLAME YOURSELF

Akemi Look is a former rhythmic dancer who was treated by Dr. Larry Nassar. Like many other elite athletes, she was sexually assaulted by Nassar. She didn't tell anyone what happened—because she felt guilty and confused.

In an interview with ABC's *20/20,* Look said, "I blamed myself for years because I was so angry. I trusted this man. I didn't want to accuse him of anything because he was this god. He was the doctor who we all looked up to, who I believed cared about me so much."

It's common to want to protect someone who hurt you—and to take the blame for that person's actions. When something goes against your core beliefs, you'll find ways to explain the discrepancy that keeps your core beliefs intact. So, if you believe someone is a great person, yet that person violates you in some way, you might reconcile that discrepancy by concluding you must have done something wrong.

It's not just traumatic events that lead to self-blame. You might also blame yourself when your situation doesn't line up with your view of the world. For example, kids are repeatedly told, "You can be anything you want if you set your mind to it." While that message sounds good on the surface, it's quite unhealthy when you look a little closer.

Perhaps your dream was to be an astronaut. Well, according to *Wired* magazine, the odds of an applicant becoming an astronaut for NASA are around one in six hundred. That means you have less than a 0.17 percent chance of reaching your dream. If you don't get picked to be an astronaut, what might you conclude? If your parents told you all you had to do was "set your mind to it," you might decide you're a loser. Or, you might think you didn't put your whole heart and soul into it or that you simply didn't want it enough.

Well, there are many other reasons you might not have made the astronaut cut. Perhaps you were up against someone who had expertise or experience you don't have. Or maybe the NASA hiring managers chose their friends to ride on the spaceship. It might not have anything to do with you at all.

When you're told, however, that you can do anything and that it's up to you to achieve your dreams, you might take 100 percent responsibility for everything that happens.

And it's not surprising that women experience higher levels of self-blame. There's a lot of pressure on women to achieve more and do more—the superwoman phenomenon. And if you aren't able to reach high levels of success, or if you can't maintain a healthy relationship or raise happy kids, you might feel inadequate.

Why It's Bad

Erin's self-blame kept her from healing, and it caused her to fall into a deep depression. During one of her weekly appointments, Erin said, "I feel like the pain I'm in is my penance for being a terrible big sister. I don't deserve to be happy."

She had started therapy at the insistence of her mother. She said, "She thinks I need medication or something. But why should I get to take pills to make my life better when I couldn't stop my brother from taking pills that led to his death?"

Before Erin could feel better, she had to believe that she deserved to live a happy, healthy life. But her self-blame was keeping her emotionally, physically, and financially stuck. She was still living with her parents, she didn't have a job, and she hadn't finished college.

No one ever gets ahead in life by blaming themselves. In fact, taking on excessive blame will prevent you from taking positive action.

SELF-BLAME TAKES A TOLL ON YOUR PSYCHOLOGICAL WELL-BEING

A new client came into my office saying, "I've ruined everything for my family." She'd quit her full-time job because she wanted to devote more time to helping her elderly parents. She'd assured her husband she could make just as much money launching a business from home and the flexible schedule would allow her to better care for her parents.

But building her own business was much more difficult than she'd predicted. She also wasn't as available for her parents as she'd hoped. Her business required a fair amount of time, but so did her parents.

She constantly felt guilty. When she was working she felt bad she wasn't helping her parents. When she was with her parents, she felt guilty she wasn't earning any money for her family.

Then one day she got a call that her father had fallen and her mother had tried to help him up, which caused her to fall too. Her mother had crawled to the phone to call for an ambulance. The physician at the emergency room called my client and said she needed to speak to a social worker, because it was clear her parents "needed more help than they were getting." The social worker recommended she look into assisted-living options.

Hearing those words caused her to feel like a complete failure. She'd quit her job in hopes of helping her parents remain in their home, but now a professional was telling her she couldn't do that. She felt too incompetent to even look into assisted-living options. She was afraid she'd mess that up too. "What if I find a place that's too expensive and they run out of money?" she asked.

She'd started descending into a downward spiral. She blamed herself for being an ineffective caregiver and an incompetent business owner. And her self-blame made it impossible to make healthy decisions moving forward. The less she was able to accomplish, the worse she felt. Fortunately, she decided to start therapy to help herself get unstuck.

Excessive guilt has been linked to a variety of problems—low self-esteem, a desire to please people, attempts to avoid criticism, and a fear of looking entitled. Excessive guilt is also a symptom of depression. But there's a chicken-or-egg question: Does excessive guilt cause psychological problems? Or does poor mental health cause excessive guilt? Researchers aren't quite sure. But they do know guilt and depression play off of one another. The guiltier you are, the worse you feel.

Research has also linked self-blame to:

- Shame
- Self-disgust
- Self-loathing
- Eating disorders
- Post-traumatic stress disorder

Self-blame also decreases your empathy for others. If you hold yourself 100 percent responsible for everything that goes on in life, you'll hold other people completely responsible as well. You'll feel less compassion for someone who is going through a tough time or someone who is struggling financially, because you'll think it's their fault or they should be able to cope better. And that lack of self-compassion can take a toll on your relationships.

TOXIC SELF-BLAME LEADS TO BURNOUT

Blaming yourself for things you can't control, like how other people behave or the entire outcome of a project you're involved in, will cause you to run out of steam and burn out. No matter how much of a positive impact you're having, accepting too much personal responsibility will cause you to feel like you're not doing enough.

Take physicians, for example. They save lives every single day. Yet surveys have found 40 to 60 percent of practicing physicians experience some degree of burnout. Burnout is defined as a prolonged response to chronic emotional and interpersonal stressors on the job, and it is characterized by depersonalization and diminished satisfaction with one's work. Burnout can lead to diminished professionalism, increased medical errors, poorer patient outcomes, and worse hospital economics.

Practicing surgeons are said to have nearly three times higher rates of alcohol use and suicidal ideation than the general population. But those numbers skyrocket when a surgeon is experiencing burnout. A 2017 study titled "Burnout syndrome in critical care team members" discovered that the average risk of depressive symptoms among physicians increases by 170 percent when burnout is present.

Researchers at the University of Pittsburgh wanted to know more about why so many physicians are burning out, so they studied internal-medicine residents to gain insight. Why are these hardworking professionals who survived medical school experiencing higher rates of psychological problems so soon into their careers?

They found that self-blame was one of the biggest contributors to burnout and emotional exhaustion. And they found that female residents were most likely to engage in self-blame.

Despite the fact that the female residents were more likely to engage in healthy coping skills, like seeking emotional support, they were also more likely to engage in "toxic self-blame." The medical students blamed themselves for things beyond their control—such as patients not following through with medical advice or an illness not responding to treatment. Their healthy coping strategies weren't enough to undo the damage done by self-blame.

Trying to solve a problem you can't fix wastes your resources and won't get you anywhere. It can cause you to put your effort into the wrong place. A woman who blames herself for being abused might put her energy into trying to be a more subservient person in hopes she can end the abuse. When her efforts fail, the cycle of self-blame will continue and she'll burn out. Or a woman who blames herself for not being a good-enough mother may waste her energy verbally berating herself. Consequently, she'll struggle to be present with her kids.

Self-blame prevents you from changing the environment. It keeps you focused on trying to fix yourself, even when there's nothing within you that needs to be fixed.

What to Do Instead

Before Erin could begin to heal from her brother's death, she had to believe that she deserved to feel OK. Otherwise, all the strategies in the world weren't going to help her deal with her grief.

Her treatment involved shifting some of her core beliefs and letting go of the thoughts that contributed to her self-blame. As she began to let go of the self-blame she'd harbored for years, the transformation was obvious. She stood up straighter, she made better eye contact, her mood was different, and even her voice sounded different. It was clear how much that burden of self-blame had been weighing her down for years.

Self-blame comes in many forms. Perhaps you blame yourself for everything. Or maybe you made a mistake and you just can't forgive yourself for messing up. Or maybe you hurt someone because you made a bad choice. Whatever the reason is that you feel bad, it's important to find a way to take appropriate responsibility without excessively blaming yourself.

HOW TO DEAL WITH SELF-BLAME
WHEN YOU'RE VICTIMIZED

Teri Hatcher is best known for her roles as Lois Lane on the TV series *Lois & Clark: The New Adventures of Superman* and as Susan Mayer on *Desperate Housewives*. But beneath her bubbly personality and bright smile, she hid a dark secret and deep pain.

In an interview with *Vanity Fair,* Teri revealed that she was molested by an uncle (through marriage), beginning at age five. She didn't tell anyone what was happening, and she partially blamed herself for the abuse. While she was repulsed by her uncle's behavior, she also felt special and craved the attention he gave to her.

When she was about eight or nine, her mother invited her aunt and uncle over for dinner. Teri got upset and her mother realized something was wrong. She never asked Teri why she was so upset, but Teri never saw her uncle again after that.

She tried to bury what happened as deeply as she could, and she never discussed the abuse. But almost thirty years later she heard that a fourteen-year-old girl killed herself after she was molested by the same man. He'd been arrested, but it didn't look like it would be an easy conviction.

Teri contacted law enforcement to reveal that she too had been a victim of abuse from the same man. With more evidence stacked against him, her abuser pled guilty and was sentenced to prison.

Although she now recognizes that the abuse wasn't her fault, Teri acknowledges the pain still affects her life. She told *Vanity Fair,* "This pain of feeling like it's your fault, and not knowing how to solve the problem . . . that's a really familiar pattern to me in my life, including when a guy stops calling you, which makes it so much more painful than what it really is, which is that this stupid guy's not calling you. There's this cycle of not being able to give yourself a break, of constantly finding an avenue to punish yourself."

She goes on to say that everyone experiences pain, and her history of sexual abuse happens to be her pain. "Women walk around feeling like everything is their fault, and if they could only be better they could get something good. What I'm trying to say is 'Hey, I've felt like that my whole life, but guess what? You don't have to lose one pound; you don't have to get a great job; you don't have to get a boyfriend—you can just start treating yourself well right now!'"

I've worked with countless women over the years who blamed themselves for being victimized. On the surface, many of them could say it wasn't a woman's fault that she was hit, or it is never a child's fault for being abused. Yet they felt like they were the exception to that rule. They'd say things like "But I chose to go back with him even though my family would have taken me in" or "I initiated the sexual contact so it wasn't his fault."

Self-blame and trauma often go hand in hand. And quite often, women don't just blame their behavior, they blame their character. They believe things like "I was assaulted because I'm reckless" or "I was abused because I'm worthless." It's tough to challenge those beliefs that are so deeply rooted from trauma.

Studies show self-blame after traumatic incidents increases the chances someone will rely on unhealthy coping strategies, like drinking or avoidance, which can lead to more problems that perpetuate the cycle of self-blame.

If you experience self-blame after being victimized, seek professional help. Talking to a professional can help you find healthy ways to manage your emotions and cope with what happened to you. Even just a handful of therapy sessions might be enough to help you let go of toxic self-blame.

SEPARATE FACT FROM FICTION

The events in your life don't cause stress. It's your reaction to those events that determines whether you grow from them or you're distressed by them. And part of that reaction involves the story you tell yourself about your accountability.

So it's important to take a step back and separate fact from fiction. Doing so will help you accept the appropriate amount of responsibility for your actions. Here are a few questions to ask yourself:

- ***Do I blame my behavior or my character?*** There's a big difference between "I made a poor choice" and "I'm a horrible human being." Blaming your behavior means you believe you made a mistake, but you can make better choices in the future. Blaming your character, however, leaves little room for change.

- **What's the percentage of responsibility I bear?** When you're blaming yourself for something, pause and ask yourself how much of the issue really is your responsibility. It's unlikely that it's 100 percent your fault, even if it feels that way. Or you might decide you're 40 percent responsible because you made a mistake or you're 75 percent responsible because you didn't take action. Whatever it is, come up with a number.
- **How might my hindsight bias affect my self-blame?** When you're looking back, it's easy to think, "I should have noticed she was sick," or "I should have recognized that he was only using me." But that's because you're viewing the situation with the information you have now. So pause for a minute and think about whether you really should have seen it coming or whether you really had the knowledge to prevent something bad from happening.
- **Is there a core belief I'm protecting?** Is your belief that the world is good or that a certain person is kind causing you to put unnecessary blame on yourself? Think for a minute about what it would mean if something wasn't your fault at all. Would that be tough to believe because it would impact the way you see the world?
- **What would I say to a friend who told me this?** It's easy to tell your friend that her child's developmental delays or her struggles with infertility aren't her fault. But it can be much harder to give yourself that advice. So take a minute to consider what you'd say to a friend and try offering yourself the same reassurance.

When thinking about how responsible you are for a situation, a problem, or an issue, keep these truths in mind:

- You can influence others but you are not responsible for their choices.

- You have no way of knowing how things would have turned out if you had done things differently.
- You made your choices based on the information you had then (not the information you have now).

The goal doesn't need to be to get your culpability to 0 percent, but it does mean you can be accountable without accepting unnecessary blame.

CHANGE THE STORY YOU TELL YOURSELF

It's easy to tell yourself a story that places the blame on you. But that's only one version: there are many ways to tell the same story.

One version of your story might be about how you lost your job, grew depressed, struggled to survive, and had to start selling purses online just to make ends meet because you're a loser and can't get hired anywhere. But, on the other hand, your story could also be that during an economic downturn there was less demand for your skills, and although that was hard for you, you weren't going to just give up. Being the scrappy, hard-working person you are, you launched your own business selling purses online. It's the same situation, just a different spin on how responsible you are for the outcome and whether you're a victim or a warrior. Here are a few examples of stories that can be spun differently:

- **Old story:** I'm a bad daughter for putting my mother in a nursing home.
- **New story:** I decided the most loving and caring thing I could do for my mother was find professional caretakers to help her.
- **Old story:** I should have recognized my child had a learning disability sooner. I'm a bad parent.
- **New story:** I'm not a professional educator. I'm a loving parent. I am doing the best I can to raise my child well.
- **Old story:** If only I had called the doctor sooner. My dad might still be alive if I wasn't such an idiot.

- **New story:** There's no proof that calling the doctor sooner would have made a difference. I did the best I could with the information I had.

Changing the way you think changes the way you feel. So when you stop telling yourself that you're completely at fault, you'll feel less guilt about your situation.

ASK FOR FORGIVENESS

Self-blame isn't always imagined or exaggerated. Sometimes, it's appropriate. Perhaps you hurt someone. Or maybe there was something you didn't do—you didn't show kindness or you didn't prevent someone from being hurt. Beating yourself up silently, however, doesn't do anyone any good.

If you are responsible for hurting someone, apologize. Acknowledge your wrongdoing and say that you're sorry. Of course, there's no use in doing this unless you plan to change your behavior. Saying "I'm sorry I don't ever visit you, Mom" and then never visiting her won't cut it. But if you've seen that you are in the wrong and you plan to change your behavior, say so.

Apologizing is hard to do. It takes courage to say "I'm sorry." But accepting responsibility and asking for forgiveness can repair your relationships and help you avoid making the same mistake again.

When it comes to apologizing, there's a formula for making your apologies effective. Researchers from Ohio State University studied why some apologies repair trust and others do not. They found that the apologies that were most effective in repairing the relationship contained the following components:

1. Expression of regret
2. Explanation of what went wrong
3. Acknowledgment of responsibility
4. Declaration of repentance

5. Offer of repair
6. Request for forgiveness

Here are two examples of apologies that contain all six components:

- *I'm sorry that I stopped returning your calls. I got wrapped up in work and my boyfriend at the time. I caused us to lose touch over the years and I'm really sorry about that. I miss you and I want to restore our friendship. If you can find it in your heart to forgive me, I'd love to start building our friendship again.*
- *I'm sorry that I said I don't care about your feelings. I was angry and hurt. But it wasn't OK to get mean with you. I need to work on managing my temper better. I don't want to ever hurt your feelings again just because I feel bad. I'd like to hear your thoughts and I promise not to interrupt this time. Can you forgive me?*

If your choices have hurt someone, apologize. That won't make what you did OK, but saying you're sorry may help you and the person you hurt move forward in a more productive manner.

If you can't apologize to the individual—like in cases where the person has passed away or when you've lost contact with someone—write an apology letter. Even if you aren't able to deliver it, writing out your apology can help you recognize that you're taking appropriate responsibility for your behavior.

MAKE REPARATIONS

One of my former clients did something fairly unthinkable to most mothers—she didn't believe her daughters when they told her their stepfather was molesting them. Consequently, child protective services removed the children from the home and placed them in foster care. But rather than fight to get her children back, she fought to clear her husband's name.

Initially, she was allowed supervised visitation with her children. But, as evidence mounted that the children were telling the truth, the state gave her an ultimatum—choose your husband or your kids. She chose her husband.

When it was clear that the children would not be able to return home, visitations ended and the children were adopted by their foster parents. Several months later, my client's husband pled guilty to the sexual abuse charges. He said he didn't want to put the children through a trial. At first, she thought this was evidence that he was a "nice guy." But slowly, over the course of a year, she began questioning his innocence.

By the time she realized her kids were telling the truth, it was too late. She couldn't get them back. She couldn't even tell them that she now believed them. Her only hope was that when they turned eighteen, they'd want to reestablish contact.

She came to therapy saying, "I became the type of person I loathe. I'm the worst kind of monster there is." She hated herself for allowing her children to be hurt. "What kind of mother allows her children to be abused and then calls them liars when they ask for help?" she asked.

Many of her statements were accurate; she'd hurt her children, she'd made big mistakes, and her choices were the reason she could not have contact with them.

But believing she was a horrible person who was incapable of redemption had a downside—it prevented her from doing anything good with her life from here forward.

Even though she couldn't make reparations with her children now (and it was uncertain whether they'd want to have contact with her when they became adults), she could still make a positive impact on the world. Over the course of several months, we identified several positive things she could do moving forward.

She decided to volunteer for an organization where she could speak to other parents about the warning signs of sexual abuse and the importance of believing children who make allegations. She said, "I want to talk to other mothers about the mistakes I made. I didn't keep my own kids safe, but I hope I can help another mother prevent her children from being abused."

Much like my client, there are many people out there who have done something that hurt someone. Sometimes it involves poor judgment, like driving while intoxicated. At other times, it involves a careless mistake, like forgetting to lock a safety gate to the swimming pool.

You might not be able to apologize to the people you've hurt, or you might not be able to fix a mistake that you made. But you can choose to make reparations going forward.

Career

Blame isn't always about some deep-seated trauma—often it's a series of smaller feelings that add up to a larger impact. Perhaps the clearest example of this is at work.

It's a widely held belief that job satisfaction depends on your ability to have some control at work. Researchers and self-help gurus have touted the importance of being able to use your skills in a way that makes you feel most effective at your job, because that's the key to managing stress.

But that's not necessarily true across the board. If you're someone who tends to take on extra responsibility, you might be better off finding a job where you have fewer decisions and less control, according to researchers from Drexel University. In a study that examined how individuals cope with job demands, researchers found that people who blame themselves when things go wrong have more illnesses when they are in a job that gives them a lot of control. They suspect the higher rates of illness stem from the stress these individuals experience when they blame themselves for the outcome of team projects or the entire company's performance.

So while on one hand you might work on reducing your self-blame, you also might look at whether your job is a good fit for you. Having too many decisions and too many options might tax too much of your mental energy.

A flexible schedule or unlimited amount of vacation days might sound like a dream. But, if you're someone who blames herself for everything, you might not be able to reap the benefits. You might feel too guilty to use those benefits in a helpful way. Or, if you're given too much free rein on projects you're assigned, you might blame yourself when things don't go as well as your boss expected.

Being mentally strong isn't about toughing it out in situations that drain your energy. Instead, it's important to create a life that helps you flourish. So while sometimes it's important to work on changing yourself, at other times it's important to change your environment. If your job makes it tough for you to take on a healthy amount of responsibility, you might decide to look for something that challenges you without depleting all your mental energy.

Family

If self-blame has become a chronic habit, it can be helpful to reflect back and think about where that tendency began. For many people, self-blame is deeply rooted in childhood.

Some kids become scapegoats. Parents who insist they have a "problem child," or those who view a child as the reason for their marital issues, place blame so they don't have to deal with what's really going on. And a child begins to believe that she's at fault for all of the family's troubles.

Self-blame is also common in people who grew up in families that wanted to appear perfect. Their parents may have put more energy into looking good rather than actually being good. The pressure to appear perfect can cause kids to think their feelings are bad and their behavior is wrong. They never feel good enough.

If you're a habitual self-blamer, tracing your self-blame back to its roots can give you some insight. And it might help you begin to change the story you tell yourself. That doesn't mean you need to blame your parents or blame all of life's problems on your upbringing—as an adult, you want to accept appropriate responsibility for your actions. But gaining a better understanding of how you developed some of your core beliefs and habits can be key to creating positive change.

Social Life

One of my former clients had a miscarriage. Although her physician assured her that it was not her fault, she was riddled with guilt. She and her husband hadn't told anyone she was pregnant yet, so they also didn't share that they had a miscarriage. She grieved privately and felt very alone when her husband seemed to be doing OK within a couple of weeks.

He was already talking about trying to get pregnant again. But the thought terrified her. She was convinced the miscarriage was her fault. She came to therapy to try to pinpoint what she'd done wrong.

She asked tons of questions, like "I used to purge in college. Could that have damaged my body beyond repair?" and "I'm a vegetarian. Do you think that had something to do with it?"

I knew there weren't enough research studies or reassuring words I could offer to put her mind at ease. I suggested she attend a support group for women who had experienced pregnancy loss. She was a little reluctant at first, but she agreed to go.

After several weeks of attending her support group, she started to feel better. She heard from other women who felt similar guilt. She found herself reassuring them that it wasn't their fault. And hearing herself console other women helped her see that she wasn't responsible either.

She also shared her story with the group. And hearing women who truly understood her pain say, "We've felt the same but you didn't do anything wrong," helped her begin to heal.

I've recommended support groups for women struggling with self-blame over a variety of issues over the years. Social support can be extremely powerful in helping women reduce their guilt.

If you are struggling with self-blame, kind words from your friends and family can make a big difference. But if those around you don't know your struggles or they don't understand what you're going through, it's important to seek out people who do. That may mean joining an in-person support group, or it may mean seeking out online support from women who know your pain.

When you are blaming yourself for something, it can be tempting to withdraw from people and to suffer in silence. But talking about the things you're going through can be key to helping you heal. Whether you join a support group, open up to your friends, or confide in a professional, gain support from other people and you'll see that you're not alone.

Accepting Appropriate Responsibility Makes You Stronger

Elizabeth Smart gained national attention when she was abducted from her home at age fourteen. For nine months, people searched for the missing teenager, and many lost hope that she'd ever be found alive.

Against all odds, Elizabeth survived. Her captors had raped and abused her and threatened to kill her family if she tried to escape. Even though she had been in public places many times, she never ran away and didn't tell anyone she needed help.

Even though people were searching for her, she wasn't recognized in public because she was made to wear a veil that covered her face. At one point, a police officer questioned her in a library about her identity. She denied being Elizabeth Smart.

Eventually, someone called the police when they saw Elizabeth and her captors walking down the street, and Elizabeth was rescued. As soon as the news broke that she was home with her family, many people started asking her, "Why didn't you run away?" Some people even accused her of sympathizing with her captors.

In an autobiography on the A&E network, Elizabeth talked about this issue. She said, "For years that question really bothered me. I eventually realized my brain was hearing it as 'You should have run. You should have tried harder. It's your fault.' Now when I come across comments like that

I feel like it's a great opportunity to talk about why I didn't. Not just why I didn't but it's very common for survivors. It's not that we don't want to or it's not that we enjoy being hurt or held in captivity. It's because the people who are hurting us are so manipulative. My captors took away everything. I made every choice to survive. Looking back, do I wish I had been rescued sooner? Absolutely. Do I wish I had been saved sooner? Absolutely. But I don't regret any decision I made because ultimately it led to my survival and the reason I'm here today."

Even when others have tried to blame her, Elizabeth didn't blame herself for what happened to her. She recognized that it was easy for someone who had never been in that situation to say what she should have done differently, but she accepted that she made the best choices she could in the circumstances she was in.

She's become a *New York Times* bestselling author, public speaker, and advocate for others who have been victimized. She encourages anyone who has been through traumatic experiences to make peace with the past and embrace the future.

You can't be the best version of yourself when you're holding on to self-blame. But when you decide to let go of unnecessary guilt, shame, and anger, you're free to move forward in a productive and healthy way.

Troubleshooting and Common Traps

Don't confuse making amends with grueling self-punishment. Giving to a worthy cause or working toward making reparations in a time-limited manner is healthy. But volunteering a hundred hours per week because you don't deserve to have fun isn't helpful. Make sure that your efforts to make reparations stem from remorse, not self-hatred.

While some women blame themselves too much, it's also possible to be too forgiving of yourself. Denying the pain you've caused others or minimizing the impact your mistakes have made won't help you to do better in the future. It's important to balance self-forgiveness with responsibility-taking.

And keep in mind that a little bit of guilt is a good thing. It means you have a conscience and you feel bad about something you've done. Shame, self-hatred, and a negative view of your character are unhealthy.

If you're struggling to let go of self-blame and it's impacting your well-being, seek professional help. Talking to a mental health professional can help you let go of the burdens you're carrying around with you.

WHAT'S HELPFUL

- Asking questions that help you establish a more realistic view of your level of responsibility
- Changing the story you tell yourself when you experience excessive self-blame
- Asking for forgiveness when you've made a mistake
- Making reparations when you have hurt others
- Gaining social support to help you deal with excessive guilt

WHAT'S NOT HELPFUL

- Engaging in grueling self-punishment
- Forgiving yourself too quickly for hurting others
- Feeling responsible for other people's feelings and actions
- Believing you are a bad person as opposed to thinking you made a bad choice

11

They Don't
Stay Silent

We realize the importance of our voice when we are silenced.
—MALALA YOUSAFZAI

Wendy walked into my office saying, "I need help managing my stress at work." I asked her what specifically was stressing her out and she said, "It's a fast-paced job and there's always too much to do. My coworkers are stressed out too, which means they're always grouchy. And my boss is a real piece of work."

Wendy worked in the finance department of a car dealership. She said her boss had a reputation for being "a dirty old man" and he was known for hiring young women. When I pressed for more details she said, "He makes inappropriate comments about what I'm wearing or he says sexual things to me. And it's not just me. I know he does it to other women too."

"He used to just say things like 'Smile, Wendy. You look better when you have a smile on your face.' Or he'd say something sort of funny, like 'Could you button that shirt any higher, Wendy? I can almost see your collarbone.' Other people laughed so I thought it was probably good for me to learn how to laugh at myself too."

"One day, he said, 'Your husband is a lucky man. You're easy on the eyes.' And he winked when he said it. Another time he threw a piece of paper on the floor and said, 'Hey, Wendy, could you bend over and pick that up for me?' That made me uncomfortable."

I asked her how much of her job stress was tied to her boss and she said, "Probably eighty percent. I don't want to ask him questions because I'm afraid he'll say something inappropriate. That creates a lot of extra work for me. I have to go through ten steps to get an answer to a simple question that he could have given me in one minute."

"Do you think you are being sexually harassed?" I asked. She said, "I don't think I'd call it sexual harassment. He's from a different generation and just doesn't know any better."

I asked if she'd ever thought of addressing the issues with her boss directly. She said that other women put up with her boss's behavior. She worried if she spoke up people would say she was too sensitive or that she was trying to get ahead in the workplace by suing her boss or something.

She said, "He's never touched me or threatened me or anything, so I don't feel like it's *that* bad. But I don't like it. I've thought about applying for other jobs, but all of them involve a much longer commute."

After learning more about Wendy's situation—and where her workplace stress stemmed from—I explained to her that her distress was a normal reaction to the situation. She *should* be stressed. And we weren't going to reduce her stress without changing her situation.

At the end of the appointment, I encouraged her to do some research on the legal definition of sexual harassment and to consider whether her boss's behavior qualified. Although I was certain it did, I wanted her to come to her own conclusion.

When she returned the following week, she said, "I don't feel like I'm a victim or anything. I just feel like he's inappropriate."

She made excuses for his behavior and doubted herself a bit too. She said, "Some of his sexual comments could be taken several ways. I am not sure it's bad enough that I should take action."

Like many women I'd worked with, Wendy was uncomfortable labeling what happened to her as sexual harassment. Using that term caused her great discomfort. So we spent a few weeks talking about it and what it really meant.

Once she came to terms with the idea that she was being sexually harassed, we discussed some of her options. She could stay silent. She could change jobs. Or she could talk to her human resources department.

I advised her to speak with an attorney to learn more about her legal rights, as I could only assist her from a mental health standpoint. At first, she said, "I'd rather not. I'm trying to avoid making this bigger than it is." So I asked, "What will life be like for you next year if you don't do anything about it?" and she said, "I'm not sure I can take this for another year."

I assured her that speaking to an attorney didn't mean she had to sue anyone. But it could provide her with clarity about her rights and her options. She agreed to contact a lawyer and begin the conversation.

She met with an attorney the following week and at the attorney's advice, she began documenting each incident. She also printed emails that contained sexual content from her boss.

Documenting each sexual comment and inappropriate gesture made her realize the extent of the situation. Every day she had at least one more thing to add to her paperwork, and seeing the papers stack up changed her perspective. She decided to take action.

With support from her attorney, Wendy approached her human resources office. Her HR director took her information and began the investigation. And Wendy held her breath to see what would happen.

To her surprise, things happened fast. Within the week, her boss voluntarily accepted a different position within the company. His new position meant he'd no longer have contact with Wendy—he'd be working in a different building altogether.

When Wendy came in for her therapy appointment the following week, she started to cry. She said, "I'm happy that it's over. But I'm sad that I didn't do it sooner. I'm angry that it happened in the first place. And I'm disgusted we live in a world where this stuff occurs."

I only saw Wendy for a few more sessions after that. She felt less stressed without her boss in the building, and she found her fast-paced job was much easier to handle once she no longer had to devote so much of her energy to protecting herself.

Do You Stay Silent?

Whether you didn't tell anyone when your rights were violated by a family member twenty years ago or you didn't speak up when people were making sexist remarks in the break room last week, we've all had times when we didn't speak up about something that was wrong. But it's not just silence about inappropriate behavior that's a problem. Many women aren't sharing their opinions and ideas at work, in their relationship, or in their everyday conversation. Do you answer affirmatively to any of the following points?

- ❐ I avoid sharing my ideas because I think other people won't value my opinion.
- ❐ In group settings, I let other people take the lead in the conversation.
- ❐ I often don't speak up because I don't want to create conflict.
- ❐ I am ashamed to tell anyone when I'm victimized.
- ❐ I want to speak up for other people whose rights are violated, but I often don't say or do anything.
- ❐ I harbor deep secrets.
- ❐ When I feel uncomfortable about the comments someone makes, I stay silent.
- ❐ I stay silent because I don't want other people to get in trouble.
- ❐ I am too afraid of what people will think or say about me to speak up.
- ❐ I worry that speaking up about things that cause me discomfort will cause others to think I'm too sensitive.

Why We Do It

Wendy did some soul-searching to figure out why she tolerated being sexually harassed for as long as she did. She said, "I never thought I'd be the kind of woman to put up with that stuff. If I get overcharged by fifty cents at the grocery store, I'm quick to complain. Or if I think a contractor is ripping me off, I'll say, 'You can't treat me like this.' So it's bizarre that I'd let my boss sexually harass me."

We spent several sessions digging deeper to uncover explanations about why she didn't speak up sooner. Understanding why she—and so many other women—stay silent was imperative to her healing process.

She finally concluded, "There was a part of me that thought if I minimized it, it wouldn't be true. I didn't want to be a victim. There was another part of me that was terrified that if I did speak up, no one would believe me. I was afraid of what people might think of me too. But I'm glad I finally said something."

There are many reasons women don't speak up about abuse, sexual assault, bullying, and other rights violations. And blaming women who can't find their voice doesn't do any of us any good. It only hurts women even more. It's important to be kind to ourselves, support one another, and stick together so that women everywhere will be able to speak up.

If you chose to stay silent, it doesn't mean you aren't mentally strong. But harboring a secret will drain you of mental strength.

BOYS ARE STRONG; GIRLS ARE SILENT

People who reference a man who talks a lot might call him friendly or an extrovert. But they might say a woman who talks a lot "can't ever shut up." Women are accused of nagging, whining, and "bitching" when they speak.

In 2017, Jameis Winston, a football player for the Tampa Bay Buccaneers, gave a motivational talk to children at Melrose Elementary in St. Petersburg, Florida. He stood in front of a room filled with third-through fifth-graders and shared his three principles for life: God, school, and the belief that you can do anything you set your mind to.

But his positive message quickly went downhill when he addressed gender issues:

"All my young boys, stand up. The ladies, sit down," Winston said. "But all my boys, stand up. We strong, right? We strong! We strong, right? All my boys, tell me one time: I can do anything I put my mind to. Now, a lot of boys aren't supposed to be soft-spoken. You know what I'm saying? One day y'all are going to have a very deep voice like this [in deep voice]. One day, you'll have a very, very deep voice.

"But the ladies, they're supposed to be silent, polite, gentle. My men, my men [are] supposed to be strong. I want y'all to tell me what the third rule of life is: I can do anything I put my mind to. Scream it!"

It didn't take long for the story to hit the media as some people took issue with the fact that he told girls to be silent. Winston responded by apologizing and saying, "During my talk, I used a poor word choice that may have overshadowed that positive message for some."

But this isn't the first time the football player's attitude toward women has come into question. In 2012, when he was a college student at Florida State University, he was accused of sexually assaulting another student. He was never charged, and his accuser filed a lawsuit against Florida State, stating the school didn't investigate the incident in an effective, timely manner. The university settled the lawsuit out of court for nearly one million dollars.

Another female student also accused him of sexually assaulting her in college, but no charges were brought against Winston for that incident either.

In 2017, he was accused of groping a female Uber driver. The NFL investigated and found the driver's account to be "consistent and credible." They suspended Winston for three games. In response, Winston apologized to the Uber driver for the "position I put you in."

Some might argue that he's never been convicted of sexual assault, so he should still be allowed to earn his big NFL salary and fans should still proudly sport his jersey. Some might even say he's still an OK role model for young kids.

But sexual assault charges aside, he's not exactly a model citizen. When he was a college student, there was an incident where he climbed on a table and yelled, "Fuck her right in the pussy!" He was suspended for half a game. During a press conference he said he wasn't a "mean person," and he apologized to his teammates because he'd have to sit out part of the game as a consequence.

The fact that he is still held in high-enough esteem that a school would invite him to give a motivational talk to children speaks volumes about our culture. The belief that women should be silent runs deep.

SPEAKING UP WHEN YOU'RE VICTIMIZED IS A BIG RISK

It's easy for people who haven't been victimized to say, "You should speak up." But clearly, women who do speak are taking a big risk. And they might face serious consequences.

More than sixty women came forward to say they were assaulted by Bill Cosby. Their stories spanned five decades, and they shared remarkably similar accounts of being drugged and assaulted by Cosby. Yet no one wanted to believe "America's dad" could be a serial rapist.

Stories like this shed light on why many women don't come forward—and discourage other women from contacting the authorities. After all, who wants to contact the police if nothing ever happens to the perpetrator?

I spoke with a twenty-one-year-old woman about her experience on a college campus. She shared this story with me:

> I was raped during my sophomore year of college. When I went to the police, I felt as though I was being interrogated even though I wasn't the rapist. I was treated as guilty until proven innocent, while my abuser was innocent until proven guilty. The detective asked me questions like "What were you wearing during the assault? What did you say to him that would make him do it? How many sexual partners have you had? Are you sexually promiscuous?"
>
> After my answers, he then asked me if I had a father in my life. When I told him my parents were divorced, he told me, "Ah, you have daddy issues. That's why you are in this situation and why

you have self-esteem issues. Your low self-esteem got you in this situation." I was hurt by his words, but because I was pressing charges just four days after my assault, I became intimidated. I felt afraid. I felt hurt because not only were people not believing me, but they were also blaming me or making me feel that it was my fault.

I was so afraid of my detective that I emailed him. I told him his language was totally inappropriate. After this, he told me that they were refusing to press charges on my offender. This was disappointing, considering the heavy evidence I had on my offender about the rape. I had a vocal recording of him explaining to me what he did to me. It was obvious to me at this time that I couldn't rely on a criminal justice system to provide justice for me along with other rape victims, when that was never the intent of the original design. The system is designed to rehabilitate the offender, and dismiss the victim.

According to the Rape, Abuse and Incest National Network (RAINN), out of every 1,000 rapes, only 310 are reported to police, and only six of those rapists are ever actually incarcerated. But of course, those statistics are only estimates. We have no idea how many women are being victimized, because so few of the incidents are actually ever reported.

It's not just sexual assault that goes unreported. The Federal Bureau of Justice Statistics estimates only about 50 percent of domestic violence incidents get reported to the authorities. And a survey by CareerBuilder found that 72 percent of people who experience workplace sexual harassment never report it.

There are many reasons why victims stay silent. Here are the most common:

- **Victims usually know the assailant**—Most women aren't victims of random crimes. They're abused or assaulted by their partners, family members, or acquaintances. Reporting the incident could affect their career, family, or social circle. Additionally, they may have conflicted feelings about the perpetrator getting in trouble.

- **Fear of retaliation**—Coming forward doesn't guarantee that the perpetrator will face justice. In fact, they might get fired, demoted, or ostracized. In cases of domestic violence, 75 percent of abused women who are murdered by their tormentor are killed after they leave their partners.
- **The legal process can be humiliating**—Telling the story to countless strangers feels embarrassing, overwhelming, and even traumatizing. And if a case goes to court, a victim may have to recount the details many times in front of many people.
- **Victims aren't always believed**—It's not uncommon for people to say things like "She's just looking for attention," or "Her story doesn't add up," when a woman comes forward.
- **Victims undergo a character assassination**—Victims are often blamed for the way they dress, the events leading up to being victimized, or their past choices.
- **First-mover disadvantage**—She who goes first is often punished. The first woman to speak out against sexual harassment in the workplace may be mistreated. Or the first person to claim her rights are being violated will likely be met with backlash.
- **Authorities aren't always helpful**—Sadly, many women are told there just isn't enough evidence for authorities to respond. Or sometimes, they're mistreated by the very people they are asking to help them.
- **Victims blame themselves**—Many victims worry that they gave mixed signals or that they didn't do enough to fend off an attack.
- **Victims don't want to believe it**—Victims sometimes minimize or deny what happened. Date rape victims, for example, often don't want to believe they were actually raped, so they try to convince themselves they had consensual sex.

- **They don't know who to tell**—It can be confusing to know who to tell or how to get the conversation started.

It's not just victims who remain silent. Sometimes, the women who witness another woman's rights being violated stay silent too. In some families, domestic violence has become so prevalent that it seems normal. Or in some companies, sexual harassment has become so entrenched in the culture that people become desensitized to it. When other witnesses aren't reacting most bystanders don't want to be the only individual to step in and say something.

Despite all of the risks and disadvantages of speaking up, people still say, "Why didn't she say anything?" or "She should have come forward sooner."

Why It's Bad

Being sexually harassed at work didn't just affect Wendy's job—it affected her personal life too. She came home from work in a bad mood, and that took a toll on her relationships with her family. She avoided asking her boss questions, including if she could get out of work early for soccer games, so she missed out on some of her kids' activities. It even affected the way she shopped. She avoided buying clothes that might give her boss any reason to comment on her outfits. And it definitely held her back from performing her best.

She knew it was happening to other women in the office too. Since they didn't say anything, Wendy didn't want to speak up for fear she'd look like a complainer. Consequently, her silence increased her suffering.

Silence allows problems to continue. It gives perpetrators the ability to keep doing what they're doing. And it embeds the problem a little deeper into the culture.

Staying silent also drains your mental strength. Hiding your secrets, denying your opinions, and burying your ideas takes extra effort. And you won't be able to put that energy into something more productive when you're busy silencing yourself.

IT TOOK ALMOST FORTY YEARS
TO GO FROM "NOT ME" TO "ME TOO"

The women of the 1980s were the "not me" generation. Despite the fact that gender discrimination was rampant, most women insisted they had never been victims.

In 1984, Faye Crosby, a psychology professor at Smith College, studied this phenomenon. Through a series of surveys, she discovered that women easily recognized gender discrimination in general. But when it came to being personally discriminated against, they didn't feel a sense of injustice. Instead, they blamed themselves.

In one of the studies, Crosby examined 182 men and 163 women with comparable education, training, and experience. Even though the women earned significantly less than their male counterparts, only thirteen felt that they were shortchanged. Almost all of them felt gender discrimination was a serious problem, however, most of them felt personally exempt. The author concluded that women were more comfortable thinking they were at fault, rather than acknowledging they may have been discriminated against.

In an article for *The University Record,* Crosby recounted an anecdote she heard about a dozen women who trained as engineers at Harvard during World War II. The school didn't offer any female restrooms at that time. The women, however, never felt they experienced gender discrimination. Even when they recounted their experiences forty years later, they didn't feel as though they had been discriminated against.

Crosby and her coauthors found that women's denial of discrimination involved many factors. Among them:

- Women wanted to think of their coworkers and supervisors as admirable.

- Acknowledging they'd been victimized meant they weren't as special as they hoped.
- Unjust treatment was unthinkable, because women wanted to feel they would be rewarded for their efforts, not subjected to undeserved misfortune.

Upon first glance, that list may look commendable. After all, women wanted to take responsibility for their behavior, and they wanted to see the good in their colleagues. But they were looking for the positive so much that they ignored reality. They were refusing to believe that they could be victims of injustice and unfairness.

We've made some progress since then in our ability to develop a more balanced outlook. But that progress is slow. It's taken forty years for women to transition from the "not me" attitude to the "me too" mind-set.

Thankfully, #MeToo and #TimesUp help women see that acknowledging you've been victimized or discriminated against doesn't make you weak. It's also nothing you need to be embarrassed about. In addition, spreading the message provides reassurance you're not alone and gives everyone a sobering look at how widespread the problem is.

The denial of personal disadvantage isn't unique to women. It's been an issue among other minority populations too. But it's clear that when we don't admit that we're victims, no one talks about it. And if no one is talking about it, nothing changes. Silence gives people permission to keep going in the same fashion.

SILENCE KEEPS WOMEN SEPARATED

I once worked with a woman whose life looked happy from the outside. She and her husband lived in a nice house in a good neighborhood. They both had great jobs and were involved in many community activities. But, behind closed doors, her life was a living hell. Her husband yelled at her, called her names, threatened to kill her, and hit her. She said, "You're the only person who knows what goes on. No one else would ever understand."

What she didn't know was that just two hours earlier, I saw another woman who lived in her neighborhood. The other woman had a very similar story—her husband punched holes in walls, threw things, and hit her. But no one knew about the torture she experienced behind closed doors.

Both women felt all alone and completely isolated. If they ever passed one another in a grocery store or on the streets, they'd have no idea that the other one was also living in her own private hell. Of course, confidentiality rules prevented me from being able to say, "Actually, one of your neighbors is in a similar circumstance." But I couldn't help but wish the two of them could at least meet for coffee to talk about what they were going through. I suspect each one of them could have said to the other, "You deserve better." And maybe hearing themselves say those words out loud could have helped them see that they both deserved better.

My therapy office sometimes felt like a revolving door of women who felt isolated. Their stories were alike, yet they felt like no one else could possibly relate to their situations.

There are support groups for victims of sexual assault or victims of domestic violence. But it can be hard to convince women to attend. And for women who are still living in unsafe situations, attending those types of groups can be too risky.

But even for women who aren't in any physical danger, attending a support group can feel like a risk. Prominent women in the community may be afraid to share their story for fear it will impact their careers. For others, telling their story and talking about what happened to them might feel too hard to do.

Although the landscape is starting to change, we have a long way to go before more women will feel empowered to come forward. Until those conversations become commonplace and women feel as though they can talk openly, women can't unite forces and fight for change.

LESS VOICE MEANS LESS INFLUENCE

Silence isn't just an issue surrounding victimization. Not sharing your ideas in business meetings or staying quiet about your opinions in relationships can also be a big problem.

A 2012 study led by researchers from Brigham Young University found that men dominate the conversation in meetings. In general, women speak 75 percent less than men in business meetings.

During the experiments, participants were placed in groups of at least five people and told they needed to decide how to distribute the money that they earned from a hypothetical task. On average, groups deliberated for twenty-five minutes and then voted by secret ballot.

When women were outnumbered by men, they were less likely to speak up and express their opinions, especially when majority ruled. When researchers told the group they needed to reach a unanimous consensus, however, things changed. Women participated more. They were more likely to see themselves as influential, and they wanted to be heard.

The authors of the study were clear that the problem wasn't just about airtime. It wasn't that women were speaking less because they were more efficient in their conversations—they weren't sharing their ideas. But when they did speak up, they were very influential. The women were more likely than men to sway other members' decisions.

The problem with women not speaking up isn't unique to boardrooms, however. It's an issue that we're seeing in schools too. Studies consistently show that girls don't talk as much in the classroom as boys.

A book published in 1994 called *Failing at Fairness: How Our Schools Cheat Girls* outlined how gender inequality plays out in the classroom. After conducting decades of research, the authors, Myra and David Sadker, made several startling discoveries about teacher biases.

They found that teachers spend up to two-thirds of their time talking to male students. Teachers are also more likely to interrupt girls but allow boys to talk over them. They spend more time prompting boys to provide deeper answers while rewarding girls for being quiet. When teachers ask questions, they direct their gaze toward boys more often—especially when the questions are open-ended.

Five years after publishing their first book, the authors teamed up with Karen Zittleman to publish a follow-up book titled *Still Failing at Fairness: How Gender Bias Cheats Girls and Boys in School and What We Can Do About It*. They discovered some minor improvements in the classroom, but overall, they found gender bias continues to be a problem.

A 2013 study that was led by a researcher at the University of Pittsburgh found that teachers reported girls had better self-regulation skills than boys—meaning they behaved better. But teachers in Asian cultures don't report the same findings. They report boys and girls have similar self-regulation skills, which leads researchers to believe that teacher bias about gender plays a big role in how children behave. Teachers in the United States are more likely to say "boys will be boys" and give them a free pass for misbehaving.

Megan McClelland, one of the authors of the study, said, "In general, there is more tolerance for active play in boys than in girls. Girls are expected to be quiet and not make a fuss. This expectation may be coloring some teachers' perceptions."

In response to the conversations about girls not getting enough recognition in the classroom, the Girl Scouts created a "Raise Your Hand" badge to encourage girls to speak up. But the problem might not be that girls aren't raising their hands. It might be that teachers aren't calling on them.

What to Do Instead

When Wendy first came to therapy, she wanted to talk about her stress level. But she didn't want to acknowledge that she was being sexually harassed. Even after she came to terms with what was going on, she said, "Saying it out loud sounds terrible."

But putting a name to it was important. Once she identified what was happening, she could move forward. Educating herself empowered her.

And the more empowered she felt, the more confident she became that she could say something.

Wendy's willingness to speak up led to positive results—and those results were fast. Unfortunately, not everyone will have that experience. Sometimes, speaking up doesn't lead to the results we want. But that doesn't mean we shouldn't do it. Even if we aren't effective in creating immediate change, our voices empower other women to speak out for positive change. And finding your voice means you'll no longer have to waste your mental energy on harboring a secret or stifling your opinion.

ACKNOWLEDGE WHAT IS HAPPENING

We've likely all had times when we've stood there listening to someone tell an offensive joke and we didn't speak up. And we've all had that one acquaintance who takes things too far and yet we don't say anything. Whether we fear appearing like a prude or we worry that we'll make things worse, we stay silent. Part of the reason we stay silent may stem from our inability to recognize when our rights have been violated or when we've been objectified.

As a therapist, I often work with parents on teaching their children the anatomically correct words for their body parts. Telling your kids about their bodies and what constitutes safe and unsafe touches is one of the best ways to protect them against a child predator. Kids who have the language to tell someone what happened to them are more likely to get help—and they may even be successful in fending a predator off.

Having the right language is important for adults too. You need to know what's happening to you so you can take appropriate action. That's not to say you can't come forward if you're not quite sure whether what happened to you constitutes sexual harassment or sexual misconduct. But knowing your rights were violated or that you were subjected to inappropriate contact is important.

That inappropriate sexual joke that your coworker emailed, the lewd comments that your neighbor makes about your sexual orientation, and the whistles you endure when you walk past a group of men on the sidewalk are just a few examples of inappropriate behavior.

Before you can talk about what has happened to you, you need the language to describe it. Naming it—whether you were sexually harassed, stalked, or raped—empowers you to be able to speak up about it.

It's important to note that just because something is legal doesn't mean it's OK. Many of our laws are archaic. It's illegal for a man to expose himself to you for the purpose of sexual gratification. But there's nothing illegal about a man sending you unwanted nude photos of himself.

There also isn't a federal law against street harassment. And studies show 85 percent of women have experienced some form of street harassment, such as catcalling. Some individual states have created legislation to help protect individuals on the streets from being subjected to harassment, but I suspect it'd have to be a major offense for police to take it seriously. Calling 911 to say a construction worker whistled at you isn't likely to be helpful.

But some of the women I interviewed for this book weren't offended when they were catcalled. In fact, one woman said, "I take it as a compliment. I'm glad men are noticing my looks." But many others mentioned how uncomfortable they felt from street harassment. One woman said, "Catcallers have actually changed the way I dress. I try to cover up my body with big jackets in the winter or I avoid wearing skirts in the summer because I don't want to draw any attention to myself. In fact, I do everything I can to try to not be noticed."

Speaking up to a street harasser isn't likely to make it stop. In fact, it might not be safe to say anything. But on the whole, women need to speak out against being objectified with crude comments or sexual gestures. It's a way men try to be dominant over women. If we make it known that it's not OK, maybe someday we can create a culture where catcalls aren't the norm.

TELL SOMEONE

You'll likely hear people say, "You have to call the police," or "You need to speak up for yourself." But that's somewhat naive advice. Speaking up to the perpetrator or going to the authorities is a decision only you can make. Your job, your safety, your income, or many other things may be at stake. And while some might say, "Money isn't worth allowing yourself to be treated that way," or "Thinking about your career is selfish," that's not necessarily true. A single mother who needs to feed her children has to think about what would happen if she speaks out. And a woman who receives threats against her life should carefully consider her options.

Not speaking up doesn't mean you are weak. If you were victimized, you had to make the best decision you could for yourself about how to proceed. And you may have decided speaking up at that time wasn't a good idea. That doesn't mean you aren't mentally strong. It means you made the best decision you could to keep yourself from being hurt more.

But harboring deep secrets forever does have consequences. Keeping your story to yourself because you are ashamed or embarrassed will drain your mental strength. It's important to tell someone what happened to you so you don't have to carry that burden around all by yourself forever.

Even if you decide not to go to the authorities or you decide not to confront the person directly (which might not be safe), that doesn't mean you can't talk about it.

Tell your physician. Talk to a therapist. Confide in a friend. Call a national hotline. Join a support group. Just tell someone.

I hear a lot of women say, "But my circumstances weren't that bad." And they don't feel worthy of joining in the #MeToo conversations. They convince themselves that being harassed, groped, or humiliated doesn't constitute a serious-enough offense to speak out.

But coming forward isn't meant to trivialize those who have been brutalized and victimized in the worst ways. Instead, it can be a way of lending support on an overall level that says, "This isn't OK."

Even striking up a conversation with a friend that says, "I was going to go on a date with this new guy I met. But listen to what he said . . . ," can get a conversation going. When you start sharing some of the things that have happened to you, you'll see how many other people have experienced similar things.

Telling a doctor or a mental health professional about being assaulted or abused is important to your physical and psychological healing. But there are some compelling reasons why you might want to speak up to friends, family, a partner, or colleagues as well:

- **To gain moral support.** Hearing other people validate your emotions and reassure you that you're not at fault can help you heal.
- **To spread awareness.** Talking about what happened to you might help someone else feel less alone. It also might address a safety issue, like telling a cousin what happened to you so she doesn't let her children around the perpetrator.
- **To explain your behavior.** Whether you refuse to take the trash out after dark or you decline to take the subway, explaining what happened to you may help those around you understand better.

If you are thinking of confiding in someone who isn't a professional—a partner, a friend, a relative, or a colleague—you might consider these questions:

1. *What is my motivation in telling?*
2. *What do I hope to accomplish?*
3. *What are the potential risks of speaking up?*
4. *What are the potential risks of staying silent?*

Even if it's been decades since something happened to you, speaking up now has value. It can help you show others that you aren't ashamed and that you know it wasn't your fault. And starting the conversation can be helpful to healing.

SPEAK UP FOR WOMEN WHO CAN'T
SPEAK UP FOR THEMSELVES

There are women across the globe who can't speak up for themselves. Women in Saudi Arabia were granted the right to drive without a guardian present in 2017. In Israel, Jewish divorce is only granted with the husband's permission. There are women all over the globe who lack rights. But you probably don't have to go to the ends of the earth to find women who aren't able to speak up when their rights are violated.

The bystander effect is a real problem almost everywhere you go. We see examples of it every day in the news. When *Today* anchor Matt Lauer's alleged sexual misconduct was revealed, many people said it wasn't a secret among other employees. And when women disclosed being assaulted by Harvey Weinstein, employees said it was widely known that he was a predator.

When you see a woman being sexually harassed at the office, speak up. Depending on the situation, you might:

- **Confront the harasser**—Step in and say, "Those comments are inappropriate and cause people to feel uncomfortable." Whether you do it in the moment or you take the harasser aside should depend on your relationship and your role in the company.
- **Save the victim**—If it's not safe for you to step in and confront the harasser, interrupt and say, "I have to talk to you about something. Do you have a minute?" Lead the victim to another room.
- **Tell a manager**—Document the incident and tell your manager or someone in your human resources department. You don't have to be the victim to be the one who reports it.

Even when you don't witness harassment, violence, or assault firsthand, you can take steps to speak up for women across the globe whose voices have been silenced. Here are just a few ways you can get involved:

- **Volunteer for an organization**—Whether you donate items for victims of human trafficking or you volunteer to operate a hotline, there are many ways to help women in your local community.
- **Get involved politically.** Call your representatives, sign online petitions, volunteer for a campaign, attend marches, and do anything that will make sure your voice is heard.
- **Keep educating yourself.** No matter how aware you feel already, keep learning about women's issues. It's easy to get so caught up in your world that you forget that women of other races, ethnicities, religions, and sexual preferences experience oppression on other levels.

Career

I often get invited to speak to women's groups about mental strength. Many of them are voluntary groups that women form to ensure their voices are heard in large male-dominated industries. And one of the things women in these groups almost always tell me is that when they get a group of women together, "the vibe is different." They feel more comfortable speaking up, taking charge, and getting things done when the men aren't present.

Once you become aware of the ways women can get silenced in the workplace, it becomes so blaringly obvious that you might question why you didn't notice it sooner. In workplaces across the globe, men are getting the bigger offices, higher pay, and better clients.

Some might argue that's because they speak up in meetings. But of course there are many factors that go into determining how much airtime anyone gets in the workplace.

Take a look around your workplace, and if you notice that women aren't speaking up, think about some of the possible reasons why. Do men talk over women in meetings? Do women get accused of nagging, talking too much, or being a bitch?

Do your part to make sure your voice is heard. Sit in the front—and save a seat for your friend. Start an email conversation. Create a list of ways your workplace could help women convey their messages better, and present it to management.

Family

One of the hardest times to speak up can be when you're dealing with family. Whether you've got an uncle who makes fun of women's rights over Thanksgiving dinner or your grandfather tells sexist jokes, saying something is hard.

But speaking up can send a message that you're not comfortable listening to those things. That's not to say you're going to change their attitudes with a single sentence, but it may make them think twice about saying something like that again.

If the behavior or comments happen in your home, you get to set the rules. You can say, "We don't use sexist language in our home." That's a good message for your kids to hear and one for you to live by.

Of course, if you're at someone else's house, you might decide to let your feet speak for you. Simply get your jacket and head for the door.

There's no sense in arguing or talking about politics. Again, you won't change anyone's mind. But you can set limits and establish boundaries that send a clear message.

Social Life

One of my friends was sexually harassed at work. She shared a few details about her experience on Facebook. She posted her phone number and said, "If something like this has ever happened to you, please call me. I'm happy to listen to you and I want to support you. I pass no judgment on what happened or how you handled it. I just want you to know you aren't alone."

She told me that she got calls from several women. Some of them were acquaintances she didn't know well. Others were women she hadn't spoken to since high school. But she listened to all of them and assured them that they weren't alone. She said just talking about it with others who could relate was really healing to her, because she had never known another woman to say she'd been sexually harassed.

Starting conversations and inviting others to talk to you is a great way to help other women find their voices. It can also help you find your own. Here are some things to keep in mind if you are talking about tough subjects, such as being a victim of sexual assault or domestic violence:

- **Listen.** Let her tell her story without any interruptions. Avoid comparing your experiences to hers and don't give her advice about what she should do.
- **Assure her it's not her fault.** No matter what happened, assure her that she didn't do anything wrong.
- **Respect her feelings.** Whether she's angry, embarrassed, scared, or depressed, validate her. Avoid saying, "You shouldn't be embarrassed." Say, "That's understandable."
- **Offer resources.** Advise her to contact her physician, a mental health professional, or an organization that serves women. Offer to help her schedule an appointment, or assist her in getting there.

Speaking Your Truth Makes You Stronger

In 2013, Taylor Swift was groped by a DJ during a meet-and-greet at a concert. Taylor told the radio station. They conducted an investigation and fired the DJ. She told *Time,* "At the time, I was headlining a major arena tour and there were a number of people in the room that saw this plus a photo of it happening. I figured that if he would be brazen enough to assault me under these risky circumstances and high stakes, imagine what he might do to a vulnerable artist if given the chance."

The DJ then sued Taylor, stating she purposely got him fired. Taylor countersued for a symbolic one dollar, accusing the DJ of assault and battery.

The jury sided with Taylor, and the case received worldwide attention. And much of the attention was focused on Taylor's blunt testimony.

When the defense attorney asked her if she was critical of her body-guard for not interfering if the DJ really reached under her skirt, she responded, "I'm critical of your client sticking his hand under my skirt and grabbing my ass."

In an interview with *Time,* Taylor referred to the trial process as "demoralizing." But she also encouraged other women to come forward by saying, "You should not be blamed for waiting 15 minutes or 15 days or 15 years to report sexual assault or harassment, or for the outcome of what happens to a person after he or she makes the choice to sexually assault you."

And it appears as though her efforts were effective. In the weekend following the trial, RAINN reported a 35 percent increase in hotline calls. RAINN's president, Scott Berkowitz, told ABC News that Taylor's case was "a great demonstration to other victims that there is strength in coming forward and pursuing justice."

Your voice is powerful. Using it to speak up for yourself or speak out against something can make a big difference in the world. And it can also make a difference for you. Staying silent will exhaust you. The more you speak up and share your voice, the more mental strength you'll have to devote toward other things.

Troubleshooting and Common Traps

Some people are concerned we're taking on a victim mentality by pointing out discrimination. That may be the case in some circumstances where women blame men for holding them back or chalk every rejection up to sexism. But, clearly, discrimination exists and it's important to acknowledge it. Dwelling on discrimination, however, will only increase your distress. It's important to find a balance between calling out incidents of discrimination and ruminating on all the ways other people hold you back.

Avoid passing blame on other women who don't speak up. Victims of assault, harassment, or discrimination have reasons for not coming forward—or not coming forward in a timely manner. Judging them for their choices isn't helpful to anyone.

Sometimes women don't speak up because they don't think their experience is *that* bad. So a woman who has been verbally harassed may think saying something somehow diminishes women who have been physically assaulted. But it doesn't matter how serious of a violation it is—you can speak up.

Another common trap is refusing to tell anyone what happened after you've had a bad experience coming forward. Perhaps your mother didn't believe you as a kid when you told her what the babysitter did to you. Or maybe your boss didn't take you seriously when you expressed concerns. Don't let those experiences silence you. Find safe people to confide in. That may mean turning to professionals to get help.

Finally, if you experienced something traumatic, seek professional support. Trauma can make it feel too scary to talk to someone. But talking about what happened is the key to reducing the impact that a traumatic experience has on your life.

WHAT'S HELPFUL

- Acknowledging when you've been victimized or discriminated against
- Telling someone about your experiences
- Speaking up for women who aren't able to speak up for themselves
- Inviting others to share their experiences with you
- Establishing clear guidelines that prevent sexism in your home
- Doing your part to ensure your voice is heard

WHAT'S NOT HELPFUL

- Assuming discrimination would never happen to you
- Allowing others to make sexist remarks in your presence without speaking up
- Staying passive about sexual harassment
- Being a silent bystander when another woman's rights are violated
- Keeping your experiences secret

12

They Don't Feel Bad about Reinventing Themselves

If you don't like the road you're walking, start paving another one.
—DOLLY PARTON

When Karen walked into my office she said, "I'm here to reassure my husband I haven't fallen off the deep end. And I guess I need some reassurance too." Karen and her husband, Bruce, had recently become empty nesters. Karen had been a stay-at-home mom, and after the kids moved out, she felt a little lost.

"I had always been a hands-on mom. I shuttled our kids to and from sports practices, I packed lunches, I was the president of the PTA, and I was always involved in fund-raising for the kids' activities. So now that they're gone, I have all this time on my hands," she said. During the early days of being an empty nester, she devoted her extra time to her youngest son, who was in college. But, after a couple of weeks of daily care packages, he told her he was running out of space in his dorm room.

She joined the Friends of the Library group as a last resort. All of the other members were at least thirty years older than she was, and they only met once a month. She hoped it would give her something to do and get her out of the house once in a while. But at their first meeting, one of the members mentioned that her daughter was holding a weekend yoga retreat. Karen asked for the details, and even though she knew nothing about yoga, she signed up the minute she got home.

She enjoyed her weekend getaway. She liked meeting new people and she was happy to learn about yoga. So when the instructor announced she was planning a trip to Cambodia for a weeklong meditation retreat, Karen said she'd like to go—but she needed to talk to her husband first.

Bruce wasn't nearly as excited about the idea as Karen was. "He knows I read *Eat, Pray, Love* so I think he's worried I'm going on some sort of quest to divorce him. But that's not the case at all," she said.

Bruce expressed concern that Karen was going through a midlife crisis. Karen said, "At first, I thought the retreat would be a great opportunity for me as I start to figure out what to do with this new phase of my life. But after Bruce's midlife crisis comment I'm wondering if it's a bad idea."

I asked her what a midlife crisis meant to her and she said, "It's when you do something stupid because you wish you were young again. Like when middle-aged men ruin their marriages for a younger woman. It's about not appreciating what you have right in front of you because you're focused on all the things you think you missed out on."

So I asked her, "Do you think going on this meditation retreat fits that definition?"

Karen said, "No, I don't *think* so. I'm not trying to build a new life. I just want to add things into my current life now that I have more time on my hands. But then again, I don't think I'd necessarily recognize a midlife crisis if I were in the middle of one." She had about a month in between her first therapy appointment and the deadline to sign up for the retreat, so she agreed to attend a few appointments to help her sort out her concerns.

We spent the next couple of appointments exploring what this meditation retreat meant for her and whether there was any deeper meaning behind her desire to embark on this new adventure.

One of the things I discovered was that Karen had spent much of her life "being busy." She found scrambling from one of her kids' activities to the next helped her feel important. And now that the kids were grown, she felt useless.

"I think I probably always felt bad about myself for not being a career woman. Having a jam-packed schedule helped me feel good about myself, even though all the things I did centered around the kids," she said.

But now, as an empty nester, she came to the conclusion that her life wasn't going to be measured by how full her calendar was. She was embracing the idea that a calmer, quieter life could be quite meaningful. She thought learning about meditation could be a good way for her to reflect more on this.

By the end of our time together, she concluded, "Things in my life have changed. So it makes sense that I would change too. That doesn't mean I'm going to change everything but exploring new things could help me learn more about what I want to do during this next chapter."

Karen decided to go on the retreat. With some further explanation about why she wanted to do it, Bruce supported her efforts. She felt confident going on the retreat was a good way to reinvent herself as she entered the next phase of her life. "I want to keep learning about how to become my best. And I think adding meditation practice to my life is a good way to kick off my quest to feel more peaceful," she said.

Are You Afraid to Reinvent Yourself?

Reinventing yourself every now and then is a great way to make sure you're learning, growing, and adapting to the changes of life. But changing something about yourself can be scary—even when you think you're changing for the better. Do any of these statements describe you?

❐ I get so caught up in day-to-day life that I don't take a look at the bigger picture to see if I'm living the type of life I want to create.

❐ I fear what other people would think if I made any major changes in my life.

☐ I figure if I haven't become the person I want to be yet, there's no hope that it will ever happen.

☐ I don't have the energy or motivation to create positive change in my life.

☐ If I made changes in my personal or professional life, I'm afraid I'd make things worse.

☐ I think it'd be a bad thing if someone said to me, "You've changed."

☐ I fear outgrowing the people around me.

☐ I live inside my comfort zone.

☐ I rarely explore new interests, think about new career ideas, or try new things.

☐ I have other things I'd like to do in life, but I always talk myself out of trying.

Why We Do It

During one of her appointments, Karen recalled a friend who struggled with aging. She said, "When she turned forty she became a health nut. She stopped drinking tap water because she thought the fluoride was bad for her. She bought every expensive anti-wrinkle cream she could find and she took dozens of supplements at every meal. She went to the gym for hours every day and her whole life centered around being fit and looking attractive. We knew she was just scared of getting old." Karen said everyone always commented on how much her friend had changed—and not for the better. And she didn't want to become someone who changed for the worse.

She said, "It sounds cliché. But I don't want to run away from my life. I want to make sure I'm running toward something." Karen was afraid that doing things differently or trying new things meant she was dissatisfied with her life or ungrateful for what she had. And she didn't want anyone to think she was making these changes because she was scared of growing old.

Even though it was only a retreat, Karen had a lot of fears about what it could mean for her life. Doing nice things for herself and embracing spirituality were out of character—and she wasn't comfortable with the idea. Even though she was excited, her fears caused her to waver.

Even if you've never aspired to learn meditation from a monk, you might have hesitated at one time or another to reinvent yourself. Whether you were uncertain about what others might think or you worried that you might somehow make your life worse, being afraid to reinvent yourself can be a common problem.

Reinventing yourself doesn't have to mean becoming a brand-new person. It could mean you simply create some simple changes in your life that help you become more like the person you want to be.

WOMEN WANT TO CHANGE HOW THEY FEEL; MEN WANT TO CHANGE THEIR CIRCUMSTANCES

You've likely heard someone say that women like to talk about problems and men like to solve problems. The different approach to problem-solving between the sexes isn't a stereotype—there's research that backs up the idea that men and women cope with distress differently. A 2008 study published in the *Journal of Depression and Anxiety* examined how each gender copes with distressing events. Researchers discovered women are more likely to use emotion-focused coping and men are more likely to use problem-focused coping.

That means when women are faced with a problem, they strive to change how they feel. They decrease their emotional distress by using strategies such as venting or changing the way they think about the situation.

Men, on the other hand, try to eliminate the source of their distress. They strive to change the environment, rather than their emotions.

Here's an example of how that might play out differently when someone dislikes their job. A woman might vent to her partner about the problems with her job, and she might look on the bright side by reminding herself of the things she enjoys about her workplace. A man might talk to his supervisor about what would make the job better, or he may apply for a new position.

The emotion-focused approach can be an advantage in circumstances that can't be changed—such as a chronic health condition. So women may cope better when faced with problems that can't be solved.

But, in situations where individuals can solve the problem—such as financial issues—problem-focused coping is a better strategy.

Researchers suspect women's tendency to use emotion-focused coping may be the reason why women have higher rates of depression and anxiety than men. Sometimes, you need to change your circumstances, not just the way you feel or the way you think about your situation. Creating change may mean reinventing yourself. Refusing to do something different might cause you to stay stuck—and that could lead to more problems.

REINVENTING YOURSELF MAY SEEM TOO CUMBERSOME, HOKEY, WEAK, OR INAUTHENTIC

Women usually enter my therapy office because they want to feel better. But when we talk about doing something different so they can feel better, I hear many different concerns. Here are some of the most common reasons women say they don't want to reinvent themselves:

- **"I don't have the energy to change."** Doing things differently does take energy. But it might require less energy than you're investing into doing the same thing over and over again when it's not working out.
- **"It sounds too new-agey."** Reinventing yourself doesn't have to involve some sort of spiritual awakening or rebirthing of your inner child. Women have been reinventing themselves for decades—they just didn't necessarily call it reinventing themselves when they went to work in the factories while the men were at war.
- **"I should be able to tolerate this."** Changing your situation, like

switching careers because you are unhappy with your current job, doesn't mean you're weak. It takes strength to do something new.

- **"I am who I am."** Reinventing yourself isn't about changing your personality or pretending to be someone you're not. But it might mean putting your best foot forward or toning down certain behaviors. You don't have to become a different person—just the best version of yourself.

Reinventing yourself doesn't mean you have to transform everything about your life. It might involve making a few simple but effective changes that enhance the quality of your life—or someone else's. Here are just a few ways you might reinvent yourself:

- **Change a habit**—Whether you want to go from being a night owl to a morning person or you want to give up smoking, identify habits you'd like to change.
- **Embrace spirituality**—Although spirituality might involve religion, it doesn't necessarily have to. It can also include finding more meaning and purpose in your everyday life.
- **Get a new job**—Most women spend a large percentage of their lives working. So you might decide it is time to change positions or shift careers altogether.
- **Meet new people**—The people you spend time with have a big influence on your life. You could get a mentor, join an organization, or simply set out to make new friends.
- **Develop a hobby**—From home improvement projects to gardening, developing a new hobby—or resurrecting one you've neglected—can bring out a new side of you.
- **Change something about your appearance**—Something as simple as a new hairstyle can do wonders for how you feel and how you act. Consider updating your wardrobe or letting your hair go gray if you want to create a physical transformation.

- **Shift your attitude**—You don't necessarily have to do anything to become different—at least not at first. You might start by shifting the way you think. Developing an "attitude of gratitude" or choosing self-compassion might be the best way to transform your world.
- **Realign your priorities**—The day-to-day hustle and bustle make it easy to get your priorities out of line. Reinventing yourself may involve deciding to spend more time with family, or it might include spending less time on social media.
- **Learn a new skill**—Take piano lessons, learn reiki, or discover how to build a website. Learning new skills expands your mind and your possibilities.

Why It's Bad

When Karen second-guessed her decision to go on a meditation retreat, she'd tell herself, "That's not me. I'm not someone who goes jet-setting with someone I barely know to learn about something I've never even cared about." When she framed it that way, it sounded sort of far-fetched.

But that statement was based on the idea that her personality, her interests, and her identity were static. She assumed she was too old to discover hidden talents or that it was too late to develop new skills. Had she stayed stuck in that mind-set, she wouldn't have experienced any growth in this new phase of her life.

Many people believe you're supposed to "find yourself" when you're twenty. Then you spend the rest of your life living according to the dreams and guidelines you set for yourself back then. But that type of mind-set could cause you to sell yourself short. Self-growth and personal change are an integral part of becoming the strongest version of yourself.

Many of the women I interviewed for this book explained how much they evolved over the years as they grew more comfortable in their own skin. One woman said, "I learned what women were supposed to be from the media when I was a teenager. I spent my twenties trying to be thin, polite, and supportive of men. In my thirties, I realized I wasn't doing myself any favors. I was only reinforcing the pressure on women to meet men's standards of the 'perfect woman.' I am now more comfortable and confident with who I am, even if I don't meet society's standards for the 'perfect woman.'"

YOUR PERSONALITY CHANGES—
AND YOU SHOULD ADJUST ACCORDINGLY

There's a notion that your personality and your identity are fairly fixed once you become an adult. And many women believe the person they were at age five is the same person they are supposed to be at age sixty-five. But the Mills Longitudinal Study found that women's personalities shift over time.

Researchers began studying women shortly after they graduated from high school. And over the course of more than fifty years, they've seen these women's personalities change. The women, who are now in their seventies, continue to show personality changes as they age. About 10 percent of the women in the study showed substantial personality change between the ages of sixty and seventy, showing that personalities grow right alongside us.

In an interview with *Psychology Today*, Ravenna Helson, the lead author of the study, said, "We have to modify our identities as we go through life. Even at 60, people can resolve to make themselves more the people they would like to become."

We used to believe your personality shaped your experiences. If you were extroverted, you might choose a job in customer service. And you might have a busy social calendar filled with a wide range of social engagements. And if you were introverted, you may gravitate toward a remote work opportunity and your calendar would include social engagements that allow you to connect with your core group of friends.

But now we know that your experiences also shape your personality. A rough divorce or two—as compared to a long-term happy marriage—could affect how you see yourself and how you interact with others.

Similarly, your job satisfaction could affect your mood, your income, your relationships, and your plans for retirement.

A 2018 study published in *Personality and Individual Differences* found that parenthood shifts women's values—but not men's values. Researchers discovered that new moms shift away from "openness to change" and begin valuing "conservation" more. That means self-direction and individual goals become less important, and women become more concerned with tradition, conformity, and security.

When your values shift, your life should shift too. The things you prioritized in one phase of your life might not be a priority in the next phase of life. Reinventing yourself might simply reflect those changes.

So whether you've gone through some major changes over the years or your life has been relatively stable, your personality has likely changed. Acknowledging and honoring that can help you get the most out of your life. And quite often, that means reinventing yourself.

YOU WON'T MAKE YOUR LIFE BETTER

One of my former clients was a nurse. And for many years, she loved working in the hospital. But things had changed since she first began her career. She was tired of hospital politics, insurance-company mandates, and ever-changing technology. She felt like she wasn't able to offer quality patient care in her current position.

There were many other opportunities out there that could give her a fresh start. She could work in home health care, a school, a doctor's office, or a variety of other settings. But she refused to look for other opportunities. Her identity was wrapped up in being a nurse on a surgical unit of the hospital.

She wanted to do good work. But her disdain for her job made it impossible for her to perform at her best. She felt stuck but she was afraid to do anything different.

I've seen many women struggle to reinvent themselves. Like this client, some stayed in jobs they hated because they didn't want to make a career shift. Others stayed in horrible relationships because they didn't want to be alone.

Sadly, they weren't able to make their lives better. Whether they doubted their ability to do something different or they worried what other people would think, many of them struggled to create positive change.

If you dig in your heels and decide that you must continue on in the same way, you'll stay stagnant. Other people will outgrow you. Your life will never change for the better.

What to Do Instead

Karen had to work through her fears. She worried other people might think she was "turning into a hippie" when she started doing yoga and meditation. And she was afraid that her desire to create positive change meant she was harboring some sort of deep-rooted discontent with life.

But she was making things much more complicated for herself. She just had to accept that she was in a phase of her life and trying new things made perfect sense. If she didn't like the retreat, she would be out some time and money, but she would have gained an experience anyway.

During one of Karen's therapy appointments, I asked her, "What would happen if you passed up the opportunity to go on the meditation retreat? What would you do instead and how might you feel?" She said, "I'd most likely spend my summer planting flowers with the eighty-year-old Friends of the Library members." After she thought about that for a bit she said, "I could do that, but I don't think I'd feel excited about life. Even though I might decide meditation isn't for me, I'd rather say I at least tried something new."

If you're thinking of reinventing yourself, you may have to face a few fears as well. And while there's no guarantee that reinventing yourself will lead to more happiness, better health, or more satisfaction with life, it will at least give you a learning experience.

ZOOM OUT AND TAKE STOCK OF THE BIGGER PICTURE

A big event may occasionally cause you to take stock of your life: a change in health, a breakup, the loss of a loved one, a milestone birthday, or a disappointing setback. In those situations, reinvention may stem from necessity or perhaps even desperation. And while creating positive change after a crisis can certainly be impactful, you don't need to wait until your life changes to change your life.

It's easy to get so caught up in the day-to-day hustle and bustle that you forget to examine if you're actually living the kind of life you want to live. But for some women, the problem isn't identifying what they want to do differently—it's taking action.

Step back and ask yourself if you're really living up to your greatest potential. Keep in mind that your greatest potential doesn't necessarily mean earning the most money, having the most prestigious job, or earning the highest achievements. Perhaps your greatest potential is something you can't quantify, such as being kind, generous, and helpful to others.

Make it a habit to check in with yourself on a monthly basis. Consider what habits you want to change or goals you want to set. To help you identify the changes you'd like to create, ask yourself the following questions:

1. ***What does the person I want to be look like?*** Take a minute to imagine what a healthy or happy person might be doing with their life. Or imagine how a great leader might behave. Think about the things those people do.

2. ***What are some steps I can start taking right now to become more like that person?*** Identify the steps you could take to become more like the person you want to be. That doesn't mean imitating or copying someone, but it may mean making some changes that feel uncomfortable at first.

3. ***What do I need to give up to reach my goals?*** Everything you gain comes with some sort of price. It's important to label the sacrifice you're willing to make. Going to the gym means less time to watch TV

in the evenings. Taking an art class means less money in the budget for dining out. Acknowledge what you'd need to leave behind if you reinvented yourself into someone new.

4. ***How will I know if I'm on the right track?*** You don't reinvent yourself in a single instance. It takes time to create positive change. So it's important to pay attention to the things you'll notice when you're on the right track. Whether you'll look different, act different, or feel different, identify the signs that will indicate you're headed in the right direction.

IDENTIFY WHAT GETS IN THE WAY OF REINVENTING YOURSELF

After caring for her ailing grandmother for several years, one of my former clients decided she wanted to give up her job in retail to start an organization that provided care for the elderly. "There aren't enough home health aides in the area to help elderly people. I want to open an agency that employs people who can help older people with cooking, cleaning, and caring for themselves so they can stay in their own homes."

She didn't know anything about how to go about starting that type of business. And when she researched it, she felt overwhelmed. "Sometimes I think I'm living a pipe dream," she said. She'd given up several times on her idea. But every time she gave up, she couldn't stop thinking about it so she'd start researching again.

But she was stressed out—and that's why she came to therapy. She said, "I don't know if this is something I have any business pursuing. I want to do it but I just can't seem to make myself move forward."

Lack of motivation wasn't her problem. She was really motivated to do this. Her problem was fear. She was afraid she was incompetent. She feared she was going to fail. And she worried that she would let people down.

Before she could move forward, she had to acknowledge those fears. There was certainly a chance her fears might turn out to be true. But until she recognized her fear, she'd keep talking herself out of trying.

Once we began talking about her fears, she was able to see that even if they came true, she was strong enough to handle it. While her fear didn't magically disappear with that revelation, acknowledging her emotional state helped her see that she could move forward despite the anxiety she felt. She knew her drive to succeed was bigger than the fear she felt.

Slowly, her description of herself as "a retail manager" shifted. And she began visualizing herself as "head of an elder care agency." She knew it was going to be a long process to get her organization off the ground. But she was determined to do all she could to make it happen.

Changing yourself—even when it's something you really want—is difficult. Motivation comes and goes, obstacles always crop up, and old habits die hard. Acknowledge the fears that threaten to sabotage your progress and your chances of success.

Here are just a few of the fears that might cause you to stay stuck:

- **Fear that you'll make things worse**
- **Fear of how others will respond**
- **Fear that you'll fail**
- **Fear that it will feel too uncomfortable**
- **Fear that you'll embarrass yourself**

Once you pinpoint your fear, ask yourself, "If my fears came true, how bad would that be?" Quite often, we avoid things because we don't want to feel afraid. But when you stop and think about it, most bad outcomes aren't all that bad. Failing, embarrassing yourself, or making things worse might be better than the regret of never having tried.

ANSWER THE MIRACLE QUESTION

I once worked with a young woman who had social anxiety. She'd been shy her whole life, but during high school, her anxiety got worse and she found it difficult to go to school. She stopped attending social events and her attendance at school became sporadic. Her parents feared she wasn't going to graduate, so they allowed her to attend online classes so she could get her diploma.

Two years after graduating, she was still unemployed and living at home with her parents. She spent most of her time watching TV and surfing the internet. She kept in contact with two of her friends from high school, but she only saw them rarely, since both of them went to college.

She wanted to go to college too and she didn't want to do it online. She wanted to attend a university in person. That's what led her to start therapy. She wanted to feel more comfortable socializing.

At first, her treatment focused on exposure therapy. She began practicing regular social interactions to face her anxiety head-on. That helped a little, but she was still far from being able to go to college on her own.

So we began working on changing some of the thoughts she had about herself. When she entered a social situation, she was convinced people were staring at her and judging her. We developed healthier scripts she could give herself so she could calm some of her anxious inner dialogue. That helped too, but not enough.

So one week, I asked her what's known as the miracle question. "Suppose tonight, while you slept, a miracle occurred. And you woke up tomorrow and your social anxiety was gone. How would you know that life had suddenly gotten better?"

She said, "The second I looked in the mirror I'd probably notice that I looked better. I'd probably dress different and wear my hair different." Over the past few years she'd stopped wearing makeup and she'd allowed her curly hair to grow really long so it would cover up her face when she looked down. She almost always dressed in black clothing.

I asked her how she'd spend her time and she said, "I'd be contacting a couple of the colleges I want to visit and I'd be making plans to go back to school."

I encouraged her to start doing some of those things—acting as if the miracle had occurred. At first she said, "I can't until I get rid of my anxiety." But I encouraged her to just try and see what happened, and she agreed.

She showed up for her appointment the following week with a noticeable spring in her step—and in her hair. She'd gotten a haircut, she was wearing a red sweater instead of her usual black, and she had a big smile on her face. She said, "Getting my hair cut and wearing bright colors again is helping me more than I thought."

Her change in appearance certainly didn't cure all of her anxiety. But it was a huge step in the right direction, and it was just the boost she needed to help her keep going. And the best news was, it was a solution she'd come up with on her own—I wouldn't have prescribed a haircut and bright colors as a treatment for anxiety. But the "miracle question" helped her find that solution for herself.

Asking, "If you woke up tomorrow and a miracle had occurred, how would you know things were better?" is a solution-focused therapy technique. It's one of my favorite ways to help people start identifying their own solutions.

Pose that question to yourself. Imagine what your life would be like if things changed for the better. How would you know things were better? What would you be doing differently? Then, go do those things.

If your "miracle" involves something that can't really happen, such as spending time with a relative who passed away, think of other people whom you might spend time with that would give you some comfort.

Many women wait until they feel different to become different. After all, women are more inclined to feel first, rather than act first. But sometimes, changing your behavior first is the key to feeling differently about yourself. You don't magically feel more confident if you aren't challenging yourself. Or you won't suddenly experience a burst of motivation unless you are already working toward a goal. Don't wait until you feel different to become different. Change your behavior first and you'll change how you feel.

Career

Reinventing yourself doesn't require you to change anything on the outside. Instead, you might make a few changes on the inside.

I once worked with a woman whose daughter had said to her, "No offense, Mom, but I want a job that adds value to the world." The mother, a hairdresser, responded by saying, "No offense taken. My job has plenty of value. Every day I give women haircuts that help them feel good about themselves."

Everyone needs meaning in their life. But your purpose doesn't have to involve changing the whole world. Instead, you might find meaning in changing just one person's world.

You also don't have to wait until the kids are grown or until you are financially stable to reinvent yourself. While you might not find it makes sense to completely overhaul your life until your situation changes, you can reinvent yourself now to find more meaning and purpose.

You don't necessarily have to go back to school to gain a new education or learn a whole new skill set. You might be able to take the knowledge and tools you have now and reinvent yourself with a career shift. And you don't always have to plan what you're going to do next. Just stay flexible and open to new opportunities as they present themselves.

That's what Annie Duke did. She was working on her doctorate in psychology when she became ill. She spent two weeks in the hospital, which caused her to lose her fellowship. She needed money, so she turned to poker as a way to earn a few dollars. Her brother was a professional poker player and she'd seen him play before. She thought she'd just play for a year, but that year turned into twenty years.

She became a world champion poker player. She won millions of dollars in poker tournaments, because she could use her knowledge of psychology to read people—and trick her opponents. She became so popular that she was invited to appear on game shows like *Are you Smarter Than a Fifth Grader?* And she became a finalist on *Celebrity Apprentice*.

In 2002, she got invited to give a talk about decision-making. She really enjoyed it, so she made another major career shift—she became an author and a speaker.

Annie never set out to reinvent herself, but she's remained flexible to whatever life throws her way. She said to me, "I have had a lot of good luck in my life, including, it turns out, that stomach illness that kept me from finishing school and getting a faculty job in 1992."

I recently had a chance to ask Annie what advice she has for women who might be afraid of reinventing themselves. She said, "It's important to get your head around the fact that if you're not satisfied with the current version of yourself, you should embrace risk and uncertainty. If you're unhappy, the bar is pretty low for the change to be an improvement. Besides, any decision to stick with the status quo involves risk and uncertainty that you're probably overlooking, especially if you're in a bad situation."

So whether you want to make a complete career shift like Annie did, or you just want to make a minor change, be open to what life throws your way. And if you're unhappy with the way things are now, take a bold step and do something different.

Family

Family can be one of the biggest reasons you might want to reinvent yourself. Your role is likely to shift often. You might become a wife, mother, caretaker, parent of a teenager, and an empty nester all within a couple of decades. And if you're like most women, you may change more than one role at a time.

But family can also be one of the biggest obstacles to reinventing yourself. Perhaps your partner isn't supportive of your dream. Or maybe your siblings aren't interested in helping care for your aging parents and the brunt of the work falls on your shoulders.

There's no question about it—your family affects your ability to create positive change. But it's important not to blame them for holding you back.

Whether you're a stay-at-home parent with few funds or you're a working mom with little extra time on your hands, the way you live your life is up to you. And while family responsibility might prevent you from trying your hand at becoming a rock star, keep in mind that you're in charge of your own happiness.

And if you value your family, keeping that in perspective is key. If you blame them for standing in your way, you'll grow bitter and resentful—which is never healthy for anyone.

Social Life

One of my former clients was never particularly concerned with her health—at least not until the doctor told her she was going to have to start taking medication for high blood pressure and high cholesterol. She'd gained a considerable amount of weight with both of her pregnancies and she never really lost it. She was too preoccupied with her kids' activities to worry about taking care of herself.

But this was a wakeup call to her, and she decided to make her health a top priority. Within a few months, she dropped several pant sizes. And while she started feeling better, her friends started making comments like "You're losing weight too fast" or "You look gaunt."

She didn't know what to make of their comments. She said, "I turn down invitations sometimes because I'm going to the gym or because I know I can't be around them eating pizza without overindulging. But I don't understand their comments. I thought they'd be happy for me."

Reinventing herself into a healthier person left her friends feeling uncomfortable. Whether her weight loss caused them to feel jealous or they were upset she wasn't as available as she used to be, it was clear that they struggled to support her efforts. Unfortunately, her experience isn't unique.

Many people find their friends less than supportive when they create changes in their lives. You might find the "new you" doesn't fit in with your social circle as well as "the old you."

But that doesn't mean you've changed for the worse. It may mean you've outgrown some people or that your new lifestyle simply doesn't fit with their needs.

That doesn't mean you should give up on having girlfriends, however. Friendships play an integral role in women's lives. Studies consistently show female friendships offer a multitude of benefits, ranging from improved psychological well-being to longer life spans.

One of the reasons female friendships are so important is because of the way social support helps women manage stress. A study conducted by researchers at UCLA found that while men experience "fight or flight" during stressful experiences, women are more likely to "tend and befriend." Women naturally seek out other women in times of stress. Social support prevents women from experiencing the same spike in stress hormones that men do when they're under stressful circumstances.

If your friends don't support the new you, don't give up on having female friends. Hold direct discussions with them about how you're feeling and what you're noticing. If they still aren't able to support your efforts, look for people who can appreciate your changes. And be aware of how you treat your friends who reinvent themselves. Certainly, you don't need to support poor choices, but pay attention to times when you may be less than supportive of them when they're trying to better their lives.

Reinventing Yourself Makes You Stronger

After being in foster care for the first year and a half of her life, Lorraine Pascale was adopted. Her adoptive parents, however, weren't stable, and she ended up back in foster care when she was eight. She bounced between several different foster homes and then, at age eleven, a charity paid for her to go to boarding school.

She flourished in the boarding school. And while she was able to engage in many activities, it was there that she discovered her passion for cooking.

When she finished school, she went into modeling. She was quite successful, and before long, she found herself alongside women like Naomi

Campbell and Kate Moss. But modeling work caused her soul to feel empty. On her website, she says, "I wanted more and to have that happiness people like my father had when he was a Spanish teacher and loved his work. I wanted to really love my work too." So, after getting married and giving birth to her daughter, she quit modeling and set out to find work that she found fulfilling.

She read *What Color Is Your Parachute?* and it set her on a path to finding her passion. She dabbled in car mechanics, interior design, and hypnotherapy before deciding to go back to what she loved doing as a child—cooking. She went back to school to learn more about the food industry, and after she graduated, she opened her own bakery.

Her bakery was so successful that offers began rolling in. She got a book deal and she appeared on multiple TV shows, such as *Worst Bakers in America* and *Holiday Baking Championship*. Lorraine says, "The only route to true happiness is to give back in whichever ways we can, no matter how small." While she finds fulfillment in baking, she doesn't hesitate to say she might reinvent herself again. She's considering going back to college to study psychology and neuroscience "as a little side extra."

On her website, Lorraine says, "I have faced many challenges in my time, like so many of us, and the way out has always been 'through.' There are no shortcuts when it comes to trying to better yourself and to heal wounds of the past."

Lorraine has never been afraid to reinvent herself—even when it meant leaving behind a lucrative career. But as she points out, doing new things can be the key to self-awareness, and it can open doors to help you live a more fulfilling life.

Troubleshooting and Common Traps

Holding on to a fantasy won't do you or anyone any good. Deciding the "new you" is going to make the Olympic track team at age sixty could do more harm than good. It's important to reflect on your goals and make sure that they're based in some sense of reality. While you may hear news stories about outliers who beat the odds or did the impossible, those stories don't cover the droves of people who weren't able to realize their dreams. So it's important to make sure that the "new you" is something you have a good chance of doing.

The "grass is greener on the other side" mentality can be a dangerous trap for people who are reinventing themselves. While a shift in career or a change to your living situation might make you happier, always thinking that something else is going to be better will leave you chronically disappointed.

If you have a habit of making bold moves in search of happiness only to find that the grass wasn't greener on the other side, reinventing yourself again isn't going to be a magical solution. You have to learn how to be comfortable in your own skin and how to be happy with what you have before you'll ever experience true contentment in life.

WHAT'S HELPFUL

- Taking a step back to examine whether you're living according to your values
- Identifying changes you want to make to be more like the person you want to become
- Acknowledging what gets in the way of reinventing yourself
- Thinking about ways you could use your current skill set to do something different
- Recognizing how your personality may have changed over time

WHAT'S NOT HELPFUL

- Getting stuck in a rut that prevents you from doing things differently

- Assuming the grass is always greener on the other side
- Refusing to change because it feels too hard
- Thinking you have to stay the same to be authentic
- Waiting until you feel like changing before changing your behavior

13

They Don't Downplay
Their Success

*Our deepest fear is not that we are inadequate. Our deepest fear is
that we are powerful beyond measure.*
—MARIANNE WILLIAMSON

Charlotte had been a sales representative for twelve years. Each month,
she consistently earned bonuses for hitting her sales incentives, and her
success attracted attention at the state and regional levels.

She had received several awards over the years for her successful performance, but she was caught off guard when she received an invitation to
become a national trainer. The promotion involved speaking at national
sales conventions and advising regional managers on sales training strategies.

The position allowed her to continue her current sales job—so Charlotte readily accepted. But almost as soon as she agreed to the promotion,
fear set in. And that's why she started coming to therapy.

During her first appointment, she said, "I should be excited about getting a promotion but I mostly feel sheer panic. I was happy in my sales
position. I'm honored they gave me this opportunity, but I don't know if
I am up for the challenge."

Charlotte didn't think she was qualified to talk about sales strategies.

"I'm not even that good at sales. I probably just get lucky and have more interested customers than other people do. What am I even going to say? That the secret to making sales is to be a nice person?" she said.

She spent the next several minutes second-guessing her success and questioning why they chose her for the position. "I feel like an idiot right now for so many reasons. I fooled people into thinking I'm great at sales and it backfired because now they want me to reveal my 'secrets' even though I have none. I feel like an even bigger fool for coming to therapy. Who needs therapy because they got a promotion?"

I assured Charlotte she wasn't alone in coming to therapy after receiving a promotion. "It's normal to feel anxious and to question your competence at a time like this," I said.

"Oh, good. So what should I do to feel more competent? I am thinking I'll start reading as many sales books as I can so I have something meaningful to say when people ask me about sales," she said.

"Do you think your bosses want you to read sales books and then regurgitate the information to other salespeople? Or do you think they want you to share knowledge based on your expertise?" I asked. Charlotte said, "Oh, I'm sure they want my expertise. But I'm afraid I don't have any expertise."

I encouraged her to put off reading any sales books—at least for now. Instead, I recommended she set up weekly therapy appointments to address her anxiety. Fortunately, she agreed.

Initially, she was convinced there were two different Charlottes; there was the person she saw herself as and the person her supervisors thought she was. We talked about how it was easier for her to assume that her boss made a mistake in thinking she was qualified, rather than accept that she might be more skilled than she gave herself credit for.

We also discussed the dangers of believing she was unfit for the position. If she didn't believe in herself, she wasn't likely to succeed.

We addressed her beliefs about being humble. She thought saying her "hard work paid off" was the equivalent of saying "I am deserving of this." To help her recognize her skills and talents, we created a list of the sales strategies she used. It only took a few minutes to fill two pages. When we were done I said, "Charlotte, based on this list I think you have plenty to share. But it doesn't matter what I think. What matters is that *you* believe it."

We spent the next few months addressing the discrepancy between her self-image and the image others held of her. We increased her self-awareness and discussed what she could do to become more confident in her ability to succeed. Slowly, Charlotte's view of herself began to shift.

It began to sink in that the reason she was picked for the promotion was because she was good at her job. Once she began believing that, her sheer panic turned into normal anxiety. She was nervous about public speaking and unsure what to expect when she advised the managers, but she felt more confident that she had the skills and the knowledge to succeed.

Do You Have Trouble Owning Your Success?

While it's no secret that failure is uncomfortable, success can also create a surprising amount of turmoil for many women. Whether you just can't internalize your success, or you fear looking like a narcissist, it can be difficult to own your success. Do any of the following statements sound like you?

- ❐ I feel unworthy of my accomplishments.
- ❐ I feel uncomfortable when people compliment me.
- ❐ When I succeed at something, I always credit external factors like good luck or help from someone else.
- ❐ I don't talk about my achievements because I don't want to sound like I'm bragging.
- ❐ I downplay my accomplishments, intelligence, or status sometimes because I don't want other people to feel bad.
- ❐ I struggle to recognize my skills, talents, and experience.
- ❐ When people say nice things to me or about me, I secretly question their sincerity.

- ❒ I often feel like I'm not as smart, talented, or skilled as other people think I am.
- ❒ I fear people are going to recognize that I'm inadequate and incompetent.
- ❒ I experience a lot of anxiety when I accomplish something great.

Why We Do It

During one of her therapy sessions, Charlotte explained that she felt insecure because everyone else on her sales team had a college degree. Sometimes, they assumed she did too and would ask questions, like what college she attended or what she majored in. She felt embarrassed when she had to reveal that she had never actually been to college.

She said, "Everyone else in my office is smarter than I am. They all have bachelor's degrees." She chalked her success up to external factors, like good luck, kind customers, and a boss who thought Charlotte was smarter than she was. She couldn't reconcile that she might have more skills or talent than people who had been to college.

I've seen many clients over the years who sought therapy not because of their failures, but because of their success. Imposter syndrome, as it is commonly referred to, is a common issue for women. While no one is immune to feeling like they're undeserving of their achievements, minorities and women are especially at risk, and it's one of the biggest reasons women struggle to own their success.

BOYS DON'T LIKE SMART GIRLS

You've likely met at least one woman who seems to "dumb herself down" when men are present. Whether she gives a man credit for the idea that she actually came up with, or she asks for help doing things she could do herself, she assures the man she's with that he's better than she is. Perhaps you've done this yourself.

A 2014 study conducted by the University of Warwick's Maria do

Mar Pereira, Ph.D., found that by age fourteen, boys had acquired the belief that girls their age should be less intelligent. The author states, "Young people try to adapt their behavior according to these pressures to fit into society. One of the pressures is that young men must be more dominant—cleverer, stronger, taller, funnier—than young women, and that being in a relationship with a woman who is more intelligent will undermine their masculinity."

After spending three months following eighth-grade students, the author found, "Girls feel they must downplay their abilities, pretending to be less intelligent than they actually are, not speaking out against harassment, and withdrawing from hobbies, sports, and activities that might seem 'unfeminine.'"

She also found, "The belief that men have to be dominant over women makes boys feel constantly anxious and under pressure to prove their power—namely by fighting, drinking, sexually harassing, refusing to ask for help, and repressing their emotions."

These gender norms that children develop at a young age don't disappear during adulthood. Researchers studying gender norms during adulthood have found:

- Men prefer female partners who are less professionally ambitious than they are.
- Men avoid female partners with characteristics usually associated with professional ambition, such as high levels of education.
- It's relatively unlikely that a woman will earn more than her husband. When she does, marital satisfaction is lower and divorce is more likely.
- Promotions increase the chance of divorce for women, but not for men.

It's no wonder that some women find it hard to own their success. High achievement could decrease your ability to find a partner or maintain a healthy, stable relationship.

Single women may be especially harmed by the notion that men don't like ambitious women. In a 2017 study of first-year MBA students, 64 percent of single females said they avoided asking for a raise or a promotion because they feared they would look "too ambitious, assertive, or pushy." Only 39 percent of women who were married or in a serious relationship said the same (and 27 percent of men). The study also found that single women were much less likely to participate in class when there were single men in the classroom.

Maddie, an eighteen-year-old college student whom I interviewed, said she's seen this problem firsthand on campus. She said, "I know girls who are intelligent but they act dumb because they think it's attractive. I would never go up to a girl and say, 'Hey, you're actually smart so why are you acting stupid,' but I would want them to know you don't have to do that to be attractive. My brothers and the guys I've met and talked to would rather date a smart girl, but some girls don't believe that. I think the most important lesson to teach young women (and one I've thankfully learned well from my own mother) is self-confidence and pride in your own ability."

Unfortunately, listing your education on your online dating profile, sharing your career aspirations on a first date, and earning more than your partner could threaten your relationship. Out of fear that they might scare a man away, many women minimize their achievement, sit quietly in the back of the room, or keep their intelligence a secret.

WOMEN DON'T WANT TO SOUND ARROGANT

There's an assumption in today's world that women lack confidence. It's a message companies market to us because product sales depend on us feeling bad about ourselves. And while body image issues are abundant, the emphasis on the low self-esteem epidemic makes it difficult for women to feel as though it's OK to be confident.

People don't expect women to feel good about themselves or to be proud of their achievements—it seems frowned upon. The fear of sounding too self-assured has led many women to downplay their success. It's become so prevalent that many women struggle to accept a compliment for fear of sounding too confident.

Researchers have found that women struggle to accept compliments in general. But this is especially true when receiving compliments from other women.

In one study, women accepted compliments 40 percent of the time. When the compliment was given by another woman, however, they only accepted their compliments 22 percent of the time.

What does "accepting a compliment" mean? The researchers considered a compliment accepted when it was acknowledged and agreed to with a response such as "Thank you." Non-accepted compliments included things like responding with a compliment in return (e.g., "No, you're amazing"); minimizing the achievement (e.g., "It was nothing"), and attributing success to someone else (e.g., "It was really my coworker who did all the work").

So why do women have trouble accepting compliments? It can feel as though saying "Thank you" actually means "Yes, I agree." When someone says "You're so smart," you might think a simple "Thank you" sounds arrogant. To sound humble, women often respond to praise with a self-deprecating statement or by minimizing their achievement.

Difficulty accepting compliments isn't always about the desire to appear humble. For many women, hearing a compliment causes them to feel distress. Here are three reasons compliments make women cringe:

1. **Low self-esteem.** Although compliments are meant to help others feel good, praise often has the opposite effect when someone has low self-esteem. It can feel embarrassing, awkward, and even insincere to hear nice things if you secretly don't like yourself.

2. **Incongruent self-image.** If the things someone says about you don't match up to the way you see yourself, they create what's known in the psychology world as cognitive dissonance. If you think you're an idiot and someone calls you smart, either you're wrong

or the person giving you the compliment is wrong. Either way, it's uncomfortable.

3. **Discomfort with big expectations.** Hearing someone say "You're so talented. I know you're going to be a huge success," puts a lot of pressure on you. The higher the expectation, the more uncomfortable you'll feel.

Why It's Bad

During Charlotte's second therapy appointment, as we discussed her promotion to national sales trainer, she said, "I think I should just come clean and tell my boss that she's mistaken. I can't teach people anything." In that moment, telling her boss, "I'm not as good as you think I am," felt reasonable to her. She almost gave up a wonderful opportunity because she wasn't sure she deserved the position.

But giving up before she even started wasn't the only danger Charlotte faced. If she had gone along with the promotion without changing her underlying beliefs, it's unlikely she would have been successful. If she didn't believe she had anything worth saying, why would anyone else listen to her? If she was going to teach people valuable lessons, she had to believe there was value in what she was offering.

Women who can't own their success end up feeling like a fraud. They never feel comfortable with their achievements and they aren't able to reach their greatest potential.

WOMEN WITH IMPOSTER SYNDROME
STRUGGLE TO SUCCEED

Imposter syndrome was first brought to light in the 1970s. At that time, psychologists thought only women experienced it, but now, we know men experience it too. While imposter syndrome isn't a clinical diagnosis, it can be a major issue in many people's lives. It's linked to self-doubt and perfectionism.

Amy Cuddy, a Harvard professor and the author of *Presence: Bringing Your Boldest Self to Your Biggest Challenges,* suggests it should be called the "imposter experience" as opposed to a syndrome. According to Cuddy, 80 percent of people feel like an imposter at one time or another. And she suggests it isn't something either you have or you don't. Instead, the feeling comes and goes.

In her book, Cuddy explains that she almost didn't mention how she felt like she didn't belong alongside successful people when she gave her TED talk in 2012. It felt too personal to bring up but ultimately, she decided to share her story. Since then, however, she's received thousands of emails from people who said that they too felt like a fake, which reinforced her position that many people feel like imposters but no one wants to admit it.

The more successful you become, the more you might feel like an imposter. A pay raise, a promotion, or a new achievement may reignite your "imposter experience" and become a roadblock to further accomplishments.

So while everyone might experience imposter syndrome from time to time, women may be more likely to be held back by it. As we discussed in the self-doubt chapter, women are more likely to allow their fears of inadequacy to affect their behavior. Here are some ways imposter syndrome can hold you back:

- **You'll convince yourself you're not good enough.** The more success you experience, the more you'll worry that you're going to have to keep up the "charade" to appear competent.
- **You'll sabotage yourself.** Imposter syndrome involves a fear of failure as well as a fear of success. Studies have found that people who experience this internal tug-of-war often sabotage their chances of success.
- **You'll assume other people overestimate you.** Compliments, awards, or promotions might actually cause you to feel worse. You'll worry that you'll never live up to the expectations people have of you.

- **You'll work really hard.** Studies show people with imposter syndrome are at a higher risk of burning out. It could cause you to push yourself beyond your limits and prevent you from being able to enjoy any of the rewards you've earned along the way.
- **You won't advance in your career.** Studies show imposter syndrome causes people to stagnate and they often feel dissatisfied with their careers. If you feel like you don't deserve your success, you aren't likely to ask for a raise or apply for a promotion.

SHRINKING YOURSELF WON'T GAIN YOU RESPECT

Some women think minimizing their accomplishments will help other people feel better about themselves, or it will at least prevent other people from being intimidated by them. But they're not really being humble. Instead, they're shrinking themselves because they aren't comfortable with their success—and they don't want to make anyone around them feel bad.

One of my friends is a popular public speaker who coaches some of the world's top CEOs. She receives phone calls from successful people across the globe who are looking for her business advice.

She divorced a few years ago, and she recently reentered the dating scene. She says the most uncomfortable part about dating is telling men what she does for a living. She said, "Sometimes men seem intimidated when I tell them what I do. One of them said, 'These rich men hire you for your looks, not your brains.' He tried to act like he was joking. I responded by saying, 'Isn't it interesting when I said I coach CEOs you automatically thought CEOs were men? Women are successful CEOs too.'" She said another man asked if her career was the reason she got divorced, because "you clearly think a lot of your job."

After a few bad experiences, she considered being vague about her career. But then she realized that if a man felt intimidated by her career, they weren't likely to have a healthy relationship. She wanted a man who was secure enough in who he was that he could handle being with a confident woman who owned her success.

Of course, it's not just professional women or single women who struggle to own their success. In response to a compliment about a child's good manners, I have heard a stay-at-home mom say, "We got really lucky with this one," as if she deserved zero credit for teaching the child how to say please and thank you.

And in response to a compliment like "You look really good. I know you've worked hard to lose all that weight," I've heard women say things like "I've got a long way to go before I get rid of these thunder thighs" or "If I could look half as good as you someday I'd be happy." They'd rather point out flaws or insist they aren't good enough so the person offering kind words won't think they deserve too much credit.

Even when women are asked to share their skills, talents, and achievements—they're not sharing them. Research on LinkedIn—the networking site where you're supposed to talk about your achievements so you can advance your career—shows men tout their skills more aggressively. When LinkedIn reviewed profiles of men and women, they found:

- Men skew their professional brands to highlight more senior-level experience, and they often remove junior-level roles altogether.
- Women have shorter profile summaries.
- In the United States, women include, on average, 11 percent fewer skills than men on their profiles, even when compared to men with similar occupations and experience levels.

In a world where each skill listed on a profile matters—members with five or more skills receive up to seventeen times more profile views—not owning your success can cost you.

Some women think they need to minimize their success to help others feel comfortable. But shrinking yourself to help others feel big isn't effective. That's not to say you need to announce your job title to everyone you meet so they know you're important, but being able to talk confidently about your talents, skills, and experiences doesn't need to be offensive.

If you feel like your success offends others, something is wrong. Your relationship might be broken, your self-worth might be damaged, or you may have some past hurts that are unhealed. Minimizing yourself won't solve those problems.

Putting yourself down won't make someone else look better any more than putting others down makes you look better. You can show that you value someone or that you recognize their importance without shrinking yourself.

YOU WON'T ADVANCE IF YOU FEEL UNDESERVING OF A PROMOTION

There's tons of career advice out there meant to help you advance, such as "Dress for the job you want, not the job you have" or "Find a good mentor." And while those strategies can be excellent tools, you also have to believe that you are deserving of a promotion. Otherwise, your insecurity will shine through and impede your progress.

A study led by researchers at the University of Texas at Austin found a link between imposter syndrome, discrimination, and mental health problems among minorities. The authors of the study suggest that minorities may feel like outsiders when members of their group aren't represented in certain areas. Feeling like an imposter can make discrimination worse. And discrimination can fuel those feelings of fraud, as well as anxiety and depression.

Since women are underrepresented in leadership, it's likely many women who do make it to the top feel like imposters. And perhaps this plays a role in the pay gap.

It's hard to ask for a raise or negotiate a higher starting salary when you're questioning whether you're actually qualified to do the work. Even if you pay the lip service and ask for more money, your body language, tone of voice, and actions will scream loud and clear that you don't really believe that you deserve more money.

If you want someone else to believe in you, you need to believe in yourself. You have to be able to show that you are capable and competent. You can't do that if you're always questioning your skills or telling yourself that you're not good enough.

What to Do Instead

During one of her appointments, Charlotte said, "Just because my sales tactics work here doesn't mean they're going to be effective for people in other parts of the country." I agreed with her and then I asked, "Do you think your boss expects you to know what will work for every geographic area, or do you think your boss wants you to share what works for you?"

"I guess she just wants me to share what works for me," she said. We talked about all the pressure Charlotte was putting on herself. She thought she needed to have all the answers all the time.

Part of her treatment focused on helping her recognize her accomplishments and her strengths while also accepting that she would never have all the answers. And that was OK. It didn't mean she was incompetent or a fraud.

Owning your success isn't about filling your head with empty platitudes or exaggerating how wonderful you are. It's about coming to terms with reality. Recognizing your strengths will help you feel confident in who you are and what you're capable of achieving.

ACKNOWLEDGE WHY YOU DOWNPLAY YOUR SUCCESS

There are two main reasons women downplay their success: they don't feel deserving of their success and they don't want to make other people feel bad.

Acknowledge the times when you struggle to own your success. Examples might include:

- Not telling anyone about your latest achievement
- Insisting your success was a fluke
- Keeping your ambitions to yourself

Keep in mind that there's a difference between being humble and not owning your success. Humility is about having a realistic view of yourself. That means acknowledging your weaknesses while also admitting your strengths.

When you notice that you are downplaying your success, ask yourself the following questions:

- ***Am I afraid of what other people will think?*** Is it a fear of how you'll be perceived? Are you afraid someone will be offended, turned off, or envious of you? Do you want people to think you're modest?

- ***Do I feel worthy of my success?*** If you don't feel like you deserve to be successful, it's impossible to talk about your achievements with confidence.

- ***Are you afraid your success won't last?*** Do you worry that someone is going to realize you didn't deserve that promotion or that you aren't good enough? If you feel as though you're going to be rejected, demoted, or terminated at any minute, you might not talk about your achievement because you won't want everyone to know.

PRACTICE OWNING YOUR SUCCESS

No one wants to run around bragging about how great they are. But everyone has expertise in something, and sharing your knowledge with others could help them. Telling someone about your success might inspire that individual to do the same, or it could give them knowledge that will help them. Here's how you can own your success without sounding arrogant:

- **Express gratitude for your success.** Saying things like "I'm grateful that I had a wonderful mentor" or "My parents had a lot to do with this. I'm thankful they taught me the value of a dollar at a young age" shows that you recognize the support you've been given. It's much different from saying you owe all your success to someone else.

- **Avoid the qualifier.** Don't bother saying "I don't mean to brag, but . . ." It makes you sound like you're about to say something hurtful and you don't care. Instead, emphasize the positive emotions and skip to the good news. Say something like "I'm excited to share . . ."
- **Skip the humblebrag.** When you feel uncomfortable you might be tempted to add a self-deprecating statement into the mix. But posting a picture of your worn-out shoes on social media and saying "I guess I should go shopping for new shoes now that I'm a manager" isn't a good idea. If you got a promotion, just say so. Studies show humblebrags will make you sound insincere.
- **Emphasize your effort.** Saying "Oh, it was nothing" when you receive praise for your latest project, or "Parenting really isn't that hard when you know what you're doing" when your child wins the spelling bee, will make you sound full of yourself. Emphasizing your effort, however, shows that you put hard work into reaching your goals. Say something more like "It wasn't easy, but it's definitely worth all the hard work it took to get here."
- **Stick to the facts.** No one wants to hear that you're the best thing that ever happened to your company or that you know more than everyone else in your college. So skip the superlatives and get right to the facts. Say something like "I doubled my sales over last year's sales" or "I got an A on my exam."

ACCEPT COMPLIMENTS GRACEFULLY

Sometimes, we think we're being polite by turning down a compliment. But when you really think about it, refusing to accept someone's compliment discounts their opinion. Or in some cases, you're essentially saying that they're a liar. Here are a few examples of common responses to compliments and what they imply:

Compliment: "You did such a great job speaking up in the meeting this morning."

Response: "Yeah, right. I'm such a bumbling idiot. Once I opened my mouth I forgot what I was going to say and just droned on and on."

What the response implies: You have no idea what you're talking about.

Compliment: "I love those pants!"

Response: "Really? I bought them on a clearance rack like ten years ago."

What the response implies: You have poor taste.

Compliment: "I'm so impressed with your weight-loss journey. You've done such a great job."

Response: "I have a long way to go."

What the response implies: I don't care what you think about my progress.

If you've gotten into the habit of refusing compliments, practice accepting them. Give yourself permission to acknowledge someone else's kind words. Simply say "Thank you," or "I appreciate that," and see what happens. It will likely feel uncomfortable at first. But it gets easier once you get into the habit.

Receiving kind words about yourself isn't arrogant. You're showing respect for the other person's thoughts. And you're showing that you're confident enough in yourself that you can listen to someone else's opinion.

When you are able to own your success, listening to compliments—as well as critiques—becomes easier because you'll be sure of who you are.

CREATE A LIST OF SUCCESSES AND READ IT AS NEEDED

Sometimes, it's difficult to recall evidence that reminds you that you deserve success. Perhaps you draw a blank, or maybe the only accomplishments that spring to mind don't actually help you feel successful—like that trophy you earned for participating on the basketball team in the third grade.

Creating a list of the reasons you are worthy of success can help. Seeing those things on paper and adding to your list regularly can keep your achievements fresh in your mind.

So write down all the things that you've accomplished that can help you own your success. Here's the beginning of a sample list:

- I graduated from college with a 3.0 GPA.
- I have fifteen years of experience as an elementary school teacher.
- I've taught some of the most challenging kids in the school.
- The principal put me on two special committees.
- I stay after school for an extra hour every day and put in the work I need to be my best.
- I've had three students say I was the best teacher they've ever had.
- I got a thank-you note from a student's mother once saying her child would have never graduated without my support.

Your list doesn't need to surround your professional life. Here's a sample list a stay-at-home mother might create to remind her that she's a good mom:

- I take care of all my kids' needs every day.
- My kids know they are loved.

- My kids have good manners.
- I let them make mistakes and I teach them how to learn from those mistakes.
- I read to my kids every day.

You might also create a list of reasons why you know you're strong. Perhaps you survived abuse, cheated death, or beat the odds. When you remind yourself of the tough things you've overcome, you'll see that accepting a compliment or sharing your good news isn't so scary.

Read over your list whenever you need a reminder that it's OK to own your success. And keep it handy so you can add new accomplishments to your list regularly. Reading over your list will help your achievements sink in so you can feel worthy of your success.

Career

About eight years into my career as a psychotherapist, I began teaching college classes in psychology and mental health. I taught in the evenings—and sometimes I taught Saturday classes—so I could work around my job as a therapist. While I was concerned that putting in more hours might be a recipe for burnout, teaching actually made me more excited than ever about my career.

In my day job, it was easy to forget how much I was learning. I treated patients every day, went to trainings, and attended meetings, but it didn't really allow me to step back and look at the bigger picture. Teaching, however, gave me that opportunity. I could share examples of how to take information from the textbook and apply it to real life. And I could field questions from eager students about psychological theories and mental health principles. It helped me own my success as a therapist, because I felt knowledgeable.

You don't have to become a college professor to share your wisdom with others, however. Mentoring someone could also remind you how much you've learned along the way. Offer to help newer professionals navigate their careers and you'll be reminded of how far you've come since you first started out.

Look for other opportunities to share your knowledge. Start a blog, write a book, or teach a workshop. But do something that will help you recognize that you have expertise, knowledge, and skills that give you a right to own your success.

Keep in mind that not owning your success will be detrimental to your career. No one wants to promote someone who can't take credit for their hard work. And customers don't want to buy a product from you if you don't feel as though you deserve to sell it to them.

Family

Author Celeste Ng sent her mother a text message that read, "Morning, mom! I thought you might want to see this week's NYT bestseller list." She then included a picture of the *New York Times* bestseller list that showed her book was number four on the fiction list. Her mother texted back, "Great, going to brunch downstairs in a little while. Love you."

Celeste shared a screenshot of their conversation on Twitter and said, "No one like a mom to keep your ego in check."

Unlike your friends, who probably have certain things in common with you—a similar level of education, values, and economic status—your family may have a different lifestyle than you. You didn't meet in college or cross paths in a Mommy and Me group. And even though you may have lived in the same house, you may have very different definitions of success.

So while some people have family who support them no matter what, others grow up with parents who are never satisfied. No matter what type of family you have, keep in mind that people who knew you when you wore diapers may struggle to recognize you as a competent, successful adult. But don't let that affect how you feel about your achievement. You can own your success even if they don't.

Social Life

On New Year's Eve, an acquaintance turned to social media to share that every year her family identified a charitable cause they wanted to help. Instead of choosing a traditional resolution, they devoted their efforts to volunteering for that charity throughout the year. She announced the charity they'd chosen and posted a picture of her family volunteering. She said, "We gain a lot by giving to others."

Most people responded positively. Some said it was a great idea and it inspired them to do something similar. But a few people reacted with anger and disgust, telling her that she was "tooting her own horn" and "bragging about her good deeds to get attention."

Not everyone appreciates good news or inspiring ideas. Someone will always be offended by something—like saying you volunteer. But that doesn't mean you shouldn't share it. It's not your responsibility to control how other people respond.

Of course, posting selfies in a swimsuit every ten minutes under the pretense that you're trying to inspire others with your beach body isn't likely to be met with favor. Showing off in an attempt to gain admiration is very different from owning your success.

Before you post your success story to social media, or before you share your latest achievement with your friends (good deed or not), consider your goal. Are you hoping to inspire others to reach their goals? Or are you looking for praise and admiration?

If your goal is to prove to other people that you're a good person or to gain validation that you're doing a good job, sharing your accomplishments might be more on the narcissistic end of the spectrum, rather than the owning-your-success end of the spectrum. But if you're hoping to inspire others by sharing your journey, posting about your achievements might motivate your friends to do the same.

No one wants to be that friend who can't stop talking about how great she is. But if you're worried that you're showing off your success too much, you probably aren't.

Owning Your Success Makes You Stronger

As an Indian-American woman, Mindy Kaling never saw anyone on TV who looked like her when she was growing up. But she didn't let that prevent her from going into the entertainment industry. Not only has she become an award-winning actress, but she's also proved she can produce, write, and direct some of the most popular shows on TV.

To say she's successful would be an understatement. From starring in *The Office* to writing and producing *The Mindy Project*, she's become a well-known celebrity. She's been nominated for numerous Emmy Awards and she's won multiple Gracie Awards. *People* magazine included her on their list of the most beautiful people—twice, *Time* named her as one of the 100 most influential people in 2012, and *Glamour* called her one of the women of the year in 2014. She's also a *New York Times* bestselling author.

In her book *Why Not Me?*, Kaling admits she's struggled with confidence at times. But she says the secret to feeling more confident was hard work. She knows she is a hard worker who has earned the right to be where she is.

However, some people don't like her because she "thinks she's great." She says, "But it's not that I think I'm so great. I just don't hate myself. I do idiotic things all the time and I say crazy stuff I regret, but I don't let everything traumatize me. And the scary thing I have noticed is that some people really feel uncomfortable around women who don't hate themselves. So that's why you need to be a little bit brave."

Owning your success may cause other people to feel uncomfortable—and it may make you uncomfortable at first. But knowing your strengths will help you feel more comfortable in your own skin. It'll also help you feel deserving of your accomplishments, which in turn can help motivate you to keep going.

Troubleshooting and Common Traps

Sometimes, people don't want to own their success because it means they'll need to own their failures too. If you take credit for the good outcomes, you have to recognize your role in the bad outcomes too. As with everything, it's all about finding a balance in how much responsibility you take. You might chalk your success up to good luck and blame your failure on the bad economy. Some things are outside of your control. But it's important to accept credit for the role you played, despite the outcome.

It's also important to be sensitive about owning your success. If you get a promotion the same day your friend gets laid off, hold off on sharing your good news. You can still own your success while being sensitive to other people's needs.

Finally, be mindful that owning your success isn't the same as flaunting your success. If you can afford a nice car or a big house, that's great. But be conscious of comments that might seem to belittle others. Saying things like "Let's take my car. It's nicer" or "Let's eat at my house. My dining room is better" might fall into the bragging category.

Owning your success should never involve belittling anyone else. If you feel the need to point out that you earn more money, look more attractive, or have a better life than someone else, you may have a self-worth issue. Like we talked about in chapter 8, putting others down won't lift you up or help you own your success. When you can acknowledge other people's strengths—especially the ones you don't possess—you'll be better equipped to talk realistically about your own strengths.

WHAT'S HELPFUL

- Recognizing when you're downplaying your success
- Talking about your achievement in a realistic manner

- Saying "thank you" when you are given a compliment
- Listing your achievements to remind yourself that you're worthy of success
- Mentoring, teaching, and training other people

WHAT'S NOT HELPFUL

- Confusing arrogance with owning your success
- Flaunting your achievement
- Minimizing yourself to try to help others feel important
- Refusing compliments

CONCLUSION

There are so many brave, strong women in the world who are making a difference. They've fought to change laws, overcome horrific tragedies, and accomplished incredible feats. We read their stories in magazines, watch them on the news, and see their talks that are broadcast to millions.

But there are also many strong women whose names we'll never know. They won't become celebrities, spokespeople, or historical figures. They won't launch businesses, write books, or be interviewed by the media. Instead, they're the women who are making a positive impact in their homes and their communities.

They're the moms who are raising their kids to be kind, the women who are working hard on healing their wounds, and the women who are helping others. You can find these women—those who are creating a ripple effect—everywhere.

Jill is one of those women. When I put the call out on social media that I was looking to interview women for this book, she responded immediately. Since reading my first book, *13 Things Mentally Strong People Don't Do,* Jill has been working hard to help other people build their mental muscles, while also building her own.

Jill was a victim of sexual assault many years ago. At the time, she felt frightened and confused and didn't know what to do. After investing many years working on overcoming the trauma she experienced, Jill signed up to become a volunteer for a sexual assault crisis service.

Before she could become a volunteer, she was required to attend a forty-hour training course that would prepare her to help victims and survivors. She had to be prepared to handle anything—from accompanying individuals who had just been raped to the hospital to listening to individuals who were struggling with flashbacks over something that happened twenty years ago.

When Jill told her friends she was planning to volunteer for the hotline, they didn't share her excitement. They said things like "Why would you want to do that? It'll be so hard." Their response caused Jill to think twice about whether it was a good idea.

She mentioned to her sixteen-year-old daughter that she was feeling nervous about the training and the things she might experience. She said, "It might be too much for me to deal with." Without skipping a beat, her daughter said, "How do you think the victims feel?"

In that instant, Jill's daughter reflected back all those things Jill had been teaching her about being mentally strong. Those words of reassurance reminded Jill that she could get involved in helping others heal even though she felt scared.

Jill said, "I smiled and was so proud of her. I think she is the voice of the future—more informed and confident."

Jill isn't just teaching her daughter how to be mentally strong. She's creating a ripple effect in her community through some of the simplest, yet kindest, actions. Following our phone call, Jill sent me this email:

> I don't have any close family around and friends are busy with their families. I've learned my self-talk is key and one of my mantras to myself when I'm feeling overwhelmed or the physical pain is unbearable is that tomorrow will be a better day. It replaces the negative thoughts with hope. I keep a list of people I know would be here in a heartbeat if they could and know their love is with me.
>
> A few years ago, I started working out at the gym after another knee surgery. A few people at the YMCA were supportive, showed me machines and helped with juggling my crutches. Not long after that, my husband and I began the divorce process. In the middle of that, my dad died suddenly.

Between dealing with a devastating divorce, post-operative pain, piles of paperwork and tests, calls from the hospital, planning my beloved dad's funeral and emptying my childhood home, I shut down.

My gym friends would take me in the back room for a short cry and hug me. I only saw them a few minutes per week but those moments of kindness made such a difference to me and gave me strength.

I wove their words into my mental motivational board and self-talk. I learned the importance of baby steps, and how empowering small acts of kindness are and to assume that everyone has hardships that they're hiding.

I started pushing myself to compliment strangers and force myself to ask neighbors for help—which in turn allowed me to be vulnerable. It eased my pain.

I taught my daughter to compliment a stranger's earrings, or make small talk and those small moments will come back to her when she needs help.

A couple of years later a woman named Ruth, who has cerebral palsy and is in a wheelchair, started coming to the gym. She looked defeated, scared, and alone—like I felt when I started there.

I pushed myself to talk to her like others had talked to me. It helps take the focus off my pain and we make each other laugh and it's just minutes a week. Now, Ruth has become an inspiration for many of us and she kindly says the same about me.

She lost 53 pounds doing just upper arm work and she became a Zumba instructor!! She is a hoot. I don't know how she does it. She takes the handicap bus to the gym, works there part time and is even on the board now.

Thank you again for helping me stay strong Amy. It's got a nice ripple effect.

Women like Jill are making the world a stronger place, one person at a time. Her example speaks volumes about how simple little changes in your life can have a positive impact on you as well as those around you.

Just like for Jill, there will be times in your life when you feel strong enough to help others build mental muscle, and times when you rely on encouragement from other women to keep you motivated. But together, we can all help each other weather life's inevitable ups and downs.

How to Keep Building Your Mental Muscles

When you give up the bad habits that are robbing you of mental strength, your good habits will become much more effective.

The best way to keep up with your mental fitness is by thinking of yourself as your own mental strength coach. Pay close attention to your habits to ensure you aren't falling into the trap of doing any of the things mentally strong women don't do. Perform regular mental strength exercises, and push yourself to build your mental strength.

Monitor your:

- **Thoughts**—Training your brain to think differently takes consistent practice. But no matter how much mental muscle you build, there will still be times when you compare yourself to others, insist on perfection, overthink everything, or let self-doubt prevent you from reaching your goals. With practice, however, you'll become better equipped to respond to those negative voices that run through your head in a more productive manner.
- **Feelings**—Your emotions influence how you think and how you behave. Becoming more aware of how you're feeling—and gaining the skills to cope with those emotions in a healthy way—takes persistence. But with practice, you'll find the courage to break a few rules that might be holding you back or let go of the self-blame that prevents you from feeling your best.
- **Behavior**—Whether you stay silent, stay stagnant, or stay stuck,

unhealthy behavior patterns can be hard to change. But the
stronger you become, the better able you'll be to recognize those
unhealthy cycles you get into. And you'll be able to create the
positive changes you need to become better.

Mental strength isn't something that either you have or you don't. It's
something you build over time, and it's something that you need to keep
working on developing. Mental muscles are like physical muscles—you
have to exercise to keep them strong.

What to Expect as You Grow Stronger

Sometimes people think being mentally strong means you'll earn millions of dollars or you'll be immune to bad days or bad moods. But those
things aren't necessarily the hallmarks of mental strength.

In fact, becoming stronger may mean saying no to lucrative financial
opportunities that aren't in line with your values. If you want to spend
more time with your family and less time in the office, working less could
be a sign of mental strength.

Similarly, if you've spent countless hours at the gym because you hate
your body, learning to love yourself more might mean working out less.
Being kinder to yourself can be a sign of increased mental muscle.

Here are the benefits you'll gain from building mental muscle:

- **Increased resilience to stress**—Although stress is part of life,
  it can take a toll on your physical and mental health if it's not
  managed well. Building mental strength buffers against those
  harmful effects of stress.
- **Improved life satisfaction**—As your mental strength increases,
  your confidence in your ability to deal with whatever life throws
  your way will soar. You'll have peace of mind that will help you find
  more enjoyment in everyday life.
- **Enhanced performance**—Whether your goal is to be a better

parent or you want to conquer your fears, mental strength will help you perform at your peak.

Of course, you'll never become an expert at anything by simply reading a book. Top musicians, athletes, and performers don't achieve success by reading a book or watching other people. They have to practice to get better. Mental strength is the same. It takes dedication and practice to become stronger.

Building mental strength is more of a journey than a destination. There will be times you'll make mistakes and times when you'll make bad choices. But there will also be times when you'll prove to yourself that you're stronger than you imagined.

ACKNOWLEDGMENTS

I'm grateful to everyone who helped make this book a reality, starting with the wonderful team at HarperCollins. Thank you to Lisa Sharkey for believing in the 13 things since day one and for supporting all three of my books. And thank you to Alieza Schvimer and Matt Harper for their assistance.

I owe a big thank-you to my wonderful agent, Stacey Glick. She contacted me after reading my article "13 Things Mentally Strong People Don't Do" and suggested I write a book in the first place.

I'm thankful to all the women who allowed me to share their stories in this book. So many of them replied to my request on social media and graciously took time out of their lives to talk to me.

I'm also grateful to Emily Morrison, the best friend anyone could have. Fortunately for me, she also happens to be an English teacher who volunteers to read through my roughest drafts. And thank you to Julie Hintgen for her support and feedback.

Of course, none of this would be possible without all my readers who want to continue to learn about mental strength.

I'm also fortunate to have encountered plenty of mentally strong people who have taught me valuable lessons over the years. There are many family members, friends, clients, neighbors, colleagues, and mentors who have left an imprint on my life and taught me about mental strength.

REFERENCES

Introduction

Harit, Shweta. 2016. *The New Face of Strength*. Kellogg's Special K. https://www
.specialk.com/content/dam/Dam/Special_K/downloads/Kelloggs-special-k
-inner-strength-whitepaper.pdf.

Chapter 1: They Don't Compare Themselves to Other People

Chou, Hui-Tzu Grace, and Nicholas Edge. "'They Are Happier and Having Better Lives than I Am': The Impact of Using Facebook on Perceptions of Others
Lives." *Cyberpsychology, Behavior, and Social Networking* 15, no. 2 (February
2012): 117-21. doi:10.1089/cyber.2011.0324.

Fardouly, Jasmine, Phillippa C. Diedrichs, Lenny R. Vartanian, and Emma
Halliwell. "Social Comparisons on Social Media: The Impact of Facebook on
Young Women's Body Image Concerns and Mood." *Body Image* 13 (March
2015): 38–45. doi:10.1016/j.bodyim.2014.12.002.

Franzoi, Stephen L., Kris Vasquez, Erin Sparapani, Katherine Frost, Jessica
Martin, and Megan Aebly. "Exploring Body Comparison Tendencies." *Psychology of Women Quarterly* 36, no. 1 (March 2012): 99–109. doi:10.1177
/0361684311427028.

Leahey, Tricia M., Janis H. Crowther, and Kristin D. Mickelson. "The Frequency,
Nature, and Effects of Naturally Occurring Appearance-Focused Social Comparisons." *Behavior Therapy* 38, no. 2 (June 2007): 132–43. doi:10.1016/j.
beth.2006.06.004.

Maloney, C. U.S. Congress. Joint Economic Committee. "Invest in Women, Invest in America: A Comprehensive Review of Women in the U.S. Economy,"
Carolyn B. Maloney, Cong. Rept. Washington: U.S. G.P.O., 2010.

Park, S. Y., and Y. M. Baek. "Two Faces of Social Comparison on Facebook: The

Interplay Between Social Comparison Orientation, Emotions, and Psychological Well-being." *Computers in Human Behavior* 79 (2018): 83–93. doi:10.1016/j.chb.2017.10.028.

Sheinin, Dave. "How Katie Ledecky Became Better at Swimming Than Anyone Is at Anything." *Washington Post,* June 24, 2016.

Want, S. C., and A. Saiphoo. "Social Comparisons with Media Images Are Cognitively Inefficient Even for Women Who Say They Feel Pressure from the Media." *Body Image* 20 (2017): 1–6. doi:10.1016/j.bodyim.2016.10.009.

Chapter 2: They Don't Insist on Perfection

Cindy Crawford. *Into the Gloss.* Accessed August 16, 2018. https://intothegloss.com/2014/05/cindy-crawford-2014/.

Curran, Thomas, and Andrew Hill. "Multidimensional Perfectionism and Burnout: A Meta-Analysis." *Personality and Social Psychology Review* 20, no. 3 (July 2015): 269–88. doi:10.31234/osf.io/wzber.

Dahl, Melissa. "Stop Obsessing: Women Spend 2 Weeks a Year on Their Appearance, TODAY Survey Shows." TODAY.com. October 14, 2016. Accessed October 1, 2018. https://www.today.com/health/stop-obsessing-women-spend-2-weeks-year-their-appearance-today-2D12104866.

Engeln, Renee. *Beauty Sick: How the Cultural Obsession with Appearance Hurts Girls and Women.* New York: Harper, 2018.

Flett, G., K. Blankstein, P. Hewitt, and S. Koledin. "Components of Perfectionism and Procrastination in College Students." *Social Behavior and Personality: An International Journal* 20 (1992): 85–94. https://doi.org/10.2224/sbp.1992.20.2.85.

Flett, G. L., P. L. Hewitt, and M. J. Heisel. "The Destructiveness of Perfectionism Revisited: Implications for the Assessment of Suicide Risk and the Prevention of Suicide." *Review of General Psychology* 18(3) (2014): 156–72. http://dx.doi.org/10.1037/gpr0000011.

Fry, Prem S., and Dominique L. Debats. "Perfectionism and Other Related Trait Measures as Predictors of Mortality in Diabetic Older Adults: A Six-and-a-Half-Year Longitudinal Study." *Journal of Health Psychology* 16, no. 7 (March 28, 2011): 1,058–70. doi:10.1177/1359105311398684.

Gray, Sophie. "Behind the Scenes of My 'Perfect' Instagram Life, My Anxiety Was Killing Me." *Marie Claire.* June 15, 2017. Accessed October 1, 2018.

https://www.marieclaire.com/health-fitness/a27708/no-more-bikini-photos
-unhealthy/.

Horne, Rebecca M., Matthew D. Johnson, Nancy L. Galambos, and Harvey J. Krahn. "Time, Money, or Gender? Predictors of the Division of Household Labour Across Life Stages." *Sex Roles* 78, nos. 11–12 (June 2018): 731–43. doi:10.1007/s11199-017-0832-1.

Kljajic, Kristina, Patrick Gaudreau, and Véronique Franche. "An Investigation of the 2 × 2 Model of Perfectionism with Burnout, Engagement, Self-regulation, and Academic Achievement." *Learning and Individual Differences* 57 (July 2017): 103-13. doi:10.1016/j.lindif.2017.06.004.

Mitchelson, J. K. "Seeking the Perfect Balance: Perfectionism and Work–Family Conflict." *Journal of Occupational and Organizational Psychology* 82 (2009): 349–67. doi:10.1348/096317908X314874.

O'Toole, Lesley. "'I Never Think I'm Thin Enough.'" *Daily Mail.* January 18, 2002. Accessed July 13, 2018. http://www.dailymail.co.uk/tvshowbiz/article -95492/I-think-Im-enough.html.

Sherry, Simon B., Paul L. Hewitt, Avi Besser, Gordon L. Flett, and Carolin Klein. "Machiavellianism, Trait Perfectionism, and Perfectionistic Self-presentation." *Personality and Individual Differences* 40, no. 4 (February 2007): 829–39. doi:10.1016/j.paid.2005.09.010.

Sherry, Simon B., Joachim Stoeber, and Cynthia Ramasubbu. "Perfectionism Explains Variance in Self-defeating Behaviors Beyond Self-criticism: Evidence from a Cross-national Sample." *Personality and Individual Differences* 95 (June 2016): 196–99. doi:10.1016/j.paid.2016.02.059.

"Survey Finds Disordered Eating Behaviors among Three out of Four American Women." Statistics—Center of Excellence for Eating Disorders. April 22, 2008. Accessed September 20, 2018. http://www.med.unc.edu/www/news archive/2008/april/survey-finds-disordered-eating-behaviors-among-three -out-of-four-american-women.

Wade, Tracey D., and Marika Tiggemann. "The Role of Perfectionism in Body Dissatisfaction." *Journal of Eating Disorders* 1, no. 1 (January 22, 2013). doi:10.1186/2050-2974-1-2.

Wong, Jaclyn S., and Andrew M. Penner. "Gender and the Returns to Attractiveness." *Research in Social Stratification and Mobility* 44 (June 2016): 113–23. doi:10.1016/j.rssm.2016.04.002.

Chapter 3: They Don't See Vulnerability as a Weakness

Dweck, C. S., T. E. Goetz, and N. L. Strauss. "Sex Differences in Learned Helplessness: IV. An Experimental and Naturalistic Study of Failure Generalization and Its Mediators." *Journal of Personality and Social Psychology* 38(3) (1980): 441–52. http://dx.doi.org/10.1037/0022-3514.38.3.441.

Elsbach, Kimberly D., and Beth A. Bechky. "How Observers Assess Women Who Cry in Professional Work Contexts." *Academy of Management Discoveries* 4, no. 2 (June 25, 2018): 127–54. doi:10.5465/amd.2016.0025.

Lewinsky, Monica. "Exclusive: Monica Lewinsky on the Culture of Humiliation." *Vanity Fair.* June 2014. Accessed October 1, 2018. https://www.vanityfair.com/style/society/2014/06/monica-lewinsky-humiliation-culture.

Meyers, Kate. "'Our Son's Autism Almost Tore Us Apart.'" *Redbook.* April 26, 2018. Accessed July 13, 2018. https://www.redbookmag.com/love-sex/relationships/advice/a6083/holly-robinson-peete/.

Salerno, Jessica M., and Liana C. Peter-Hagene. "One Angry Woman: Anger Expression Increases Influence for Men, but Decreases Influence for Women, During Group Deliberation." *Law and Human Behavior* 39, no. 6 (December 2015): 581–92. doi:10.1037/lhb0000147.

Chapter 4: They Don't Let Self-Doubt Stop Them from Reaching Their Goals

Andrews, Travis M. "Annie Glenn: 'When I Called John, He Cried. People Just Couldn't Believe That I Could Really Talk.'" *Washington Post.* December 9, 2016. Accessed October 1, 2018. https://www.washingtonpost.com/news/morning-mix/wp/2016/12/09/to-john-glenn-the-real-hero-was-his-wife-annie-conqueror-of-disability.

Bian, Lin, Sarah-Jane Leslie, and Andrei Cimpian. "Gender Stereotypes about Intellectual Ability Emerge Early and Influence Children's Interests." *Science* 355, no. 6323 (January 27, 2017): 389-91. doi:10.1126/science.aah6524.

Constans, Joseph I. "Worry Propensity and the Perception of Risk." *Behaviour Research and Therapy* 39, no. 6 (June 2001): 721–29. doi:10.1016/s0005-7967(00)00037-1.

Ede, Alison, Philip J. Sullivan, and Deborah L. Feltz. "Self-doubt: Uncertainty as a Motivating Factor on Effort in an Exercise Endurance Task." *Psychology of Sport and Exercise* 28 (January 2017): 31–36. doi:10.1016/j.psychsport.2016.10.002.

Ehrlinger, Joyce, and David Dunning. "How Chronic Self-views Influence (and Potentially Mislead) Estimates of Performance." *Journal of Personality and Social Psychology* 84, no. 1 (January 2003): 5–17. doi:10.1037/e633872013-215.

Lerner, Jennifer S., Deborah A. Small, and George Loewenstein. "Heart Strings and Purse Strings. Carryover Effects of Emotions on Economic Decisions." *Psychological Science* 15, no. 5 (May 2004): 337–41. doi:10.1111/j.0956-7976.2004.00679.x.

Mirels, Herbert L., Paul Greblo, and Janet B. Dean. "Judgmental Self-doubt: Beliefs about One's Judgmental Prowess." *Personality and Individual Differences* 33, no. 5 (October 2002): 741–58. doi:10.1016/s0191-8869(01)00189-1.

Petry, Ashley. "A Conversation with Cheryl Strayed." *Booth: A Journal.* July 25, 2014. Accessed October 1, 2018. http://booth.butler.edu/2014/07/25/a-conversation-with-cheryl-strayed/.

Richard, Erin M., James M. Diefendorff, and James H. Martin. "Revisiting the Within-Person Self-Efficacy and Performance Relation." *Human Performance* 19, no. 1 (November 2009): 67–87. doi:10.1207/s15327043hup1901_4.

Vancouver, Jeffrey B., and Laura N. Kendall. "When Self-efficacy Negatively Relates to Motivation and Performance in a Learning Context." *Journal of Applied Psychology* 91, no. 5 (September 2006): 1146–153. doi:10.1037/0021-9010.91.5.1146.

Woodman, Tim, Sally Akehurst, Lew Hardy, and Stuart Beattie. "Self-confidence and Performance: A Little Self-doubt Helps." *Psychology of Sport and Exercise* 11, no. 6 (November 2010): 467–70. doi:10.1016/j.psychsport.2010.05.009.

Chapter 5: They Don't Overthink Everything

Deyo, Mary, Kimberly A. Wilson, Jason Ong, and Cheryl Koopman. "Mindfulness and Rumination: Does Mindfulness Training Lead to Reductions in the Ruminative Thinking Associated with Depression?" *EXPLORE: The Journal of Science and Healing* 5, no. 5 (September/October 2009): 265–71. doi:10.1016/j.explore.2009.06.005.

Lareau, Annette, and Elliot B. Weininger. "Time, Work, and Family Life: Reconceptualizing Gendered Time Patterns Through the Case of Children's Organized Activities." *Sociological Forum* 23, no. 3 (July 21, 2008): 419–54. doi:10.1111/j.1573-7861.2008.00085.x.

Michl, Louisa C., Katie A. McLaughlin, Kathrine Shepherd, and Susan Nolen-

Hoeksema. "Rumination as a Mechanism Linking Stressful Life Events to Symptoms of Depression and Anxiety: Longitudinal Evidence in Early Adolescents and Adults." *Journal of Abnormal Psychology* 122, no. 2 (May 2013): 339–52. doi:10.1037/a0031994.

Nolen-Hoeksema, Susan, Blair E. Wisco, and Sonja Lyubomirsky. "Rethinking Rumination." *Perspectives on Psychological Science* 3, no. 5 (September 2008): 400–24. doi:10.1111/j.1745-6924.2008.00088.x.

Sio, Ut Na, and Thomas C. Ormerod. "Does Incubation Enhance Problem Solving? A Meta-analytic Review." *Psychological Bulletin* 135, no. 1 (2009): 94–120. doi:10.1037/a0014212.

Strick, Madelijn, Ap Dijksterhuis, and Rick B. Van Baaren. "Unconscious-Thought Effects Take Place Off-Line, Not On-Line." *Psychological Science* 21, no. 4 (February 26, 2010): 484–88. doi:10.1177/0956797610363555.

Thomsen, Dorthe Kirkegaard, Mimi Yung Mehlsen, Søren Christensen, and Robert Zachariae. "Rumination—Relationship with Negative Mood and Sleep Quality." *Personality and Individual Differences* 34, no. 7 (May 2003): 1293-301. doi:10.1016/s0191-8869(02)00120-4.

Verkuil, Bart, Jos F. Brosschot, Kees Korrelboom, Ria Reul-Verlaan, and Julian F. Thayer. "Pretreatment of Worry Enhances the Effects of Stress Management Therapy: A Randomized Clinical Trial." *Psychotherapy and Psychosomatics* 80, no. 3 (2011): 189–90. doi:10.1159/000320328.

Winfrey, Oprah. "What Oprah Knows about the Power of Meditation." Oprah.com. Accessed July 13, 2018. http://www.oprah.com/spirit/what-oprah-knows-about-the-power-of-meditation.

"Women Have More Active Brains Than Men." *Journal of Alzheimer's Disease.* Accessed July 13, 2018. https://www.j-alz.com/content/women-have-more-active-brains-men.

Chapter 6: They Don't Avoid Tough Challenges

"Billie Jean King: Accomplishments." Billie Jean King Enterprises. Accessed July 13, 2018. https://www.billiejeanking.com/biography/.

Chan, Amanda. "How to Be Brave, According to 8 Insanely Courageous Women." *Real Simple.* Accessed July 13, 2018. https://www.realsimple.com/work-life/life-strategies/how-to-be-brave.

Harris, Christine, and Michael Jenkins-Guarnieri. "Why Do Men Take More

Risks than Women?" *Judgment and Decision Making* 1, no. 1 (July 2006): 48–63. doi:10.1037/e511092014-212.

Kay, Katty, and Claire Shipman. *The Confidence Code: The Science and Art of Self-Assurance—What Women Should Know.* New York: HarperBusiness, an Imprint of HarperCollins Publishers, 2018.

"Learning New Skills Keeps an Aging Mind Sharp." Association for Psychological Science. Accessed July 13, 2018. https://www.psychologicalscience.org/news/releases/learning-new-skills-keeps-an-aging-mind-sharp.html.

Leibbrandt, Andreas, and John A. List. "Do Women Avoid Salary Negotiations? Evidence from a Large-scale Natural Field Experiment." *Management Science* (2014).

Morgenroth, Thekla, Cordelia Fine, Michelle K. Ryan, and Anna E. Genat. "Sex, Drugs, and Reckless Driving." *Social Psychological and Personality Science* (2017). 194855061772283 doi: 10.1177/1948550617722833.

Steinman, Judith L. "Gender Disparity in Organ Donation." *Gender Medicine* 3, no. 4 (2006): 246–52. doi:10.1016/s1550-8579(06)80213-5.

Chapter 7: They Don't Fear Breaking the Rules

Bowles, Hannah Riley, Linda Babcock, and Lei Lai. "Social Incentives for Gender Differences in the Propensity to Initiate Negotiations: Sometimes It Does Hurt to Ask." *Organizational Behavior and Human Decision Processes* 103, no. 1 (June 2005): 84–103. doi:10.1016/j.obhdp.2006.09.001.

Brauer, Markus, and Peggy Chekroun. "The Relationship Between Perceived Violation of Social Norms and Social Control: Situational Factors Influencing the Reaction to Deviance." *Journal of Applied Social Psychology* 35, no. 7 (2005): 1,519–539. doi:10.1111/j.1559-1816.2005.tb02182.x.

Brescoll, Victoria L., and Eric Luis Uhlmann. "Can an Angry Woman Get Ahead?" *Psychological Science* 19, no. 3 (March 2008): 268-75. doi:10.1111/j.1467-9280.2008.02079.x.

Feldblum, Chai, and Victoria Lipnic. "Select Task Force on the Study of Harassment in the Workplace." Report. U.S. Equal Employment Opportunity Commission. June 2016. https://www.eeoc.gov/eeoc/task_force/harassment/upload/report.pdf.

Flood, Alison. "Judy Blume: 'I Thought, This Is America: We Don't Ban Books. But Then We Did.'" *The Guardian.* July 11, 2014. Accessed July 13, 2018.

https://www.theguardian.com/books/2014/jul/11/judy-blume-interview
-forever-writer-children-young-adults.

History.com staff. "Eleanor Roosevelt." History.com. 2009. Accessed July 13, 2018. https://www.history.com/topics/first-ladies/eleanor-roosevelt.

History.com staff. "Susan B. Anthony." History.com. 2010. Accessed July 13, 2018. https://www.history.com/topics/womens-history/susan-b-anthony.

Huh, Young Eun, Joachim Vosgerau, and Carey K. Morewedge. "Social Defaults: Observed Choices Become Choice Defaults." *Journal of Consumer Research* 41, no. 3 (October 2014): 746-60. doi:10.1086/677315.

Mohr, Tara. *Playing Big: Find Your Voice, Your Mission, Your Message.* New York: Avery, an Imprint of Penguin Random House, 2015.

Montag, Ali. "'Shark Tank' Judge Lori Greiner's Daily Routine Sets Her Up for Success." CNBC. October 5, 2017. Accessed July 13, 2018. https://www.cnbc .com/2017/09/18/shark-tank-judge-lori-greiners-daily-routine.html.

Reuben, E., P. Sapienza, and L. Zingales. "How Stereotypes Impair Women's Careers in Science." *Proceedings of the National Academy of Sciences* 111(12) (2014), 4403–08. doi: 10.1073/pnas.1314788111.

Schumann, Karina, and Michael Ross. "Why Women Apologize More Than Men." *Psychological Science* 21, no. 11 (September 20, 2010): 1,649–55. doi:10.1177/0956797610384150.

"Supplemental Material for Student Characteristics and Behaviors at Age 12 Predict Occupational Success 40 Years Later over and above Childhood IQ and Parental Socioeconomic Status." *Developmental Psychology* 51, no. 9 (September 2015): 1,329–40. doi:10.1037/dev0000025.supp.

"The Real Story." Kathrine Switzer: Marathon Woman. Accessed July 13, 2018. http://kathrineswitzer.com/about-kathrine/1967-boston-marathon-the-real -story/.

Chapter 8: They Don't Put Others Down to Lift Themselves Up

Brown, Anna. "The Data on Women Leaders." Pew Research Center's Social & Demographic Trends Project. March 17, 2017. Accessed July 14, 2018. http:// www.pewsocialtrends.org/2017/03/17/the-data-on-women-leaders/.

Buss, David. *Evolution of Desire: Strategies of Human Mating.* Perseus Books Group, 2016.

"Civility in America VII: The State of Civility." Report. https://www.weber

shandwick.com/uploads/news/files/Civility_in_America_the_State_of_ Civility.pdf.

Dezső, C., D. Ross, and J. Uribe. "Is There an Implicit Quota on Women in Top Management? A Large-sample Statistical Analysis." *Strategic Management Journal* 37, no. 1 (2015): 98–115.

Feinberg, Matthew, Robb Willer, and Michael Schultz. "Gossip and Ostracism Promote Cooperation in Groups." *Psychological Science* 25, no. 3 (January 24, 2014): 656–64. doi:10.1177/0956797613510184.

Feinberg, Matthew, Robb Willer, Jennifer Stellar, and Dacher Keltner. "The Virtues of Gossip: Reputational Information Sharing as Prosocial Behavior." *Journal of Personality and Social Psychology* 102, no. 5 (2012): 1015-030. doi:10.1037/a0026650.

Forrest, Sarah, Virginia Eatough, and Mark Shevlin. "Measuring Adult Indirect Aggression: The Development and Psychometric Assessment of the Indirect Aggression Scales." *Aggressive Behavior* 31, no. 1 (2005): 84–97. doi:10.1002/ ab.20074.

Khazan, Olga. "The Evolution of Bitchiness." *The Atlantic.* November 20, 2013. Accessed October 1, 2018. https://www.theatlantic.com/health/archive /2013/11/the-evolution-of-bitchiness/281657/.

"These Are the Women CEOs Leading Fortune 500 Companies." *Fortune.* June 7, 2017. Accessed September 20, 2018. http://fortune.com/2017/06/07/fortune -500-women-ceos/.

Vaillancourt, Tracy, and Aanchal Sharma. "Intolerance of Sexy Peers: Intrasexual Competition among Women." *Aggressive Behavior* 37, no. 6 (November/ December, 2011): 569–77. doi:10.1002/ab.20413.

Valen, Kelly. "My Sorority Pledge? I Swore Off Sisterhood." *New York Times.* December 2, 2007. Accessed October 1, 2018. https://www.nytimes.com /2007/12/02/fashion/02love.html.

Valen, Kelly. *The Twisted Sisterhood: Unraveling the Dark Legacy of Female Friendships.* New York: Ballantine, 2010.

Velasquez, Lizzie, and Catherine Avril Morris. *Dare to Be Kind: How Extraordinary Compassion Can Transform Our World.* New York: Hachette Books, 2017.

"Women Presidents Profile—American College President Study." The American College President Study. Accessed September 20, 2018. http://www.aceacps .org/women-presidents/.

Chapter 9: They Don't Let Others Limit Their Potential

Barlow, Rich. "BU Research: A Riddle Reveals Depth of Gender Bias." *BU Today*. Boston University. January 16, 2014. Accessed July 14, 2018. http://www.bu.edu/today/2014/bu-research-riddle-reveals-the-depth-of-gender-bias/.

Brands, Raina A., and Isabel Fernandez-Mateo. "Leaning Out: How Negative Recruitment Experiences Shape Women's Decisions to Compete for Executive Roles." *Administrative Science Quarterly* 62, no. 3 (December 15, 2016): 405–42. doi:10.1177/0001839216682728.

Chen, Gina Masullo, and Zainul Abedin. "Exploring Differences in How Men and Women Respond to Threats to Positive Face on Social Media." *Computers in Human Behavior* 38 (2014): 118–26. doi:10.1016/j.chb.2014.05.029.

Correll, Shelley, and Caroline Simard. "Research: Vague Feedback Is Holding Women Back." *Harvard Business Review.* April 29, 2016. Accessed July 14, 2018. https://hbr.org/2016/04/research-vague-feedback-is-holding-women-back.

"From Upspeak to Vocal Fry: Are We Policing Young Women's Voices?" NPR. July 23, 2015. Accessed July 14, 2018. https://www.npr.org/templates/transcript/transcript.php?storyId=425608745.

Graham, Heather. "Heather Graham: Harvey Weinstein Implied I Had to Have Sex with Him for Movie Role (EXCLUSIVE)." *Variety.* October 10, 2017. Accessed October 1, 2018. https://variety.com/2017/film/columns/heather-graham-harvey-weinstein-sex-for-movie-role-1202586113/.

NDTV Profit. "Classmates Said I Sing Like a Goat, Owe Career to Parents, Shakira Tells Prannoy Roy." YouTube. January 17, 2017. Accessed July 14, 2018. https://www.youtube.com/watch?v=w1HGWyumfek.

Kay, Andrea. "At Work: To Succeed, Learn to Take Criticism." *USA Today.* February 16, 2013. Accessed July 14, 2018. https://www.usatoday.com/story/money/columnist/kay/2013/02/15/at-work-criticism-sensitivity/1921903/.

Lebowitz, Shana. "After Getting a Brutal Rejection, Barbara Corcoran Spent 8 Minutes Writing a Powerful Email Defending Herself—and It Changed the Next 9 Years of Her Life." *Business Insider.* November 8, 2017. Accessed July 14, 2018. http://www.businessinsider.com/barbara-corcoran-almost-rejected-from-shark-tank-2017-11.

Pappas, Stephanie. "Male Doctors, Female Nurses: Subconscious Stereotypes Hard to Budge." Live Science. June 20, 2016. Accessed July 14, 2018. https://www.livescience.com/55134-subconscious-stereotypes-hard-to-budge.html.

Wood, Dustin, Peter Harms, and Simine Vazire. "Perceiver Effects as Projective Tests: What Your Perceptions of Others Say About You." *Journal of Personality and Social Psychology* 99, no. 1 (July 2010): 174–90. doi:10.1037/a0019390.

Chapter 10: They Don't Blame Themselves When Something Goes Wrong

Effron, Lauren. "Former Gymnast Says She 'Trusted' Larry Nassar: 'I Blamed Myself for Years.'" ABC News. January 26, 2018. Accessed July 14, 2018. https://abcnews.go.com/Sports/gymnast-trusted-larry-nassar-blamed-years /story?id=52608992.

Elizabeth Smart: Autobiography. A&E. November 12, 2017.

Etxebarria, I., M. J. Ortiz, S. Conejero, and A. Pascual. "Intensity of Habitual Guilt in Men and Women: Differences in Interpersonal Sensitivity and the Tendency Towards Anxious-Aggressive Guilt." *Spanish Journal of Psychology* 12, no. 2 (2009): 540–54.

Glinder, Judith G., and Bruce E. Compas. "Self-blame Attributions in Women with Newly Diagnosed Breast Cancer: A Prospective Study of Psychological Adjustment." *Health Psychology* 18, no. 5 (1999): 475–81. doi:10.1037//0278-6133.18.5.475.

Kelly, Megyn. *Settle for More*. New York: Harper, 2016.

Malaquin, Stéphanie, Yazine Mahjoub, Arianna Musi, Elie Zogheib, Alexis Salomon, Mathieu Guilbart, and Hervé Dupont. "Burnout Syndrome in Critical Care Team Members: A Monocentric Cross Sectional Survey." *Anaesthesia Critical Care & Pain Medicine* 36, no. 4 (August 2017): 223–28. doi:10.1016/j.accpm.2016.06.011.

Mann, Adam. "Your Odds of Becoming an Astronaut Are Going Up." *Wired*. April 22, 2013. Accessed July 14, 2018. https://www.wired.com/2013/04 /astronaut-applications/.

Lewicki, Roy J., Beth Polin, and Robert B. Lount. "An Exploration of the Structure of Effective Apologies." *Negotiation and Conflict Management Research* 9, no. 2 (April 6, 2016): 177–96. doi:10.1111/ncmr.12073.

Lutwak, Nita, Jacqueline Panish, and Joseph Ferrari. "Shame and Guilt: Characterological vs. Behavioral Self-blame and Their Relationship to Fear of Intimacy." *Personality and Individual Differences* 35, no. 4 (September 2003): 909–16. doi:10.1016/s0191-8869(02)00307-0.

Schaubroeck, John, James R. Jones, and Jia Lin Xie. "Individual Differences in Utilizing Control to Cope with Job Demands: Effects on Susceptibility to Infectious Disease." *Journal of Applied Psychology* 86, no. 2 (April 2001): 265–78. doi:10.1037//0021-9010.86.2.265.

Spataro, Brielle M., Sarah A. Tilstra, Doris M. Rubio, and Melissa A. McNeil. "The Toxicity of Self-Blame: Sex Differences in Burnout and Coping in Internal Medicine Trainees." *Journal of Women's Health* 25, no. 11 (November 2016): 1,147–152. doi:10.1089/jwh.2015.5604.

Chapter 11: They Don't Stay Silent

"Be Bold. Be Brave. Raise Your Hand." Girl Scouts: Nation's Capital. Accessed July 14, 2018. http://www.gscnc.org/raiseyourhand.

Bianchi, Mike. "Jameis Winston Message to Girls: Be Quiet and Let the Boys Show You How Strong They Are." *Orlando Sentinel.* February 24, 2017. Accessed July 14, 2018. http://www.orlandosentinel.com/sports/open-mike/os-jameis-winston-fsu-tampa-bay-bucs-elementary-school-20170223-story.html.

Crosby, F. "The Denial of Personal Discrimination." *American Behavioral Scientist* 27, no. 3 (1984): 371–86.

Dockterman, Eliana. "'I Was Angry.' Taylor Swift on What Powered Her Sexual Assault Testimony." *Time.* December 6, 2017. Accessed July 14, 2018. http://time.com/5049659/taylor-swift-interview-person-of-the-year-2017/.

Farmer, Olivia, and Sara Smock Jordan. "Experiences of Women Coping with Catcalling Experiences in New York City: A Pilot Study." *Journal of Feminist Family Therapy* 29, no. 4 (October 2, 2017): 205–25. doi:10.1080/08952833.2017.1373577.

Jones, Jeffrey S., Carmen Alexander, Barbara N. Wynn, Linda Rossman, and Chris Dunnuck. "Why Women Don't Report Sexual Assault to the Police: The Influence of Psychosocial Variables and Traumatic Injury." *The Journal of Emergency Medicine* 36, no. 4 (May 2009): 417–24. doi:10.1016/j.jemermed.2007.10.077.

Karpowitz, Christopher, Tali Mendelberg, and Lee Shaker. "Gender Inequality in Deliberative Participation." *American Political Science Review* 106, no. 3 (August 2012): 533-47. doi:10.1037/e511862012-001.

McClean, Elizabeth, Sean R. Martin, Kyle J. Emich, and Todd Woodruff. "The Social Consequences of Voice: An Examination of Voice Type and Gender on

Status and Subsequent Leader Emergence." *Academy of Management Journal,* September 14, 2017. doi:10.5465/amj.2016.0148.

Niemi, Nancy S. *"Still Failing at Fairness: How Gender Bias Cheats Girls and Boys in School and What We Can Do about It,* by David Sadker, Myra Sadker and Karen Zittleman." *Gender and Education* 22, no. 1 (January 2010): 142–43. doi:10.1080/09540250903464773.

"Perpetrators of Sexual Violence: Statistics." RAINN. Accessed July 14, 2018. https://www.rainn.org/statistics/perpetrators-sexual-violence.

Sadker, David Miller, Myra Sadker, and Karen Zittleman. *Still Failing at Fairness: How Gender Bias Cheats Girls and Boys in School and What We Can Do about It.* New York: Scribner, 2009.

Schad, Tom. "Jameis Winston Suspended for Three Games, Apologizes for Uber Incident." *USA Today.* June 28, 2018. Accessed August 15, 2018. https://www.usatoday.com/story/sports/nfl/buccaneers/2018/06/28/jameis-winston-suspended-tampa-bay-buccaneers-uber/742691002/.

Wagner, Laura. "FSU Pays $950,000 to Woman Who Accused Jameis Winston of Sexual Assault." NPR. January 25, 2016. Accessed July 14, 2018. https://www.npr.org/sections/thetwo-way/2016/01/25/464332250/fsu-pays-950-000-to-woman-who-accused-jameis-winston-of-sexual-assault.

Wanless, S. B., M. M. McClelland, X. Lan, et al. "Gender Differences in Behavioral Regulation in Four Societies: the United States, Taiwan, South Korea, and China." *Early Childhood Research Quarterly* 28 (2013): 621–33. doi:10.1016/j.ecresq.2013.04.002.

"Women in Elective Office 2017." CAWP: Center for American Women and Politics. Eagleton Institute of Politics, Rutgers University. Accessed July 14, 2018. http://www.cawp.rutgers.edu/women-elective-office-2017.

Chapter 12: They Don't Feel Bad about Reinventing Themselves

"About." Lorraine Pascale. Accessed July 14, 2018. https://www.lorrainepascale.com/about/.

Bryan, C. J., G. M. Walton, T. Rogers, and C. S. Dweck. "Motivating Voter Turnout by Invoking the Self." *PNAS: Proceedings of the National Academy of Sciences of the United States of America* 108, no. 31 (2011): 12,653–56. http://dx.doi.org/10.1073/pnas.1103343108.

Gersick, Connie J. G., and Kathy E. Kram. "High-Achieving Women at

Midlife." *Journal of Management Inquiry* 11, no. 2 (June 2002): 104–27. doi:10.1177/10592602011002005.

Helson, Ravenna, Constance Jones, and Virginia S. Y. Kwan. "Personality Change over 40 Years of Adulthood: Hierarchical Linear Modeling Analyses of Two Longitudinal Samples." *Journal of Personality and Social Psychology* 83, no. 3 (September 2002): 752–66. doi:10.1037//0022-3514.83.3.752.

Kelly, M. M., A. R. Tyrka, L. H. Price, and L. L. Carpenter. "Sex Differences in the Use of Coping Strategies: Predictors of Anxiety and Depressive Symptoms." *Depression and Anxiety,* 25(10) (2008): 839–46. http://doi.org/10.1002/da.20341.

Lönnqvist, Jan-Erik, Sointu Leikas, and Markku Verkasalo. "Value Change in Men and Women Entering Parenthood: New Mothers Value Priorities Shift Towards Conservation Values." *Personality and Individual Differences* 120 (January 2018): 47–51. doi:10.1016/j.paid.2017.08.019.

"Meet Annie." Annie Duke. Accessed July 14, 2018. http://annieduke.com/meet -annie-duke/.

Roberts, B. W., R. Helson, and E. C. Klohnen. "Personality Development and Growth in Women Across 30 Years: Three Perspectives." *Journal of Personality* 70 (2002): 79–102.

Webber, Rebecca. "Reinvent Yourself." *Psychology Today.* May 6, 2014. Accessed October 1, 2018. https://www.psychologytoday.com/us/articles/201405 /reinvent-yourself.

Wu, Qiong, Natasha Slesnick, and Jing Zhang. "Understanding the Role of Emotion-oriented Coping in Women's Motivation for Change." *Journal of Substance Abuse Treatment* 86 (February 2004): 1–8. doi:10.1016/j.jsat.2017.12.006.

Chapter 13: They Don't Downplay Their Success

Bertrand, Marianne, Claudia Goldin, and Lawrence F. Katz. "Dynamics of the Gender Gap for Young Professionals in the Financial and Corporate Sectors." *American Economic Journal: Applied Economics* 2, no. 3 (2010): 228–55.

Bertrand, Marianne, Emir Kamenica, and Jessica Pan. "Gender Identity and Relative Income within Households." *Quarterly Journal of Economics* 130, no. 2 (2015): 571–614.

Bowley, Rachel. "Women's Equality Day: A Look at Women in the Workplace in 2017." Official LinkedIn Blog. Accessed August 28, 2017. https://blog

.linkedin.com/2017/august/28/womens-equality-day-a-look-at-women-in -the-workplace-in-2017.

Brown, Stephanie L., and Brian P. Lewis. "Relational Dominance and Mate-Selection Criteria: Evidence That Males Attend to Female Dominance." *Evolution and Human Behavior* 25, no. 6 (2004): 406–15.

Bursztyn, Leonardo, Thomas Fujiwara, and Amanda Pallais. "Acting Wife: Marriage Market Incentives and Labor Market Investments." *American Economic Review* 107, no. 11 (2017): 3,288–319. doi:10.3386/w23043.

Cokley, K., L. Smith, D. Bernard, et al. "Impostor Feelings as a Moderator and Mediator of the Relationship between Perceived Discrimination and Mental Health among Racial/Ethnic Minority College Students." *Journal of Counseling Psychology* 64, no. 2 (2017): 141–54.

Cokley, Kevin, Shannon McClain, Alicia Enciso, and Mercedes Martinez. "An Examination of the Impact of Minority Status Stress and Impostor Feelings on the Mental Health of Diverse Ethnic Minority College Students." *Journal of Multicultural Counseling and Development* 41, no. 2 (April 2013): 82–95. doi:10.1002/j.2161-1912.2013.00029.x.

Cuddy, Amy Joy Casselberry. *Presence: Bringing Your Boldest Self to Your Biggest Challenges.* New York: Back Bay Books, 2018.

Fisman, Raymond, Sheena S. Iyengar, Emir Kamenica, and Itamar Simonson. "Gender Differences in Mate Selection: Evidence from a Speed Dating Experiment." *Quarterly Journal of Economics* 121, no. 2 (2006): 673–97.

Folke, Olle, and Johanna Rickne. "All the Single Ladies: Job Promotions and the Durability of Marriage." IFN Working Paper 1146. 2016.

Greitemeyer, Tobias. "What Do Men and Women Want in a Partner? Are Educated Partners Always More Desirable?" *Journal of Experimental Social Psychology* 43, no. 2 (2007): 180–94.

Kaling, Mindy. *Why Not Me?* New York: Random House, 2015.

Sezer, Ovul, Francesca Gino, and Michael I. Norton. "Humblebragging: A Distinct and Ineffective Self-Presentation Strategy." *SSRN Electronic Journal* (August 2017). doi:10.2139/ssrn.2597626.

University of Warwick. "Girls Feel They Must 'Play Dumb' to Please Boys, Study Shows." *ScienceDaily.* Accessed July 12, 2018. www.sciencedaily.com /releases/2014/08/140805090947.htm.